I Remember

Experiences Growing Up in Small-town America 1911-1929

by
Jessie E. Davenport

Edited by Hal Lewis

Jessie Elizabeth *Davenport* Lewis/Raimondi (1911-2000)

This photo is believed to be when Jessie was eighteen, which means it was shortly after she married Harold Lewis, probably late 1929 or early 1930.

Sadly, no one in the family can find photos of her or her siblings during their childhood years and hardly any during their adolescence either. We just have to rely on our imaginations as we read her memoir, but the photos on the following pages may in some cases help us visualize some parts of the Introduction and Afterword.

I have respected her preferences for title and authorship as evidenced by what she wrote on the first page of her manuscript. The only title she listed was "I Remember", so I have used that with an appropriate subtitle. She listed authorship by her maiden name, "Jessie E. Davenport".

Jessie's mother, Elizabeth Mary *Fitzpatrick* Davenport ((1883-1929)

Jessie's father, William Alexander Davenport (1884-1971)

MARJORIE L. DAVENPORT

912 W. State Street

Home Room Basketball 5; The Wreck of the Hesperus 3; Lady of Shalott 3; O Lovely Night 4; King Harold 4; Senior Stunts 4; Dramatic Club 4.

Rose White and Rose Red of the fairy tale will indeed have to bow to this angelic little fairy princess! It was Rose White, wasn't it, whose disposition was so sweet and good? Well, she was something like Marjorie but not quite; for under her apparent angelic temperament Marjorie is not too good and sometimes can be quite a scamp. Did you see her in the Frolic? If you did all your ideas of perfection have been ruined. Well, she is plenty good enough, and those children who follow wisdom's way under her guidance after she finishes Normal School—Oh, what a darling teacher they will have!

Jessie's sister, Marge (1909-1984)
Ithaca HS yearbook photo
The only sibling to finish
high school and go on to college

ALEXANDER T. CONNELL
82.

William's Uncle Alex (1861-1947)
Twice mayor of Scranton
Entrepreneur and gold prospector
From *Prominent Men: Scranton and Vicinity,* 1905

Jessie's first husband, Harold Lewis
(1905-2003)

Harold as a boy of 7. 1912

Harold & Jessie
Perhaps the summer they married, 1929,
ages 24 & 17

Jessie & Harold in 1938,
ages 26 & 33
Woman on right is possibly one
of Jessie's sisters, maybe Claire

v

Jessie's second husband,
Tony Raimondi (1922-1986)

Jessie's maternal grandfather,
Michael Fitzpatrick (1855-1909) with his
8th child, Veronica (1899-1968) in 1900.
He was by then the fire boss in the
Connell's Shamokin-area colliery and well
respected in that community.

Jessie's future father-in-law, George F.
Lewis (1881-1962) taken in front of his
Hawley Street grocery in downtown about
1911. Mr. Mitchell put up much of the
capital, but George ran the shop.

George F, Lewis with his horse, Midget,
and grocery delivery van in front of his
downtown Washington Street store about
1921.

Aloysius Noel (1835-1900) who was a great-grandfather of Jessie (maternal grandfather of her mother, Elizabeth). Served as a private in 1862 and 1863 in Company F of the 165th Pennsylvania Infantry, one of three of Jessie's great-grandfathers who fought to preserve the Union and free the slaves. A small man, about 5'0" tall. (The Springfield 1861 rifled musket he held was 4'8" long without the bayonet, nearly as tall as he was.) Of Pennsylvania Dutch (German) heritage, partly of Alsatian descent. Aloysius (pronounced AL-oh-ISH-əs) was once a popular name of German and Latin origins and means "famous warrior".

I remember Marge and I wore pink sailor dresses and the top had a
little pocket. I had a nickle in the pocket (riches) and I promptly
lost my nickle down between the keyes of their piano. Of course I put
up a howl. Well the lady got the hired man and he got the nickle out for
me. It was all for nothing as I lost the nickle when I was playing in
the field. No amount of crying could bring it back/. We had a
wonderful week running around all day in good country air, and eating
fresh vegatables and fruits. I hated to go home at the end of the
week but I think the lady was glad to see us go.

One thing that happened at the farm concerened Helen, Mary
abd Bill. They had a good time roaming through the fields and woods
One day they dressed up in some old clothes that the farm lady said
they could play with. So they went into the BARN and got into some
paint that was stored there in cans and streaked thier faces until
they looked like something from a horror movie. They were in the
wood near the road when they heard voices. They peered out of the bushes
and saw three small children walking hand in hand. They were going to meet
thier father. They ranged in age from about eight down to the smallest
one who was about two years old. I don't know what possesed my brother
and sisters but they jumped out of the bushes screaming and yelling and mak
making horrible faces. The poor kids were so scared they ran as fast
as they could down the road. The littlest one was pulled along so fast
her feet never touched the ground. HELEN and her partners in crime were
scared about what they had done. They went hurriedly down to the
creek and scrubbed the paint from thier faces. They took off the
costumes they were wearing and got into thier own clothes. It was

Sample page from Jessie's first draft

Contents

Cast of Main Characters

The Author:
- Jessie Elizabeth *Davenport* Lewis/Raimondi 1911-2000

Jessie's parents:
- William Alexander Davenport 1884-1971 (referred to as William or possibly Will, but never as Bill)
- Elizabeth Mary *Fitzpatrick* Davenport 1883-1929

Jessie's older siblings:
- Helen Evelyn *Davenport* Hawley 1904-1990 (author of *Sister Helen's Stories*)
- Mary Jemima *Davenport* Clark 1906-1942
- William Alexander Davenport, Jr. 1907-1969 (Bill)
- Marjorie Teresa *Davenport* Moruzzi 1909-1984 (Marge)

Jessie's younger siblings:
- Claire Catherine *Davenport* Wyman 1913-2010
- Carmel Connell *Davenport* Condinho 1915-1986
- James Edward Davenport 1917-1993 (Jim)
- Richard Raymond Davenport 1919-1950 (Dick)

Sibling spouses who appear in the book:
- Earnest Hawley 1902-1972 (Helen's husband, Jack)
- Ralph Clark 1903-1972 (Mary's husband)

Jessie's grandparents (never personally known to her):
- James Edward Davenport 1857-1914
- Jemima Elizabeth *Connell* Davenport 1858-1906
- Michael Fitzpatrick 1855-probably 1910
- Mary *Noel* Fitzpatrick 1862-1911

Other relatives discussed by Jessie:
- Alexander Thomas Connell 1861-1947 (Uncle Alex, maternal uncle of William, twice mayor Scranton)
- Helen *Davenport* Janes 1893-1964 (Aunt Helen, younger sister of William)
- Frederic Janes 1891-1972 (Aunt Helen's husband)
- Harriet *Fitzpatrick* Neibauer 1884-1940 (Aunt Hattie, closest sister of Elizabeth)
- John Joseph Neibauer 1881-1963 (Uncle John, husband of Hattie)
- John Joseph Neibauer, Jr. 1905-1925 (Cousin Joe, first of the nine children of Hattie and John)
- Agnes *Neibauer* Yazisko 1912-1963 (Cousin Agnes, "Aganess", fifth of the nine children of Hattie and John)

Introduction

There is value in learning more about the daily lives of ordinary people in earlier generations. We can thereby put our present-day lives into clearer perspective, and we might even find the process entertaining. This book is about the life of a girl growing up in small American cities in the 1910s and 1920s. It records what experiences were meaningful to her and what she felt about them in an exceptionally personal way. In her eightieth year, my paternal grandmother, Jessie *Davenport* (Lewis) Raimondi, sat down at an old manual typewriter with a worn-out ribbon and churned out a 135-page manuscript of the memories of her life up to the age of seventeen. The core of this book is an edited version of that effort. What I have tried to add to the core has also been personal. As far as I know, Jessie never went further than that first rough-draft manuscript, and it isn't even quite clear who her intended audience was. My first assumption was that she meant for it to be read only within the family, and I started this project with just that audience in mind. But as I reflect on it more, I feel she would have welcomed the attention of a more general audience, if there are those who might find it interesting.

Even if just for the entertainment value, my grandmother's story is worthwhile reading. She was an excellent storyteller with her own idiosyncratic sense of humor, and I think these characteristics come through even better in her writing than they did when she spoke. We feel drawn into her story and might even feel as we read it some of the same emotions she describes. I have felt more joy than I would have expected in reading and rereading it, including even the messier and less pleasant parts. All children engage in shenanigans, but what is unusual about my grandmother is that she remembers hers so clearly and explains them well and honestly. I am proud of her for that.

Not everyone feels the same way about it, but there is general value in learning more history. I have been informed by those who know more about the social sciences than I that there is an emphasis in those fields on the concept of *path dependency*. This, I am told, is the concept that it is impossible to understand fully how and why things work the way they do now unless we understand what led up to the current circumstances. If something people are doing now is illogical and incomprehensible when viewed only in terms of the present, we will likely understand it better with a historical perspective. Some of us have intuitively understood this concept all along, and it is one of our prime motivators in seeking more historical knowledge.

For those with a family connection to Jessie and her stories, I add that genealogy is nothing so much as the personal side of history. With few exceptions, we are all deeply influenced, for better or worse, by our parents, and we know that is largely unavoidable. We only need to project backward one more step to see that our parents were likely just as much influenced in turn by their parents. And with the knowledge that habits, attitudes, and even vices tend to become traditions that perpetuate themselves through several generations, it might even be worth digging further into the past. Genealogy can be a tool for deeper self-discovery.

But a frustrating aspect of genealogy, or history in a more general sense, is that the knowledge we gain is often less substantial than we would like it to be. Discovering key dates and locations of births, deaths, marriages, and the like is not superficial information, but it still leaves us short of the deeper understanding we wish we had. What was a day like for a particular family of ancestors trying to earn a living, and how hard was it for them? How did they see their place in the wider world and God's creation? Did they live in fear of attack by nearby enemies, and did they worry about wars in the news from farther away? When did they meet and choose their marriage partners, and how did they raise their children? How did they bear up under the prevalence of disease and early death when medical science was less advanced than today? If we see that a family of ancestors moved from one location to another, why did they move, and how difficult was the journey for them?

Usually, even our speculations on these questions only get us as far as gross generalizations. Almost certainly, our ancestors' lives were harder than ours in most respects. Centuries ago, there were only limited choices of potential marriage partners since they probably had few chances to meet people beyond the nearby villages. Migrating usually had something to do with finding affordable land in earlier centuries or finding better job opportunities in more recent times. Those kinds of answers are reasonable assumptions, but even if they're entirely true, they still provide only a very general kind of understanding of our past.

What we would really like to have, but only rarely do, is a detailed personal narrative of someone from an earlier generation. When these do exist, they can help us more than any other source in answering the detailed questions we want to ask. These are treasures. This alone is sufficient reason for seeing Grandma Jessie's memoir as valuable.

I should explain how this volume developed. It must have been in 1990 or early 1991 that my grandmother sat down and typed out her rough manuscript. I am not sure how many weeks it took her to produce those 135 double-spaced pages. It is probable that part of Grandma Jessie's inspiration came from a similar, earlier effort by her eldest sister, Helen *Davenport* Hawley. Great-aunt Helen had written a twelve-chapter memoir of her childhood, organized more around topic area than chronology. She titled this *Sister Helen's Stories* and included with it a collection of her poems and drawings. Those who know of this within the family usually refer to it now as "Aunt Helen's book". Whereas that book is quite well known within the family circle, and several relatives have their own photocopies, very few of us knew that my grandmother had attempted a similar project. Certainly, I didn't. And while *Sister Helen's Stories* is a more-or-less finished product, Grandma Jessie never got beyond a first draft, at least as far as I know.

My grandmother passed away in Binghamton on December 21, 2000, about a decade after writing that draft, so why didn't more of us know about it? Well, to start with, for many of us in the family, our relationship with Jessie was a complicated one. Speaking now for myself, I didn't feel that she and I were estranged, but we were not particularly close either. Part of this had to do with some difficult aspects of the family history. Another factor is that she didn't always act or talk in ways that would seem typical of a grandmother. As I reflect on this now, I see that that aspect of her character is understandable, at least to some extent. Jessie never had a chance to meet any of her grandparents, and therefore lacked a model for the grandparent role. When I was a child, my father took us to see his mother from time to time, but not as often as to other close relatives. As an adult, I think I continued in a similar pattern. When I did see her, her manner of speaking seemed to me to be overly frank on some topics and unnecessarily reticent on others. I was living overseas for most of the decade leading up to her death, but that is not really an explanation for why I didn't know about the draft, since we did exchange several letters during that period.

A few decades later, I was gradually becoming more intensely interested in genealogy, but at first, I did not put as much focus on the Davenport branch of my family tree as I did some of the other branches. Then some months ago, it became clear to me that, at the age of eighty-six my father was developing a keen interest in knowing more about the maternal side of his heritage, and this became my motivation to make more efforts in that direction. Among the actions I took, I corresponded via email with a few Davenport-side second cousins whom I had never met before. One of these is exceptionally knowledgeable of our shared family history. To my surprise, she sent me via mail my grandmother's 135-page manuscript, which up to then had been in her possession. I suppose my cousin believed that I, as a direct descendant, would value this the most, and I am ever so grateful for her thoughtfulness.

It was obvious that this manuscript was a first draft. Whatever the age of the typewriter she used, it is clear at least that the ribbon was almost used up, since the type is faint and gets fainter as the pages go on. Toward the end, it is just barely legible. In the usual manner of revising text in the days before word processors, my grandmother had made handwritten comments in margins for either corrections or notes on intended modifications. It would be unfair to expect a draft written on a conventional typewriter to be as nearly error-free as what we can easily accomplish with the aid of a word processor and spell checker, especially for someone whose career is something other than a writer or stenographer. Typos and some misspellings are to be expected, and it would be natural to see phraseology that could be improved. Even so, I was mildly surprised that Jessie made as many spelling errors as she did, given that she was a lifelong avid reader. Overall, my grandmother expressed herself remarkably well, but there are some points where it takes a while to see her point or to put her narrative into context. And as should be expected in a first draft, even some of the more understandable sentences are clumsily constructed.

After receiving the manuscript, I quickly went to work scanning the pages and printing out a copy for my father to read. For passages where I could add comments that I thought might explain context or help clarify Jessie's meaning, I wrote up a set of notes on separate pages. My dad was pleased to receive both the copied original pages and my notes and began reading them. Soon, however, he began to complain that the copied pages were difficult for him to read, in part due to the faint type caused by the old typewriter ribbon. He expressed the wish that someone should retype them.

The "someone" meant me, so though not a speedy typist, I took this up as the natural next step in the process. Obviously, I would attempt to repair the spelling errors as I went along, but I quickly arrived at the conclusion that having gone that far, there was no reason my editing efforts should end with spelling. It would be just one more step to restructure Jessie's sentences and paragraphs to try to make it easier to follow her narrative. My goal was to strike a balance between improving the clarity while maintaining as much as possible of my grandmother's style in phrasing her thoughts. In the end, I arrived at a policy I would follow. I changed the wording of sentences where I thought best. I sometimes changed the order of the sentences within a paragraph or broke up long paragraphs, but I would never change the order of paragraphs or the order of the anecdotes in which Jessie wrote her story. Retyping and editing the manuscript also allowed me to incorporate the notes directly as footnotes.

One example can illustrate what I mean by preserving Jessie's writing style. For most of the years I lived overseas, it was the days before email, and so I kept in touch with relatives and friends back home by writing letters the old-fashioned way. One common pattern I noticed in all the letters I received from relatives that were of my grandparents' generation was that they habitually used "as" in places in sentences where they might have used "because", as in "The corn isn't growing so well this year *as* we didn't get enough rain in June." Apparently, this manner of wording was more common among people who grew up in the early 20th Century than it is now, and it therefore doesn't surprise me that my grandmother routinely used "as" in this way. For the most part, I decided not to change that aspect of how she wrote her sentences when expressing causation.

I worked on one chapter at a time and gave copies to my dad and a few other of my closest relatives. I received some useful comments that led me to improve some of the footnotes. I also got the sense that those people curious enough to read Jessie's story would be happy to receive more background material as well. For that matter, I too was curious and had already been trying to piece together a family history going back to as many earlier generations as was readily possible. This was the first motivation for adding this lengthy introduction as well as an afterword that will follow.

I should mention here my general approach for naming the many individuals we will meet in the book. Throughout the rest of the introduction, in the footnotes, and in the afterword, I will typically refer to people simply by their given names or nicknames. This is merely because that is the most straightforward way to name them. It is in no way intended to show disrespect toward my elders. It would quickly become tiresome especially for readers who are not connected to the story in the same way I am if I were to keep referring to "my grandmother" or "Grandma Jessie". So, most of the time she will be just "Jessie". Similarly, it will be "Helen" rather than "Great-aunt Helen" and "William" instead of "Great-grandfather William". In a few places I might add birth years as a suffix if there is a part of the discussion where I need to refer to two people who always used the same given name, such as "Jessie-1911" in contrast with "Jessie-1891". When necessary for quick reference, I have added a list of the cast of main characters. I will nonetheless mention briefly here that Jessie's parents were William and Elizabeth. Her four older siblings were Helen, Mary, Bill, and Marge; and her four younger ones were Claire, Carmel, Jim, and Dick. In the past, these names had little significance to me, since I never met most of them, but as this project progressed, I began to feel I knew them each quite intimately.

I grew up hating the confusion caused by people having the same names. On the one hand, it is a fine custom to honor the grandparents, aunts, uncles, and other relatives by naming one's children after them, but arrogantly naming sons Jr., or even worse III, is going much too far. It is a terrible, terrible custom, and I urge young people starting their own families not even to consider it when they have sons. In the case of Jessie's family, "Bill" apparently always meant her brother, never her father. As far as I have seen, her father is everywhere referred to as "William" or sometimes "Will". That at least makes things better. If you are going to engage in the dreadful custom of naming a son Jr., at least have the good sense to use different nicknames.

As one last point about names, when I need to give full names of married women, I will use the convention of listing the maiden names in italics before their married surnames. Thus, Jessie's mother's full name I write as "Elizabeth Mary *Fitzpatrick* Davenport". In family tree charts, I will just list their maiden names, so in this case, I will show Jessie's mother as "Elizabeth Fitzpatrick".

On one other point, it is worth remembering that genealogical research is not generally an exact science. Often it involves carefully weighing evidence and coming to the most probable conclusions. I do my best to state as fact only what has a very high probability of being true, and I indicate as only probable what I arrive at as an educated guess. In most cases, documentary evidence and established historical facts should be given greater weight than what the family has traditionally believed. Human memories are imperfect, and when stories are passed down through generations, there is even more room for error, like what happens with the old parlor game. Still, family tradition is valuable not just for filling in the gaps, but also for helping to understand the motivations behind what people did in the past. It is also true that in a few cases, documents can be in error, so on rare occasions there may be reasons to trust traditions over documents. Another important source is just looking into general history as a way of putting the family history into context. Furthermore, I continue to emphasize that Jessie's and Helen's stories each help us put the other in clearer context.

Jessie seems to have intended her book to be like Helen's in some ways, but somewhat different in others. Jessie generally wrote in a more personal way. Helen put more emphasis on how various experiences influenced the whole family, though certainly she did have her personal opinions as well, and she did sometimes share deeply personal experiences. But Jessie reflected more centrally on what the experiences meant specifically to herself. Jessie's book was organized around what I'll call her four chapters for the four different towns her family lived in while she was growing up—Scranton, Dalton, Ithaca, and Binghamton. This makes the story chronological in the big-picture sense, but not on a detailed level, since within each chapter her narrative seems to be based more on stream of consciousness recollections rather than following any detailed timeline. As for the specific events the two books record, there is some overlap, but since the two sisters were nearly seven years apart in age, it is natural that both the events they remembered and the perspectives they had about them might differ significantly, and they indeed do. Overall, the two books complement each other to a very substantial degree. Helen's book helps us understand better what Jessie wrote in hers, and vice versa.

Elizabeth's mother (Jessie's maternal grandmother) was Mary *Noel* Fitzpatrick. Mary was born in July of 1862 in Adams County, Pennsylvania to Aloysius (1838-1900) and Maria (or Mary) E. *Biedler* (1839-1924) Noel. The Noels were a large family and lived mostly in that area around Gettysburg by that time, though in earlier generations they lived near York and various other parts of southeastern Pennsylvania. In 1854, when Aloysius was a teenager, his family moved in mass to Grand Rapids, Michigan, where some of them became wagon-makers as well as farmers. However, over the next few decades, most of the young Noel men returned to Adams County for various purposes. They usually came back to marry women they knew there with similar family backgrounds, and they enlisted in Pennsylvania regiments during the Civil War. In most cases, they eventually resettled back to the Gettysburg area to spend the rest of their lives. Thus, for most of the family, the move to Michigan was only temporary.

On October 15, 1862, twenty-seven-year-old Aloysius Noel enlisted as a private in Company F of the 165th Pennsylvania Infantry Regiment as a substitute for a man named John Stanley. Company F was one of the units raised from Adams County men, and it appears that four of Aloysius's brothers and cousins joined the same company at the same time, perhaps also as substitutes for men who were drafted and had paid them to be their substitutes. Aloysius, who was one of my 3xgreat-grandfathers, was a small man. The enlistment records show he was 5' 0" tall, which didn't meet the official minimum height requirement, but apparently this was overlooked. The 165th Regiment served mainly in Virginia, where they were attached to the 2nd Brigade of the 1st Division of VII Corps, and as such, the main engagement in which they participated was the Siege of Suffolk. By Civil War standards, the unit's casualty rate was low. The whole regiment was mustered out on July 28, 1863. Is it ironic that a regiment recruited in Chambersburg and Gettysburg, didn't fight at Gettysburg? Throughout his adult life, Aloysius listed his occupation as carpenter. He and Maria had four children. There is some inconsistency in the records as to whether their daughter Mary (the future Mrs. Fitzpatrick) was eldest or if one of her brothers was older.

The Noels were predominantly of German descent, with a little bit of Welsh blood several generations back. Most of their ancestors arrived in Pennsylvania in the early 18th Century from Alsace (thus the French-sounding name) and other regions near the middle Rhine. In her *Sister Helen's Stories*, Helen describes her maternal grandmother as of Pennsylvania Dutch background. When Helen was small, she spent a lot of time with her grandmother and mentions learning from her to recite the Lord's Prayer in German. Indeed, there does seem to be some evidence that when the Noel ancestors first arrived in Pennsylvania in the early 1700s, they were mostly

Mennonites, but the belief systems within the family apparently had become a somewhat more complex story by the 19th Century, a generation or two before Mary was born. Judging from what is found in some of the records, several of the Noel relatives had become Quakers, but several others had converted to Catholicism, and are described in places as very dedicated to the Catholic faith. Indeed, Helen describes her grandmother in just that way. Culture might have been a bit of an issue, but religious beliefs were not at all an impediment for Mary to marry an Irish Catholic Fitzpatrick, and she surely played a major role in raising Elizabeth and her other children to be strong Catholics.

Noel Family Connections

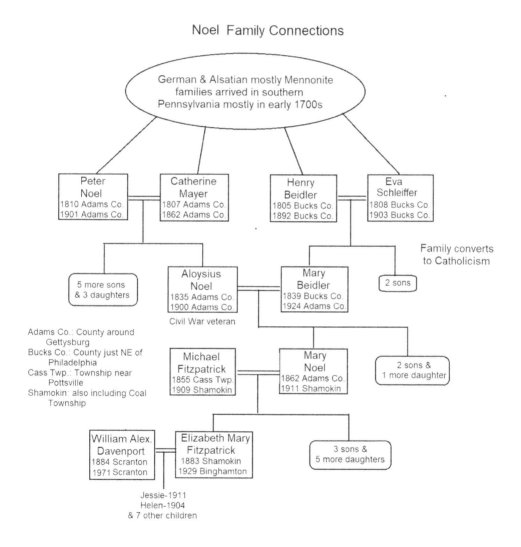

Mary passed away in February of 1911, a half year before Jessie was born, and is buried in St. Edwards Cemetery near Shamokin. Though Jessie never met her grandmother, she surely experienced her grandmother's influence indirectly through her mother and perhaps through Helen as well. Helen had fond memories of her time as a small child living next door to her maternal grandparents and her Aunt Bernadette (Michael and Mary's youngest child), who was only three months older than she was.

Elizabeth's father was Michael Fitzpatrick. It appears that some of his grandchildren and others in the family believed him to have been born in Ireland. We can be certain based on available records that that is not quite true. Both of his parents were Irish immigrants, but we have solid evidence that he and all his siblings were born in coal-mining towns in Pennsylvania within a few decades of when their parents arrived. All the same, there is good reason to believe Michael and all his family were very Irish. It is also clear that they represent an excellent example of the tendency for immigrant families to work hard and attain upward mobility in their new country, especially if that country is America. Very likely, when Michael's parents arrived, they were impoverished. Some records also suggest they were illiterate, which was not at all unusual for those born in early 19th Century Ireland. At the time they arrived, the Irish were at the very bottom rung of the work hierarchy in the coal mines and elsewhere, and the best they could hope for were the most menial jobs at near starving wages. But they rose quickly. By the time Elizabeth was born, and certainly by the time she came of age, the Fitzpatricks were highly respected and even approaching elite status in their community.

We can know quite a lot about the arrival of our line of Fitzpatricks in America, but some of the details will likely remain a little hazy. One of the difficulties is that there were often other families with the surname Fitzpatrick, though not closely related, in the same towns where they lived. To make it worse, they often had common given names. When looking up old records, it is often hard to be sure which Michael or John or Mary Fitzpatrick is the right one. And even when we do have the right records, they are not always perfectly accurate. We can, however, be quite certain on some points.

Michael's father (Elizabeth's grandfather and Jessie's great-grandfather) John Fitzpatrick was born in Ballyadams Parish in 1820. Ballyadams is located about fifty miles southwest of Dublin, fairly close to the center of Ireland. This parish, also known as Ballyadams Barony, is part of what was then called Queen's County, which was a name imposed by the British. After 1922, the name was changed to County Laois, which I am told is pronounced LEESH. John married Harriet Brennan. Harriet was born about 1828, and we can be certain that was also in Ireland. They probably married about 1845, but I am not sure whether this was before they left Ireland, in which case she was probably from Ballyadams or a place close by it. For that matter, I don't know of any documents indicating specific arrival dates for either of them. This is not surprising because many such records were lost from that time. There are arrival records for young men named John Fitzpatrick, but these must be for other men of that name since they don't match up well for age or other factors. What does seem

Fitzpatrick Family Connections

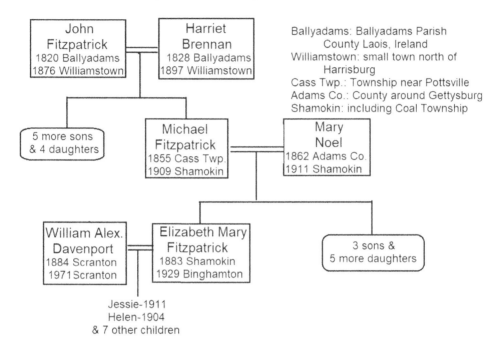

John Fitzpatrick	Harriet Brennan
1820 Ballyadams	1828 Ballyadams
1876 Williamstown	1897 Williamstown

Ballyadams: Ballyadams Parish County Laois, Ireland
Williamstown: small town north of Harrisburg
Cass Twp.: Township near Pottsville
Adams Co.: County around Gettysburg
Shamokin: including Coal Township

5 more sons & 4 daughters

Michael Fitzpatrick
1855 Cass Twp.
1909 Shamokin

Mary Noel
1862 Adams Co.
1911 Shamokin

William Alex. Davenport
1884 Scranton
1971 Scranton

Elizabeth Mary Fitzpatrick
1883 Shamokin
1929 Binghamton

3 sons & 5 more daughters

Jessie-1911
Helen-1904
& 7 other children

certain is that John and Harriet arrived sometime before 1846, because their first child was born that year, and she is clearly claimed to have been born in Schuylkill County. This means they left Ireland either before or at the very start of the great potato famine, and at the very beginning of the period of peak Irish immigration.

The first place we find John and Harriet Fitzpatrick living in the New World is in Schuylkill County near the City of Pottsville,[1] specifically in Cass Township, and later in Minersville. Their first neighborhood in Pennsylvania is obviously the "patch village" of a colliery. That is, they were living in the cluster of shanties owned by the coal company. Nearly all their close neighbors were Irish immigrants with their Pennsylvania-born very young children. Men working in the coal mines had to attain a certain level of experience to qualify officially as "miners". A miner was essentially a team leader and had an assistant going down into the mine with him. The men and boys who went down in the mines to do the nearly equally backbreaking work of

---

1 The Pottsville area is known to many of us as where Yuengling Beer comes from, but it stands out for other reasons as well. Besides playing a key role in the development of the anthracite coal industry, it was also the hometown of the once famous author John O'Hara (1905-1970) and was the setting for many of his novels and short stories. His literary works tended to focus on the dark undercurrents of life, and many readers found them quite addictive. He was considered a controversial figure, apparently both for his conservative political views and his alcohol-fueled bad temper.

assisting the miner, are typically listed in the census as just "laborers". In the coal-mining jargon a miner's assistant was called his *butty*. A butty hoped to gain enough experience working with the miner to someday become a miner himself. As of the 1850 census, only a minority of their Irish neighbors had attained the title of miner. John and most of his neighbors were still listed as mine laborers, though that would not last.

Many of us living to the north might associate the anthracite region with northeastern Pennsylvania, specifically areas around Scranton, Wilkes-Barre, and Carbondale. What we are thinking of is just the northern end of the anthracite region. Anthracite mining began farther to the south, in a central eastern part of the state, within 100 miles of Philadelphia. Schuylkill County specifically was the center of many of the earliest collieries. For much of the history of Pennsylvania coal mining, most of the labor force, whether as miners or mine workers with other titles, was composed of immigrants. The countries of origin for the bulk of the immigrants changed over the decades, and there would later be periods when new recruits were Italian and Eastern European immigrants. In the early days, Welsh, English, and Irish immigrants made up the labor force, but the Welsh and English miners were given much more respect than the Irish at first, partly because they typically arrived in Pennsylvania as already experienced coal miners from their home countries, whereas the Irish typically did not. Thus, the Irish started out in a particularly lowly position. Add to this that many of them were illiterate and faced the general discrimination against Irish Catholics in the 19th Century, and it is easy to see they had a hard struggle in their first decades in America.

John was soon promoted to miner; and he, Harriet, and their rapidly growing family remained in the Pottsville area for about twenty years. Sometime around the Civil War, probably about 1864, the family moved about 25 miles west to a new settlement called Williamstown. This is a small borough in the same county as the state capital, and today is officially considered part of the Harrisburg metropolitan area. But due to the mountainous terrain and the odd shape of the county, it is even now a nearly one-hour drive from Harrisburg. It is effectively a remote little community onto itself, and at the time it had a growing economy with its own anthracite mines and other industries including hosiery mills. There is no reason I know of to believe that the war had a direct bearing on the decision to move, and it was most likely that the family was seeking greater job opportunities. John and Harriet had six sons and four daughters. My ancestor, Michael, born in 1855, was the fourth of the ten children and the second son. There is no record of any family member serving in the Union army during the war, and this is probably because no one was in the right age range. Being in his forties didn't necessarily preclude John from joining, but with such a large family to support, it wasn't likely. And even the eldest son, Richard, would have been only sixteen at the end of the war.

There is no evidence that suggests that the Fitzpatrick family was even involved with the allegedly militant radical group known as the Molly Maguires. The Mollies had been active for some time in Ireland in support of tenant farmers, but their greatest notoriety in Pennsylvania was for their alleged violence in the 1870s in some of the anthracite collieries of Schuylkill County. Since the Fitzpatrick family had moved to another county by then, it is highly improbable that they ever joined the Mollies.

Though the use of child labor was nearly universal in earlier centuries, historians claim that the use of boys in Pennsylvania coal mining did not become a major part of the industry until the late 1860s as part of a drive toward greater efficiency. Anthracite coal was typically extracted in large clumps with chunks of slate and other materials intermixed with the coal. The general term for the slate and other waste material was *culm.* In the earliest mines, the miners themselves and their butties were expected to break up the clumps and pick out most the culm while still in the mine, leaving the waste material in the mine and bringing only the cleaned coal to the surface. In the new approach, mine operators erected large structures above ground called *breakers*, where the large clumps were broken up mechanically, and the broken pieces were sent down several chutes. Rows of *breaker boys* as young as eight sat on planks over the chutes. Their job was to pick out the pieces of culm. They sat with their feet in the chute to control the flow of the coal, allowing it to slide down the chutes to more rows of boys below them picking the coal still cleaner. Strict *breaker bosses* enforced a rapid pace of the work, and typically the boys were not permitted to wear gloves based on the rationale that their sense of touch helped them better distinguish between the chunks of coal and the chunks of culm. Though this work was above ground, it was nearly as dangerous as going down in the mines. Interestingly, breaker boys eventually developed a reputation for fierce independence and standing up to authority, and as young as they were, they played a major role in the labor union movement.

Once the boys were about twelve, they were often sent down into the mines for some of the more basic tasks. As part of the intricate systems for maintaining the flow of fresh air down below, doors had to be installed across the tunnels at various strategic locations. Twelve-year-old boys called *nippers* were stationed at each of these doors to open and close them to permit the passing of the mule-drawn coal cars hauled along the rails. Boys a little older, if they were good at working with animals, might be ready to start their careers as mule drivers, starting out working just one mule at a time, and later graduating to working with multiple mules in tandem. They didn't use reins and had to control the mules solely with voice commands, so they had to have a good rapport with their animals. Some boys thought of the mules as their pets. A lamp was attached to the harness of the lead mule to light the way.

The nimblest boys might become *spraggers.* For stretches of track where the goal was to transport the coal cars to a lower level, the cars could be allowed to roll, letting gravity do the main work, but the spraggers' job was to prevent the cars from rolling too fast. They had the very athletic and quite dangerous job of running along beside the cars and shoving poles into the spokes of the wheels at just the right place to allow for sufficient braking. The whole time they were racing along beside the rolling cars, they had to avoid crashing into the tunnel walls or low ceilings and avoid crushing their fingers. It's amazing they didn't all end up maimed.

In their mid- to late-teens, boys could start working as butties, assisting the miners in a variety of ways, especially by loading the cars with the coal that the miner had extracted, largely by blasting with black powder. Finally, in their early twenties, after already having faced perhaps more than a decade of dangerous work and exposing their young lungs to coal dust, they might be ready to take on the role of miner. In the late 19th Century, boys in the patch villages, as small as their wages might be, were playing a significant role in supporting their large families. Life was also a struggle for the women and girls maintaining their households under the miserable conditions in the patches.

What we can see in the 1870 census and other records is particularly interesting and illustrative of the times. Forty-nine-year-old John was then a miner. Since he didn't own real estate, apparently the family was living in company-supplied housing in the "patch", with their $200-worth of worldly possessions. Forty-two-year-old Harriet was obviously working very hard to raise her family under these conditions. Daughter, Ann, at seventeen, was surely a great help to her mother, but Ann was soon to marry a mule-driver named John Punch, and they would have their first child the following year. Richard, at nineteen, along with (Jessie's grandfather) Michael, at fifteen, were laborers in the mines, and since they are shown as literate, they must have had the chance to attend school when they were small. Their younger brother, James, at the age of only twelve, was already a mule driver in the mines, and he is shown as illiterate. Was there some reason he didn't have the chance to attend school when he was small, or did he just resist all attempts at formal education? Fortunately, nine-year-old Thomas had not been sent to work in the breakers yet and was still attending school, along with his seven-year-old brother, John. Patrick and little Harriet, at ages five and three, respectively, were still at home. Eldest daughter, Elizabeth, then twenty-two, was no longer living with them. She had married twenty-eight-year-old Emmanuel Noel and their first child was one month old on the date the census was taken. Emmanuel was a younger brother of Aloysius, the father of the Mary Noel who would later marry Michael Fitzpatrick. Emmanuel had the important job of stable boss, managing the mule stable in one of the mines, and he and Elizabeth had a more prosperous life than the rest, living in their own $1750 home outside the patch. They owned $350-worth of personal possessions.

My ancestor, Michael Fitzpatrick, soon became licensed as a coal miner, and along with the rest of his family remained in Williamstown throughout the 1870s. I believe it was sometime in the second half of 1879 when he married Mary Noel. He would have been about twenty-four, and she about eighteen. We can speculate on how they met. Perhaps Mary traveled north from Adams County to visit with her Uncle Emmanuel as well as other uncles and cousins then living in Williamstown. A very plausible scenario is that she met Michael during a social event involving the in-laws of her Uncle Emmanuel. Michael and Mary lived in Williamstown for the next few years, and Michael continued working as a coal miner there. John (a common name in the family) seems to have been their first child, and he was born in June of 1880. Elizabeth Fitzpatrick (Jessie's mom) we believe was born in August of 1883, and she was the second child, or at least the second to reach adulthood. She had two younger brothers and five younger sisters.

Not being able to find records specifically relating to her birth, I am not sure whether Elizabeth was born in Williamstown or Shamokin, because it was sometime around 1883 that the young couple moved north. Shamokin is about twenty miles to the north of Williamstown as the crow flies, but nearly thirty on the winding roads through the intervening ridges.[2] It was then a thriving community not only due to the anthracite mines, but also because of the silk mills and thriving printing industry it would soon have. Two of Michael's younger brothers; James and John; also moved there at about the same time or perhaps a few years later. Their parents and their other siblings remained in Williamstown, and most were buried in the old Catholic cemetery there and later at Sacred Heart Cemetery after the original cemetery flooded. As far as I can tell, Mary was not joined in Shamokin by any of her Noel relatives. She might have returned to both Adams County and Williamstown to visit them from time to time.

The best assumption as to a reason for the move of these young Fitzpatricks was to seek better job opportunities. The record trail for the late 19th Century is not as complete as we would like it to be, partly due to the massive loss of 1890 census records in a 1921 fire in Washington, D.C. But it is nonetheless clear that before the dawn of the new century, the Fitzpatricks of Shamokin were attaining at least a moderately high level of prosperity and respect in the community. Michael, with his many years of mining experience, became a *fire boss*. This was an important position with responsibilities essentially akin to being the chief safety inspector for a mine. A fire boss got up very early and went down in the mine before the shift started to check for any safety concerns—pockets of carbon monoxide or flammable gases, potential cave-ins, etc. Michael's brother James was a successful grocer in Shamokin. He married a woman named Anna, a daughter of immigrants from England, in about 1882, but this couple remained childless. Another brother, John "Jock" Fitzpatrick was a coal miner. He married Mary Ann Conrey, a daughter of Irish immigrants, and they had four children.

Upper mobility continued into the next generation, which is to say Elizabeth, her siblings, her cousins, and their spouses. Some worked as miners or other respectable and quite well-paying blue-collar occupations. Many eventually owned nice houses in the Shamokin area. And quite a few entered professional roles. Not just Elizabeth, but also her brother Richard, became schoolteachers. Even if the requirements for becoming a teacher were different at that time, surely, they had far more education than was typical for those born in the 1880s and growing up in Shamokin. There is some indication that Richard became a school principal.[3] Incidentally, of Richard's sons (who were among Jessie's first cousins) two became well known priests; one became one of the most esteemed dentists in Harrisburg; and one entered what was then called the Pennsylvania Motor Police Force. Another Richard Fitzpatrick was Elizabeth's cousin, a son of John "Jock" Fitzpatrick. From a young age he entered the

---

2 Much of the time the family was located not in the Borough of Shamokin *per se*, but rather in the surrounding Coal Township. For the sake of simplicity let us refer to these collectively as Shamokin.

3 In her book, Helen mentions both of her mother's younger brothers becoming teachers, and one becoming a principal. Richard clearly did become a teacher, but all the records indicate that her other younger brother, James, made a career as a coal miner.

15

field of telegraphy. He started work as a telegraph operator for the railroads, and later became the same for a silk company based in Shamokin. He eventually rose to become an executive in that company. It is true that he fell on hard times during the depression, likely because the silk company went under, but it is an impressive career, nonetheless.

The point is that it would be a mistake to take a stereotypical view of Elizabeth's upbringing as that of a poor, humble daughter of a downtrodden Irish coal miner. By the year 1900, the Fitzpatricks of Shamokin were an upstanding Irish Catholic family, rightfully proud of the success and respect they enjoyed in the community. A large proportion of the Shamokin community was Catholic, and it seems clear that the Fitzpatricks were esteemed as faithful parishioners. The patriarch Michael's job as fire boss was a respected one in the area's most important industry. The family certainly is not of the wealthy class or owners of large companies, but they generally seem to be above average in prosperity by local standards. They owned their home. Elizabeth and some others in her family had much more than an average level of education for their time.

Clearly, the most significant influence on Jessie as a child and on her ways of thinking was her mother. To understand why Jessie looked at the world the way she did, it is necessary to understand Elizabeth as well. As I read and reread *Sister Helen's Stories*, it strikes me that one of Helen's main themes throughout the book is her mother's powerful sense of pride. Obviously, pride is not necessarily a bad thing, but Helen repeatedly frames it in such a way that she believed it sometimes made her mother her own worst enemy. Helen describes Elizabeth as often acting against her own best interests or even violating her own firmly held beliefs, for the sake of pride. On the other hand, what sometimes is interpreted as pride is better described as self-respect and self-confidence, and all the best people have those. There are many good sides to the way Elizabeth thought about the world and the way she brought up her children. On another point, Helen suggests that her mother had been raised in quite a privileged way, and that made it more of a challenge to adapt to married life and raise a large family without the benefit of domestic servants.

The record is confusing when trying to sort out the date of death of Michael Fitzpatrick. One challenge with this and some of the other details is that there were two Michael Fitzpatricks in Shamokin of nearly the same age; they were both married to women named Mary; and they both were buried in Saint Edward's Cemetery. However, there are clues that make it quite clear that my ancestor was not the Michael who passed away in 1920. The cemetery record that does point to the right person unfortunately must be pointing to the wrong date. It shows the year of death of the other Michael Fitzpatrick (the right one) as 1904. But since it also indicates an unmarked grave, it means that there is no gravestone to verify that they have that date correct, and it appears that the death certificate was lost. Our best bet then is to rely on what is implied by *Sister Helen's Stories*. Helen has many clear memories of spending time as a small child with her grandfather, a kind and gentle man who adored children. Since she was born in November of 1904, this makes a 1904 date for her grandfather's passing at least a few years too early. Later in the same chapter, when Helen describes the stabbing incident (which I will come back to later) she makes it clear that her grandfather was alive at the time, which would be June of 1909, and describes the shame of that incident as precipitating a decline in his health leading up to his death apparently a few months later. We do know that Michael's wife, Mary is shown to be a widow in April of 1910. Weighing all the evidence, I think the best assumption is that Michael Fitzpatrick died sometime in the second half of 1909. Concerning the death of Mary *Noel* Fitzpatrick, I do believe we can trust the date of February 2, 1911, found in the cemetery records, is indeed accurate.

This means that both of Jessie's maternal grandparents were gone before she was born. Helen, on the other hand, spent her earliest years living next door to them, and remembered them very fondly. She wrote of her grandfather as a proud Irishman, as a great storyteller, and as very loving and gentle. She also remembered spending much time with her kindly grandmother and her playmate Bernadette. Bernadette was an aunt to Helen, but only a few months older. Helen, and perhaps to some extent the other older siblings, must have benefited from the sense of connection grandparents can provide, but Jessie missed out on this. Another implication is that when we read in Jessie's narrative about Elizabeth sometimes taking trips by train to visit relatives back in Shamokin, these would be to see her siblings, but not her parents, since they were already gone.

The Davenports almost certainly had been in America for many generations by the time William was born, likely well back in colonial times. But we cannot yet trace them back very far with any degree of certainty. The earliest we can know for certain is that William's grandfather, Edward E. Davenport was born in 1836 in Sparta Township, Sussex County, New Jersey. Sussex is that county in the far northern corner of New Jersey that borders on both Pennsylvania and New York State near Port Jervis. Some of my other ancestors lived in this same tri-state area. It seems to be a region where many families lived for a generation or two as they moved in stages to the west. There were a surprisingly high number of people named Davenport living in the various townships of Sussex County at that time, but I can't determine specifically who Edward's parents were. It appears that these several Davenport families had settled there a generation or so before Edward was born, and that they came there from the mid-Hudson Valley. As is true of many other branches of my family tree, several were married to Dutch women and worshiped in Dutch Reformed churches. There is a good chance that Edward had a mix of English and Dutch ancestry and cultural heritage. We can only guess how many generations earlier they had arrived in the New World or specifically where they came from. One possible hint is that the surname Davenport is known to originate from a place name in the English county of Cheshire. Edward married Margaret Jane Smith, who was born March 10, 1838, also in Sussex County. The date of their marriage was almost certainly 1856 or early 1857. There is little we know about Margaret's background either except that her father was named Abraham, and she had a younger sister named Caroline.

Edward seems to have moved on his own in his mid-teens some distance to the south within New Jersey. The 1850 census shows a fourteen-year-old Edward

17

Davenport Connections

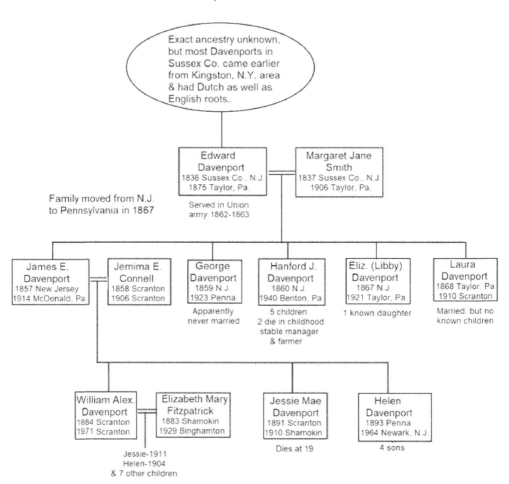

Exact ancestry unknown, but most Davenports in Sussex Co. came earlier from Kingston, N.Y. area & had Dutch as well as English roots.

Edward Davenport
1836 Sussex Co., N.J.
1875 Taylor, Pa.

Margaret Jane Smith
1837 Sussex Co., N.J.
1906 Taylor, Pa.

Family moved from N.J. to Pennsylvania in 1867

Served in Union army 1862-1863

James E. Davenport
1857 New Jersey
1914 McDonald, Pa.

Jemima E. Connell
1858 Scranton
1906 Scranton

George Davenport
1859 N.J.
1923 Penna.

Apparently never married

Hanford J. Davenport
1860 N.J.
1940 Benton, Pa.

5 children
2 die in childhood
stable manager
& farmer

Eliz. (Libby) Davenport
1867 N.J.
1921 Taylor, Pa.

1 known daughter

Laura Davenport
1868 Taylor, Pa.
1910 Scranton

Married, but no known children

William Alex. Davenport
1884 Scranton
1971 Scranton

Elizabeth Mary Fitzpatrick
1883 Shamokin
1929 Binghamton

Jessie Mae Davenport
1891 Scranton
1910 Shamokin

Dies at 19

Helen Davenport
1893 Penna.
1964 Newark, N.J.

4 sons

Jessie-1911
Helen-1904
& 7 other children

Davenport living with the Meeker family in Rockaway, New Jersey, apparently as a live-in hired farm hand. Perhaps he already was seeking opportunities in a part of the state that was a little more densely populated than Sussex County. It is possible he was an orphan, but this is not necessarily so since it was common then for boys to leave home and find work from an early age. He might have returned to Sussex County to marry Margaret, whom he perhaps knew from childhood. Shortly after marrying, the couple moved still further south since the best evidence is that their first child, James Edward Davenport (William's father), was born in New Brunswick, New Jersey on October 25, 1857. They must have moved back to Rockaway within the next year or so, since their next three children we know of; George (born 1859),

18

Hanford (1860), and Elizabeth (1867, often listed as Libby); were all born there. Edward may have been supporting his family as a farm laborer, but there is some hint that he was working in the Hibernia Iron Mines that were then very active in that part of New Jersey. It appears that, at least when they were young, the resources of this family were very limited.

During this time, at the age of twenty-six, Edward left his family behind for a time to serve in the Union Army. The 27th New Jersey Infantry Regiment was raised in Morris and Sussex Counties. Edward became a private in Company L, which was raised specifically in Rockaway. The regiment was mustered in on September 3, 1862, and trained in Newark before serving both in the eastern and the western theaters of the war. They fought in the Battle of Fredericksburg. In addition to their losses in combat and to disease, the regiment lost many men to drowning while attempting to ford the Cumberland River in Kentucky. They were recruited for a term of just nine months, but the regiment as a unit volunteered to remain in service for one extra month at the time Lee was preparing to invade Pennsylvania. Even at that, the timing was less than perfect since the regiment was mustered out on July 2, 1863. Some of the veterans of this unit later volunteered to join another regiment under the same colonel, but this did not include Edward who had to go back to supporting his family. There is no evidence, and it seems unlikely, that Edward Davenport joined the Union army as a substitute for a richer man. And records from long before the war show his surname had always been Davenport. It might be though that a recruitment bonus played a role in him joining the army. Thus, any family traditions about an Irishman ending up with the surname Davenport as a result of serving as a substitute in the war are definitely in error.

The family moved to Taylor, Pennsylvania in 1869, apparently with the desire to find opportunities in anthracite mining. Taylor is the suburb adjacent to southwestern Scranton. Laura, their youngest child was born there in December of that year. I haven't found records to verify this, but it seems likely Edward was working as a miner in Taylor during this period. We don't have the details, but he died in 1875, tragically just thirty-nine years old. It is easy to imagine it could have been due to either a disease or a mining accident. The widow Margaret would live on until September 10, 1906, when she died in Taylor at the age of sixty-nine, after suffering for some years from the heart disease, myocarditis. I have not found any record showing where Edward and Margaret are buried, perhaps at a cemetery in Taylor or possibly in Forest Hill Cemetery on the other side of Scranton in Dunmore. Several of their children would later be laid to rest there. The death of Edward at such a young age must have resulted in much hardship for the family, financially as well as in other ways. James as the eldest son was only eighteen, and though he surely had a job, it must have still been a struggle supporting the family after the loss of their father's wages.

I have found only limited information about the careers of James and his siblings during the period they were young adults, though there is some indication that they were moderately successful in the end. After his marriage into the Connell family, James may owe much of his eventual career as a mine foreman to nepotism. The best information we have on him shows that he was just a farm hand before he met his wife. I'll come back to him more after discussing the Connell family history. The third brother, Hanford, is cited later in life as a successful man. His main job is described as stable manager for the DL&W Railroad. Apparently, even a steam-powered railroad had some need for horses or mules. The sister Elizabeth (or Libby) must have received a good education and entered the teaching field, because we find out that at the end of her life, she was a school principal in Taylor. She died of breast cancer in 1921 at the age of only fifty-one. She had married a man named Thomas Jones, but at the time of her death she is listed as a widow, so Thomas presumably died at a still younger age. I have not yet found much on the careers of second brother, George, or second sister, Laura.

I have also not found much information about the faith traditions of the Davenport family. Some of the earlier Davenports found in Sussex County were baptized in the Dutch Reformed Church, especially those who had Dutch mothers. There is one vague reference that Libby Jones (née Davenport) was affiliated with a Presbyterian church in Scranton. Since James married a devout Methodist woman, it is likely that in the end he had at least some degree of connection with the Methodist church.

The background of the Connell branch is the most dramatic part of Jessie's family tree. Unfortunately, it is also the branch most confused by family traditions that are mistaken about several of the details. Although those traditions can serve as a useful starting place, we are obliged to reject the parts that are clearly contradicted by available documentary evidence. Chapter 1 of *Sister Helen's Stories* is one source we can use, and even if Helen is clearly off on several of the details, there are some general truths in her overall flow of the story. Helen starts the narrative with her "Great-Grandfather McGinnis" who "came from Ireland". She goes on to describe him and his wife, Elizabeth (née English), as the ones who were shipwrecked off the shores of Nova Scotia[4], but were able to save the famous heirloom violin. The great-grandfather she is referring to here was the man who appears in all available records as Thomas Connell. He was born June 14th, 1833, not in Ireland, but in the city of Sydney on Cape Breton Island, part of Nova Scotia. He is listed in most records as one of the four sons of James (1800-1883) and Susan (1802-1881, née Melville) Connell, but in some places, reference is made to him being the one and only adopted or foster child among the four Connell sons. Helen goes on to describe her great-grandfather being asked in 1860 to take the place of one of the rich Connell sons who was drafted into the army during the Civil War with the promise that should he die in the war, they would treat his wife and children as generously as if they were their own descendants, but we'll see that some of these details are certainly incorrect.

As for the Connells, we do have a pretty good idea of how they arrived in the New World. Though I have not found the primary sources myself, some have claimed that the father, James, was born in Aberdeen, Scotland in 1800. Presumably, at the age of twelve or thirteen and penniless, he ran away from home, supposedly mainly

---

4 Helen repeatedly referred to Newfoundland, but she must have meant Nova Scotia.

Connell Family Connections

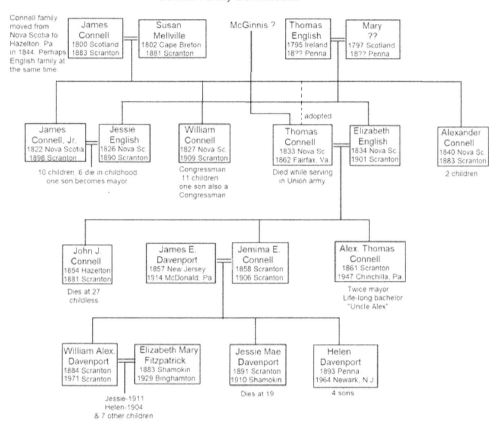

because of mistreatment by his stepmother. He signed on to a British merchant ship, and a few years later settled in what was then called the Cape Breton Colony[5] of British America, or as we now call it, Canada. James Connell eventually married Susan Melville, who was born there on Cape Breton Island, and they started raising a family. He apparently began working in the Cape Breton coal mines, which were under development at that time. In 1844, already an experienced miner, James moved with his family to Hazelton, Pennsylvania and eventually Scranton where he

---

5 In the same way that a few centuries earlier Plymouth Colony was not originally part of Massachusetts Bay Colony, and New Haven Colony was not originally part of Connecticut, Cape Breton Colony was for a time considered a separate entity from Nova Scotia before rejoining the same in 1820.

would be the patriarch of one of the most prestigious and wealthy families in the entire history of that city. His wife, Susan (née Melville), was born in 1802. In addition to their adopted son, Thomas (born 1833); their three biological sons; James (1822), William (1827), and Alexander (1840) were also born on Cape Breton Island.

The 1850 U.S. federal census is very useful in adding both verification and clarity to the story. In that year, we find the household of James and Susan Connell living in Hazelton. Fifty-year old James is shown as a miner born in Scotland and his wife, the forty-eight-year-old Susan, shows Nova Scotia as her birthplace. The offspring living with them, all born in Nova Scotia, are William, twenty-three, working as a miner, Thomas, seventeen, already also a miner, and ten-year-old Alexander. Unfortunately, unlike later censuses, the one in 1850 did not explicitly list household relationships (such as "head", "wife", "son", "daughter", "daughter-in-law", "boarder", "servant", etc.), but what is clear is that Thomas's surname is listed as Connell. Thus, assuming that it is true that he was adopted, the adoption was clearly long before the Civil War, and very likely back in Nova Scotia. He was already definitely considered a son. (Eldest son, James Connell, Jr., is not listed with them because he was married in 1846, and he and his wife had their own household.)

Thus, we have well documented facts that contradict several aspects of the family tradition, but other aspects of the legend still are probably true. We know for certain that a Stradivarius violin was passed down in the family, because we have records of it being sold (with deep regrets) in 1957 by William Davenport late in his life to cover medical expenses. The story about a shipwreck off the coast of Nova Scotia and of ancestors managing to rescue the violin along with themselves is not the sort of tale that would have been made up out of whole cloth. Also, even though no one, as far as I know, has ever found a single document linking Thomas to the name McGinnis, it is the sort of detail that would not come out of thin air.

I think the most reasonable interpretation would go something like the following. The family tradition as recorded by Helen, once again, has some aspects of the story right, but is off by a generation or two and on some of the other particulars. (The parts about the violin and the shipwreck are particularly confused, but since they are not a core part of the story anyway, we won't focus on them here.[6]) Even if we cannot find documentation to prove it, it is plausible or even probable that he began life with the name Thomas McGinnis, or at least some surname similar to McGinnis. After all, early sources do seem to make it quite clear he was adopted, and the family memory of the McGinnis name must come from somewhere. But at the same time, the legend must

---

6 It is most likely that Helen's description is off target by two generations, and even the way William described the story to the reporter for the Scranton newspaper, *The Tribune*, in 1957 must have been off by one generation. The indirect ancestor who supposedly bought the violin during a tour of the Continent from his home in Ulster could not have been a brother of Elizabeth (née English) as Helen describes, nor even Elizabeth's uncle as William describes. He was most likely a great-uncle to hers. The couple who saved the violin in the 1802 shipwreck could not have been Thomas and Elizabeth (born 1834), nor even Elizabeth's parents (Thomas and Mary English, small children at the time), but most likely were Elizabeth's paternal grandparents (given names unknown to me at this time).

be off target in suggesting that he had come from Nova Scotia all on his own, and that he met the Connell family only at the start of the Civil War. We know for certain he was adopted as a Connell long before the war, and he likely moved from Nova Scotia to Pennsylvania as already a part of the Connell family. Most likely his parents died of disease when Thomas was still a small child, and the Connells adopted him as a young orphan. It is possible that the part of the family tradition about him serving in the place of another Connell might still have some small element of truth. He may have volunteered, possibly out of gratitude for his adoption, to serve in the place of a brother. But it is more likely that the entire story about Thomas serving as a substitute is mistaken. Perhaps the legend as passed down in the family comes from conflating his army recruitment with that of Aloysius Noel, who really did serve as a substitute for a draftee. Thomas Connell's military record seems to indicate that he enlisted simply as a volunteer, not as a substitute.

In any case, Thomas did indeed already have a family by the time the war started. Elizabeth English was born in 1834 in Bridgeport, a small town also on Cape Breton Island (again, clearly not in Ireland). But Thomas and Elizabeth were married, not while they still both lived in Nova Scotia, but rather in Hazelton, Pennsylvania on March 10th, 1854. Their first child, John, was born July 25th of the same year in Hazelton. (As we all know, gestation periods were much shorter in those days.[7]) William Davenport's mother, Jemima Elizabeth (sometimes written as Elizabeth Jemima) was their second child. She was born in Minooka, now a neighborhood in Scranton, on August 27th, 1858. Their third child, Alexander, was born in Scranton shortly after the start of the war on June 12th, 1861.

Now, here is where it all gets even more interesting if we go back to the 1850 census record and study it more carefully. There are two people with surnames other than Connell listed as living in the James and Susan Connell household. One is a thirty-year-old miner from Ireland, named Isaac Smith, and we can assume he was just a boarder at the time and has little to do with our story. But the other is Elizabeth English, who would have been about sixteen and is listed as born in Nova Scotia.[8] Surely this is the woman Thomas would marry four years later and have a child with a few months after that. Since the 1850 census lacked a household relationship column, we must guess as to how the family thought of her role as part of their household. Could they have considered her a hired servant? They might have been thinking of her as living with them as an in-law. As already mentioned, the eldest son, James, Jr. had married back in 1846. The name of the woman he married was Jessie MacGregor English, born on Cape Breton in 1826. Undoubtedly, she was an older sister of this Elizabeth. Complicating matters a little bit more, living next door to the Connell, Sr. family were an Irish-born fifty-five-year-old miner named Thomas English with his Scottish-born fifty-three-year-old wife, Mary, and their eleven-year-old Nova-

---

7 OK. Old genealogy joke.

8 Her age is listed in this census as 18, which must be a mistake, because everywhere else her age is listed in ways consistent with an 1834 birth.

Scotia-born daughter, also named Mary. We can assume these are the parents and baby sister of both Jessie and Elizabeth English. Even knowing that she was an in-law, we can only speculate what the exact reason is that sixteen-year-old Elizabeth is staying at the Connell house rather than with her parents next door. Perhaps she is helping Susan in the busy household, or perhaps her parents' living quarters are extra cramped and the Connells have a little more space in their house.

Incidentally, based on their surnames and the pattern of intermarriages, it seems clear that the various people listed here as born in Ireland were Ulster-born British-Irish Protestants, what in America are often called the "Scots-Irish" or "Scotch-Irish", and the British typically call "Ulster-Scots".[9] This is considered by most people to be a distinct ethnic group from the mostly Catholic indigenous Irish. This might even apply to the name McGinnis. Though that spelling is originally of Irish origins, it is believed that in some families now writing their name that way, this is a spelling modification over the generations from the Scottish name McInnis. Indeed, immigration records for Nova Scotia show several families named McInnis arriving in the early 19th Century. It is reasonable to assume that Thomas could have been the orphaned child of one of those McInnis families.

Thomas Connell served as a private in Company B of the 48th Pennsylvania Infantry. This is known to be a regiment raised in Schuylkill County, and indeed the record does show him enrolling at Pottsville, even though it also identifies his place of residence at the time as Scranton. We can only guess what reason he had for traveling across a few counties to enlist in a town seventy miles away. Perhaps the 58th was a regiment that offered a particularly good sign-on bonus. He was twenty-seven years old when he enlisted in September 1861. The record lists Thomas's occupation at the time of enlistment as engineer, as is also shown in an earlier record. This might be interpreted in multiple ways, but my guess would be that he was operating steam engines used in the operations of the mines, or possibly railroad locomotives. A generation later, several members of the Connell clan would be attaining advanced educational levels and becoming physicians, teachers, bankers, lawyers, judges, and politicians, as well as mine owners and mining engineers in the modern sense. But in Thomas's case, I suspect "engineer" is used here in the old sense to mean steam engine operator. Thomas was of light complexion, 5'8" tall, and had dark hair and grey eyes. Unlike the regiments with terms of a year or less, the 48th Pennsylvania served until the end of the war. However, Thomas would die within a year. Military historians tell us that during the Civil War, far more troops died of disease than were killed in combat. Thomas died in a Union army camp in Fairfax, Virginia on August 21st, 1862. His cause of death is listed quite unpoetically as "chronic diarrhea", which seems to me to be stating more a symptom than a cause.

Though the place of the Connell family was rising rapidly in Scranton society at the time of Thomas's (Nova-Scotia-born) brothers, it was in the next (Pennsylvania-born) generation that the family rose to its greatest prominence. They would become highly educated for their time; hold prestigious professions; own and operate some of

9 See the several books listed in the Scots-Irish section of the bibliography, especially *The Scotch-Irish: A Social History*, by James G. Leyburn.

the major local companies and banks; hold high political office; and play major roles in local society and philanthropy. I have not yet made a complete study of Connell family history, but already it seems overwhelming. In the economic realm, they owned, operated, and served on the boards of multiple mining and railroad companies and banks. They also founded and owned a variety of manufacturing companies making products as diverse as buttons and blasting powder. The button company was one of the largest in the world. They controlled insurance companies, at least one newspaper, and a textbook-publishing firm. They owned prosperous retail firms such as jewelers and furniture stores. There were two Connells who represented northeastern Pennsylvania in the US Congress; and two more who became mayors of Scranton, each for two terms. Connells also held a variety of other political offices. Some played a role in endowing churches and educational institutions. In terms of politics, they were Republicans, and in terms of faith, they were predominantly Methodists, but also with a few Presbyterians.[10]

The Connell family was both fortunate and unfortunate at the same time. Overall, they were wealthy by the end of the 19th Century. Some of the educational institutions they attended were prestigious and expensive, such as University of Pennsylvania and very exclusive boarding schools that charged much more in tuition and fees than the average person made in wages. The Connells lived in some of the finest homes in the city, and I have found more than one example of a Connell family with three live-in Irish servants, which seems like plenty for homes with only two or three children.

But in those days, wealthy families were apparently just about as likely as poor families to lose children and young adult members to disease—tuberculosis, scarlet fever, typhoid, heart disease, and so on. The Connells were particularly unfortunate in this regard, losing a number of children that was disproportionally high even for the times. For example, James Connell Jr. and his wife Jessie, lost six out of their ten children to disease before the age of 20. In the next generation, their son William Lawrence Connell Sr. was one of the four to survive. He would become a mayor of Scranton, but he lost one out of the three children he had with his first wife. He also lost her. When she died, he married her sister, and three out of the four children they had also died in childhood. This is overwhelmingly tragic to the point of being horrifying. These might be the worst cases, but there were many losses in other branches of the Connell family too. And even among the Connells who survived to adulthood, too many died as young adults. I don't know what the explanation is for one extended family facing so much heartbreak. It makes me wonder. Could William Davenport's angry and volatile attitudes toward life have been influenced by a fatalistic awareness that death was so likely to come early in his family?

It does appear that the Connell extended family provided Thomas and Elizabeth's three children with similar chances to succeed in life to what their many

---

10 Although most Scots-Irish arrived in North America as Presbyterians, some of the histories of this ethnic group indicate that it was a common pattern for them to shift over to the Methodist or Baptist denominations a generation or two later.

cousins had. (On the other hand, early on they may not have lived as wealthy a lifestyle as the rest.) The widowed Elizabeth never remarried, and we can assume that until her death in January of 1901, she continued to play a role in the Connell family at large. It may have helped that her sister was married to the eldest of the other Connell brothers.

John J. Connell, born in 1854, was the first child of Thomas and Elizabeth. In at least one place, his occupation is listed as engineer, and since he is soon after listed as the superintendent of one of the anthracite mines owned by the Connells, I assume he had received some formal education as a mining engineer. Sadly, John was to die of typhoid fever at the age of twenty-seven, two days after Christmas in 1881.[11] His death certificate indicates he was then Superintendent of Mines for the "Connell Mines Meadow Brook". There is still a location, apparently long abandoned, labeled on some Scranton city maps as the "Meadow Brook shaft" in a southern part of the city. Surely that is the location of a colliery John once managed. The death certificate shows him as married, which must mean a recent marriage since he was still single eighteen months earlier. Unless more records turn up somehow, we might never know anything about his bride. It is unlikely they had any children. Interestingly, the doctor who signed the death certificates was Alexander James Connell, M.D, one of John's first cousins. One of the reasons it is extra sad that John died so young is that young William Davenport might have benefited from having two prominent maternal uncles to guide and help him in his youth rather than just one.

William's mother (our Jessie's grandmother) was the second child of Thomas and Elizabeth Connell. Jemima E. Connell was born in Minooka in 1858, and except when her husband was working in Shamokin, she apparently spent her whole life in Scranton.[12] Jemima's father left for the army just after her third birthday, so perhaps she had vague memories of him. I have found only limited information about her life before she married, but we do know she was a schoolteacher and must have had a quite good education for her time. She was about twenty-four when she married James Davenport sometime in 1882. I'll write more later about what little we know about their family life, but just to mention the main points, their three children; William, Jessie, and Helen (this Jessie and Helen being aunts of the Jessie and Helen whose memoirs we have) were born in 1884, 1891, and 1893, respectively. Jemima died in

---

11 I remember my grandmother once talking to me about how it is extra sad for a family when a member dies during Christmas time. I wonder now about her family being particularly conscious of this because it happened quite often in the family history.

12 Helen, in her book, refers to her paternal grandmother in some places as Elizabeth rather than Jemima. That part is not an error. Although most records list her name as Jemima Elizabeth, a few records list the names in the other order. But since Jemima is most often represented as the first name, and at the end of her life she is always called Jemima (or "Gemima") I will stick with that. It is less confusing that way anyway since there are so many other Elizabeths in our history. Helen is definitely incorrect though on some of the other particulars. She refers to her grandmother being a small child when she was adopted into the Connell family. We have seen already that, if anyone, it was Jemima's father, Thomas, who was adopted as a small child into the family and was listed under the Connell name for decades before Jemima was born.

Scranton on March 26th, 1906, at the age of only forty-seven after suffering for about two years of consumption (tuberculosis). We can imagine that as sad as her funeral must have been, it was also a truly major affair with a large presence of both the Connell extended family and the Elm Park Methodist Episcopal Church. The family had a long connection to that church, and Jemima was an active member. At least four of the pallbearers were her Connell first cousins, including one who was a former mayor. The funeral was officiated by the Rev. Dr. George Clarke Peck who was apparently a grandson of Rev. George Peck, the famous Methodist circuit-riding preacher of the early 19th Century. Yes, the Connells were very, very Methodist.

The third child of Thomas and Elizabeth was the Honorable Alexander Thomas Connell, born in 1861. He is a man who lived a fascinating life and was the uncle who played a major role (though perhaps not major enough) in the life of Jessie's father, William. I hope to get the chance to research more details of his remarkable life than what I have learned so far. Since the 1880 census shows the eighteen-year-old Alex at school, and since his two elder siblings held professional jobs, we can be confident that the Connells ensured that he had the opportunity of an advanced level of education for the times. Alex was coming of age at a time when his uncles and cousins were becoming major players in the industries and politics of northeastern Pennsylvania, but that didn't necessarily mean he would start at the top. It is believed that one of his first adult jobs was as a bookkeeper for a local steel company, which must have been connected to the Connell family in one way or another; and I suspect he held a variety of similar positions during the 1880s and early 1890s. It might have been during this time that he started a company to manufacture blasting powder for use in the mining industry. His relatives owned coal mines, but it was gold that Alexander became most interested in mining. It must have been about 1897 as a man in his mid-thirties that he caught gold fever and ran off to join the Klondike gold rush. Like most participants, he bore many hardships there and never struck it rich. He returned to Scranton still full of energy, got into politics, and won two terms in the Pennsylvania State Legislature, before winning his first term as Scranton mayor from 1903 to 1906. His second term as mayor was from 1918 to 1922. I do not yet know all that he did in the twelve years between the two terms, but apparently, he failed in his run for Lackawanna County Sheriff at some point during this time. He may have been running his blasting powder company and attending to other of his business interests. Alex was in his late fifties during his second term, older than most mayors. He joked about himself as "the old grey mayor".

I may be mistaken, but my impression is that Alex Connell was an unusually idealistic politician, serving well the best interests of his constituents. He oversaw the construction of the largest sewer system project in Scranton history and several other public works. He fought for better schools. Despite being from a family of coal-mine industrialists, he fought hard against the coal companies to prevent cave-ins in the city. His second term coincided with the catastrophic Spanish flu pandemic, and the mayor seems to have served his city well in coordinating healthcare in the crisis. Alexander lived on for another quarter century after his second term as mayor. I guess that once a person catches gold fever, it never goes away. In 1931, at the age of seventy, Alex

27

moved to Colorado to oversee the development of a gold mine there. I don't yet know how successful that attempt was. Alexander died in 1947 at the age of eighty-six at the home of friends in a village called Chinchilla in the Scranton suburbs.

I don't know why Alex T. Connell never married. Some men are too full of energy, idealism, and sense of adventure ever to settle down to family life, and I would like to think his is that kind of case. William, as his only nephew and Helen (the one born in 1893) as his only surviving niece, were the closest he had to surviving direct descendants and potential heirs. But knowing those two to be quite rebellious and wild youths, he must have hesitated to endow them too readily financially. He was also obviously such a busy man that he did not have the opportunity to spend as much time with them and their families as he might have liked.

I wish we had more of a documented historical record of the early years of the James and Jemima Davenport family, especially as relates to the childhood and youth of their son, my Great-grandfather William. Unfortunately, the last two decades of the 19th Century are difficult to trace, partly due to the loss of the 1890 census, and partly because fewer documents of other types survive from this period than would be true in some other periods. We can hope that we won't be too far wrong in relying on a combination of family tradition and what we can deduce or infer from the records we do have.

James and Jemima married about 1882. Leading up to that time, Jemima had been teaching school and was living on Breck Street in Scranton with her widowed mother and her two brothers. The last record I can see for James leading up to that time shows him a live-in farm hand with a family in Newton Township some miles west of Scranton. It is certainly true that James was "marrying up". The Davenport family was not really living in poverty up to then, but they were certainly nothing close to wealthy either. And they did not hold positions of high prestige. His fortunes rose after he married, but as far as I can tell, James was never given a job as superintendent of an entire colliery as is sometimes stated. For sure though he did hold some relatively cushy positions a little lower than that in the Connell coal-mining business, surely due to his status as an in-law. He apparently was at some points running the company stores at various collieries and later was a foreman in one or more of the Connell mines. As foreman, James would have reported to the superintendent of the mine. Since the miners not only supplied their own tools and supplies but were accustomed to working in isolated locations in the chambers, they thought of themselves as almost independent contractors and did not take well to day-to-day meddling in their work. So, unlike a foreman in a factory who would be busy overseeing every aspect of production, a mine foreman had an easygoing sort of job, mainly just going around the chambers every few days and checking in with the miners. At some points, James's job is described as outside foreman or outside supervisor, which means he oversaw the above-ground operations of the colliery including the breaker, the hoists, the culm banks, etc.

Helen's book suggests that the family was living together with Jemima's mother. That possibly could have been true at some points in the marriage, but it does not seem to be the general pattern. The widowed mother Elizabeth Connell was living in Scranton with her bachelor son, Alexander, at most times during this period, and the family of James and Jemima were living near whatever Connell colliery James was working at the time. At least for some periods, that was as far away as Shamokin.

I believe Helen is generally correct when she suggests that her father, William, was pampered and spoiled as a small child, and this contributed to his attitudes and temperament as an adult. For his first seven years, William was the only child of James and Jemima, the only grandchild of Elizabeth, and the only nephew of his bachelor Uncle Alex. Even after his two sisters were born, he might still have been treated special as the only boy. We don't have any hard documentation relating to William's schooling, but I suspect Helen does describe it quite accurately. As she presents it, Uncle Alex was willing to finance an elite education for William. After being kicked out of multiple private schools for pranks and general misbehavior, William was sent to Valley Forge Military Academy with hopes that the stricter discipline would do him good, but he managed to get kicked out of even there. Jessie mentions thinking that her father was still going to college when he met her mother. It seems doubtful that he went to any place officially called a college, but perhaps he may have been getting some advanced technical training at some point in what was to be his career with steam power. I also don't know of any solid evidence to back up the story that he ran away to Chicago, became a bellhop there, and dropped a trunk on his toe. But we can probably believe it is essentially true since it is the sort of story a child might have heard told many times about a parent's earlier life and therefore would remember accurately. We do know that according to the 1900 census, sixteen-year-old William was still in school and was living with his parents and two younger sisters near Shamokin. I don't know if the interlude in Chicago would have come before or after that.

We know that most of William's working career, from about 1910 on, was with the Delaware, Lackawanna, & Western Railroad, but clearly, he had been working for several years prior to taking that job. The best information we have on his early career comes from the set of recommendation letters that he presented when he applied to the DL&W RR and are still there in his personnel file. Since we believe he and Elizabeth married in 1903, his pre-railroad career would probably include a few years of his working life while he was still a bachelor as well as the first several years of their married life. Apparently for all this time he was living and working in Shamokin. Based on the recommendations, we know that for some of those years, William was working as a steam-shovel operator and at other times operated the stationary steam engine powering the breaker in the Connell colliery at Shamokin. During that time, he seems to have reported to his own father, which would make sense since James Davenport's occupation is stated about that time as outside foreman. There are also references to him working for some time as a brakeman on the electric hoist for another mining company as well as working for a well-drilling company. Clearly, for his entire career, William's stock in trade was his mechanical ability, and in the era when his career began, this typically meant steam power. Notwithstanding the various negative traits, we might assign to him for other aspects of his character, a fair evaluation of the evidence would indicate that he was always a hard worker, took his work seriously, and had a high degree of technical skill.

Obviously, there were several key events in the family life during the first decade of the century. A few years after the 1903 wedding of Elizabeth and William, William's mother would die in March of 1906, and I already mentioned the grand funeral the Connell family had for her at that time. This would be another grandparent that Jessie was born too late to know. Even Helen would have been under eighteen months and probably had no real memory of her Grandmother Jemima. The widower James Davenport would go on living with his two daughters at the home they were renting at 906 North Orange Street in Shamokin and working as a foreman in the Connell-owned Shamokin mine until at least 1910.

As far as we know, in the time up to his marriage, William was living with his parents and two sisters in Shamokin,[13] and presumably Elizabeth was similarly living with her family in nearby Coal Township. From Helen's book, we know that up until their move to Scranton in 1910 or 1911, William, Elizabeth, and their first four children were living in a small cottage next door to a larger house belonging to Elizabeth's parents. Apparently, this was always a difficult arrangement for William, since Helen suggests that from the start, he was quite unpopular with his in-laws. He must have thought often that he would have preferred to live elsewhere, but it was a convenient arrangement for Elizabeth. She was in familiar surroundings and able to visit, perhaps daily, with her parents and siblings. Helen also emphasizes that since her mother had been raised in a way that she hadn't learned much about cooking or other homemaking skills, living next door to her mother was very helpful when she needed practical advice.

The notorious stabbing incident happened at that cottage in 1909. Helen was about four and a half at the time, which was apparently old enough to have a vivid memory of what happened. Her account of this episode in her book is well written and completely consistent with the stories in the newspapers at the time. Just to repeat the main points here, the problem was with Elizabeth's only older sibling, John Francis Fitzpatrick. He was apparently the black sheep of this respected family. John is described as not only generally ornery, but also as a mean-spirited drunk. One evening in June, William was working late, and Elizabeth had spent much of the evening at her parents' house along with her first three children, all toddlers at the time. And she would have been six-months pregnant with Marge at the time. At about ten PM, she took the children back across the yard to their cottage. Shortly thereafter, while she was putting the children to bed, John showed up at the cottage very drunk, let himself in, and became verbally abusive toward his sister. Several minutes later, William returned home from work, and naturally the two brothers-in-law exchanged words. John refused to leave the house. William grappled with him and managed to push him out as far as the front porch. While the two men continued their struggle out there, John pulled a knife and stabbed William both in the abdomen and the chest,

---

13 If Helen is correct that her Grandfather Davenport moved the family to Scranton about the time William planned to marry, it must have been only a temporary move. There are records showing clearly that he and his daughters were living in Shamokin as late as 1909 and 1910.

30

once barely missing his heart. Witnessing this violence was obviously traumatic for the children. When the authorities arrived, William was rushed to the hospital and John was carted off to jail. If William had ended up dying of his wounds, certainly John would have been charged with homicide. Obviously, William did recover, but it took a while.

The way Helen describes the upshot of this incident is quite ironic, and this is probably based primarily on how she heard her parents describe the outcomes when she was a little older. Apparently, even though William was not at fault and even though he graciously refused to press charges, the result was that he became even less popular with his in-laws. Remember that the Fitzpatrick family was rightfully proud of their status in the Shamokin community as upstanding and moderately prosperous citizens. They were very ashamed to have a son/brother/nephew who had committed a vicious stabbing and was sent to jail. And Helen informs us that, as unfair as this was, they blamed William for this circumstance. It must have been a very difficult situation for Elizabeth as well. As discussed above, Elizabeth's father, Michael, probably died in about the second half of 1909. Helen also explains that her grandfather's declining health leading to a stroke he suffered at the mine and his subsequent death was perceived to be brought on by the shock and disgrace of having a son sent to jail. And this was even more reason for the rest of the Fitzpatrick family to resent William. One more reasonable assumption Helen makes is that her Grandmother Fitzpatrick's decline and eventually death in early 1911 were due to the incident itself as well as the loss of her husband. By about 1910 it must have been an obvious decision for William and Elizabeth to make plans for moving their young family elsewhere. William's position with the Fitzpatrick family in Shamokin must have seemed by then untenable, and it couldn't have been comfortable for Elizabeth either. Probably William wished they had moved to Scranton much earlier.

Of course, life was also going on for William's family of origin, which after his mother's death in 1906 means just his father, James Davenport, and two young sisters. We know from *Sister Helen's Stories* that young Helen did have some opportunities to get to know her Grandfather Davenport. She never lived next door to him, so the time they spent together was much more limited than the interactions she had with her maternal grandparents, but the impressions she had of him were almost equally positive. She describes him more than anything else as a charming man, and he apparently directed much of this charm toward his little granddaughter.

Four years after Jemima's death, more tragedy came to the Davenport home. In January of 1910, Jessie, the older of the two daughters, died of tuberculosis just days after her 19th birthday in her father's home on Orange Street in Shamokin. She had been suffering from that disease for about a year. She had been working at the cigar stand in the rather fancy Hotel Graemer in Shamokin, and possibly she was still going to school as well. My grandmother was born about a year and a half after this tragic early death, and although there were several other women in the family tree named Jessie, I believe she was named after this recently deceased young aunt of hers.

Helen writes of her charming paternal grandfather's departure "for parts unknown". This was after Jessie's death, probably not too long after, sometime in late

1910 or in 1911. The parts unknown turns out to be a small Pennsylvania town named McDonald to the southwest of Pittsburgh. I am not sure what kind of work James was doing there over the next few years, but I have found that he married as his second wife a woman named Mary Foringer. She was about thirty-nine years old at the time. After James died in January of 1914, Mary would be the "young, comely woman" Helen describes in her book who brought his casket back to Scranton to the house on South Hyde Park Avenue before his burial in Forest Hill Cemetery in Dunmore. Even though they had been married just a few years and Mary was still quite young, she never remarried. She went back and lived out the rest of her life as a widow in McDonald until she died at the age of seventy-eight in January of 1950.

I am not sure what the exact motivation was for James Davenport, then in his mid-fifties, to move away to a distant part of the state. Perhaps it had something to do with the grief of losing a daughter a few years after losing his first wife, or perhaps he had already somehow met the woman who would be his second wife. In her book, his granddaughter, Helen, implies that it was a sort of abandonment of his family, and maybe it would be fair to some degree to think of it like that. But he was not abandoning small children. His only son was already well into adulthood and raising his own family, and his only surviving daughter was approaching adulthood. (In an attempt to avoid confusion here, I will distinguish these two Helens by using their birth years as suffixes. Thus, Helen-1893 means the sister of William, and Helen-1904 means the daughter of William and Elizabeth and the author of *Sister Helen's Stories*.) Helen-1904 seems to be remembering her Aunt Helen-1893 as a few years younger than she actually was at the time. Helen-1893 would have been about seventeen by the time her father moved away, not abandonment of a young child in any case.

I do assume Helen-1904 is correct on some of the other points though. Apparently, the extended family assumed that the best plan would be for Helen-1893 to move in with the family of William and Elizabeth shortly after they moved to Scranton. Since William was working at a job that took him away from home for days at a time, this meant twenty-seven-year-old Elizabeth, almost on her own, and with four small children to raise and a fifth child on the way, was expected to care for and supervise her seventeen-year-old sister-in-law as well. Even under the best of circumstances this would not have been the ideal arrangement. If, as we see from *Sister Helen's Stories,* Helen was a carefree, self-centered adolescent, and Elizabeth was a woman of strict moral standards, it seems that the circumstances were downright unsustainable. Keep in mind that the two sisters-in-law did not even come from the same religious backgrounds. Elizabeth was a strong Catholic and Helen was raised as a Methodist. It could be that the trauma of losing both her mother and her only sister led Helen to act out even more than she otherwise would have. It must have been very difficult for the two of them even to try to get along. We also read in *Sister Helen's Stories* that Helen-1893 kept all to herself the generous allowance her Uncle Alex made for her rather than sharing it with Elizabeth as part of her room and board in the Davenport household.

Undoubtedly, Helen-1893 did indeed meet her future husband, Frederic Janes, while she was staying at William and Elizabeth's home in Scranton. Helen-1904 does not seem to be correct though in stating that her aunt was already four-months pregnant when she married Fred. The marriage record shows that the marriage was in September of 1912, and the first of their children was not born until April of 1914, so unless there was a miscarriage, the shotgun marriage scenario must be in error. Fred and Helen Janes eventually had four sons. They continued living in the Scranton area over the next few decades and had a variety of interactions with William and Elizabeth's family, as discussed by the writings of both Helen-1904 and Jessie-1911. The Janes family, including their adult sons, moved to Newark, New Jersey sometime around World War II, and Helen-1893 died there in 1964, followed by Fred in 1972. Helen and Fred are buried back in Scranton though, at the Washburn Street Cemetery.

Well then, having gone through so much detail on family history starting in the early 19th Century and leading up to about the time of Jessie's birth, how might it all relate to Jessie's life and how she represented her childhood in her writing? I suppose that for most people, our extended families and our family backgrounds influence us both directly and indirectly. What I mean here by direct influence is what we learn by spending time with our grandparents, uncles, aunts, cousins, and other relatives. Indirect influences, on the other hand, are the family traditions, habits, mindsets, cultural patterns, religious beliefs, moral principles, etc. that are passed down to us through our parents and other authority figures within the family.

When it comes to extended family, it strikes me that the direct influences on Jessie were relatively limited. Unlike Helen, Jessie was too young to meet any of her grandparents. On the Fitzpatrick side, Jessie and her siblings had several aunts and uncles, and many cousins. But in most cases, Jessie seems to have had few chances to spend time with them. Most of the Fitzpatrick relatives were living quite far away in Shamokin. We learn that Elizabeth was in the habit of going back to Shamokin quite often to visit her siblings, in-laws, nieces, and nephews, but it seems that Jessie went along on these trips only on rare occasions. Jessie does write of one time when her Aunt Hattie (Elizabeth's sister, Harriet), Uncle John (Harriet's husband, John Neibauer), and just one of their several children (Cousin Joe) visited her family in Dalton, but it doesn't seem as though visits *from* Shamokin relatives were very frequent either. The cousin Jessie writes most about is the dreaded Agnes, and the sense of antagonism is so strong there that it is doubtful that anything good came from that connection.

On Jessie's father's side, Jessie's only surviving close relative was her Aunt Helen-1893. We do know, from what both Jessie and Helen-1904 wrote, that their father's baby sister did indeed play a significant role in their lives, but they generally look on that role as negative. Based on what we know from what Helen-1904 wrote about the troubled, self-centered teenager Helen-1893, and how many problems this created for Elizabeth, the daughters already thought ill of their aunt out of sympathy toward their mother. After Helen-1893 married, she and her husband, Fred, seem to have lived in the same neighborhood as the Davenport household for most of the Scranton years. Jessie wrote that when her parents were experiencing their most extreme marital strife, they sometimes separated, and her father lived with Helen and Fred during these periods. To be fair, a few positive points come out too. Jessie seemed to admire the skill of her Aunt Helen playing the piano for the silent movies. She also was grateful that Fred went to the trouble of sending the family crockery with minor defects when he was working in the ceramics shop. But overall, we get the sense that Helen-1893 was not a positive influence. We also read nothing about her four sons, the only first cousins Jessie and her siblings had on their father's side. Among the more distant relatives, the influential Uncle Alex and the wealthy distant Cousin Jessie reached out helping hands at times, but they seem generally to be hands that stayed in the distance. We don't read much about spending time with the distant relatives.

Familial relationships are a relative thing, so I might be overthinking this, but from my perspective, I would summarize Jessie's family life by saying that she had a tight and extra-large inner family circle combined with a very limited and somewhat negative outer family circle. Having eight siblings makes for a large nuclear family, especially by current standards. And it is obviously clear in Jessie's mind that she has an enormous collection of shared experiences with her brothers and sisters as well as with her parents. But outside that inner circle of the immediate family, I am struck by how much less fortunate she was than I. My childhood was rich with time I could spend with all my grandparents and some of my great-grandparents. Of my thirty-four first cousins, I had a bond with all the ones close to me in age and at least a nodding acquaintance with the rest. I knew all my aunts and uncles. When I was growing up, on some branches of my family, I knew several of my great-uncles, great-aunts, and a few of my second and even third cousins. I wonder if Jessie's experiences of extended family had been more like mine, perhaps she would have felt more secure and confident of her place in the world. On the other hand, she might have felt her life was richer for having had more siblings than most people do to share her childhood with, though with five siblings I had an inner circle not much smaller than hers.

When it comes to indirect influences, these can really all fall under the heading of culture if we define that word broadly. There is a tendency in our family to think of the part of our family trees that Jessie represents as almost entirely Irish. It might be true, but not necessarily in the way people think. Cultural heritage is, of course, a major part of who Jessie was, so it is not belaboring a point to examine this a little more.

In terms of genetics, bloodlines, descent from the old countries, however we want to think of it, the evidence shows clearly that Jessie and her siblings were nothing close to entirely Irish. Since each of her grandparents represents a quarter of Jessie's genetic makeup, most of this is easy to summarize based on what we already discussed:

- Maternal grandfather: Michael Fitzpatrick: Both parents immigrants from Ireland and certainly Irish of the most indigenous sort. Irish contribution to Jessie's bloodline: **25%**.

- Maternal grandmother: Mary Noel: Descended almost entirely from Pennsylvania Germans going back several generations: Irish contribution to Jessie's bloodline: **0%**.
- Paternal grandfather: James Davenport: Most likely of English and likely partly Dutch, descent from ancestry living several generations in Hudson Valley. Irish contribution to Jessie's bloodline: **0%**.
- Paternal grandmother: Jemima Connell: Entire family tree arrived in North America by way of Cape Breton Island, almost certainly a combination of Ulster Scots, Lowland Scots, and northern English, all Protestants (i.e., Scots-Irish). Irish contribution to Jessie's bloodline: **??% (depends on definition of Irish)**.

Thus, we know that Jessie was certainly at least one-quarter, and certainly something less than one-half, Irish, but settling it more precisely than that leaves us wrestling with a controversial semantic issue.

Even authors of books on Irish culture often appear to be nervous when it comes to the definition of just who should be included. They know this is a messy question, sure to get them in trouble no matter what they write. One related memory I have is US History class in high school under the tutelage of Mr. Gahagan. One day he asked the class how many of us were Irish. When he further queried one of the girls who had raised her hand, she hemmed and hawed a bit and finally said that her family had told her she was Scotch-Irish. Mr. Gahagan's reaction was to inform us in no uncertain terms that that did not make her Irish. On the other hand, we can consider the scholar, Jay P. Dolan, most definitely an authority to be respected on the subject. For many years he taught a course on Irish American history at the University of Notre Dame, considered by many to have the best program in Irish studies of any school in North America. In the book he wrote[14] based on the course, he clearly does include as Irish those, primarily Presbyterian, descendants of peoples who were transplanted to the "Ulster Plantation" in the time of James I. There is no pleasing everyone. I've noticed among Protestants I've met from Northern Ireland, that they're not even consistent themselves. Even the same person might refer to himself as Irish in one conversation and insist that he is not Irish in the next.

So how much we say Jessie is of Irish descent depends in part on whose definition we want to follow. If we go with Mr. Gahagan, I believe we have to say she is exactly one-quarter Irish, no more, no less. If instead we follow Professor Dolan, Jessie is more than one-quarter Irish, but still less than one-half, since some of Jemima's ancestors arrived in Nova Scotia not from Ireland, but from Scotland and possibly northern England. But bloodlines are not what is really the main point anyway.

What should interest us most are cultural influences, and it might be argued that what came down to Jessie was very largely Irish in that sense. And the argument is not even really a hard one to make. First, Jessie's mother clearly had much more influence in how Jessie and her siblings were brought up than their father did.

---

14 Listed in the bibliography along with other books on the subject.

Elizabeth was obviously not only Jessie's role model, but also her main source of guidance. Throughout her narrative, Jessie very frequently writes about her mother forbidding her to do one thing or her mother allowing her to do something else. Due in part to his work, William was not even around all the time, and though he may have set some of the rules, Elizabeth was the one who set the patterns for their day-to-day lives. For one thing, obviously, she was the one who saw to it that the children were raised as Catholics. And going back a generation, though Elizabeth's mother was of German descent, we can still imagine the Fitzpatrick household was mainly subject to Irish cultural influences. It appears that Mary *Noel* Fitzpatrick was not joined in Shamokin by any of her Noel relatives, and it would seem inevitable that she would have assimilated over the decades to a largely Irish ethos there. I can imagine that most of her friends and peers, both at church and in the neighborhood, would have been Irish American women of roughly the same age. Also, we know from *Sister Helen's Stories* that Elizabeth had been influenced by her Fitzpatrick uncles, and probably aunts as well. It thus seems fair to say that both Jessie's mother and Jessie herself were raised in households where Irish American culture predominated.

So, any claim that Jessie was purely Irish is incorrect if it is meant in the genetic sense, but essentially correct if meant culturally, and that's what really counts after all. And if we assume that Jessie had the most significant influence on how any of her children were raised, it might be fair to say they are not just half-Irish, but more than half.

But how specifically do we characterize what we mean by Irish cultural influences? This too is a dangerous question. I have my own well-formed concepts of what traits are implied, and though many of those traits are positive ones, to describe them in detail runs the risk of engaging in stereotyping. If you have your own set of ideas, they are likely similar to mine, so taking the coward's approach, I'll just ask you to think in those terms. I will only go so far as to say that if your set of Irish characterizations include an overriding sense of romanticism and even a penchant for melodrama, that might help explain a lot about Jessie.

Other questions worth exploring a little more are what kind of financial means did Jessie's family come from and what was their standing in the community? We already have a sense that the answers are rather complicated and depend to a large degree on what generation and what branch we are looking at. Without a doubt, life was often a particularly difficult struggle for William and Elizabeth when they were raising their nine children. As far as I could find, they never owned their own home and their tight budgets left little room for luxuries. A job as a locomotive engineer was still a working-class job even if it was a relatively skilled and respectable one, and at the time it was hard to raise a large family on the sort of income it provided. No matter how William might work and how hard Elizabeth might work at economizing, or even when the adolescent children were working to help with family finances, we learn from Jessie and Helen's books that it was an ongoing struggle. Some of what we glean from William's personnel file with the railroad shows that he often owed money and was pursued by creditors. He had dreams of coming up with a successful invention, developing a career as a writer, or even becoming a hypnotist. I suspect these were not so much quests for fame and fortune as they were desperate searches for relief from the family's ongoing financial challenges. But, alas, all those dreams were frustrated. In terms of prestige, perhaps the high point was when William was foreman at the railyard in Ithaca, but that lasted only a few years, and seems to have boosted the family's standing in the community only in a minor way if at all.

On the other hand, the family was not the poorest of the poor either. We rarely read about them going hungry, and in fact rich desserts such as pies and fudge seem to have been routine. It was probably a struggle for the parents at Christmas time, but the children received quite nice presents every year. Jessie wrote much about clothing, and it is clear that sometimes she had the fashionable apparel she wanted even if not always. In a family of avid readers, there were never enough books around, but their home library was far from bare. Children had to share bedrooms and even beds, but they did have generally adequate housing even if it was always rented. By the standards of the times, they might even have been of slightly above average means for a large working-class family, but that still meant that life was always a struggle.

Going back one generation, both Elizabeth and William grew up in more fortunate circumstances than they experienced as married adults. In the modern world, and especially in America, we think of each generation of a family having a higher standard of living than the one before, but of course there are exceptions. I have already mentioned some of the points Helen made in Chapter 2 of her book about the quite privileged life her mother had experienced before marriage. We can read of the rings with emeralds, diamonds, and opals she received from her uncles along with a lady's gold watch on a gold chain. She won whole sets of books in contests and acted in traveling shows put on by her uncle. The way Helen describes it makes one think that Elizabeth was being raised with the expectation that she would marry well and have a fine house with servants. Her father's job as a fire boss was a quite prestigious one. It appears that much of Shamokin society at the time was Irish and Catholic, and if the Fitzpatricks weren't in the upper crust, they were at least close to it for their time and place. In her book on Shamokin society, anthropologist Janet MacGaffey indicates that by the turn of the century the Irish were becoming the bosses and foremen, and "they were replaced at the lower end of the hierarchy by later comers—Poles, Lithuanians, Ukrainians, and Italians."[15]

It is all the more clear that William grew up in a privileged way. Even if not everyone associated with the Connell family was equally wealthy, surely by the time of his generation none of them were anything close to poor. And there must have been a great deal of prestige attached to anyone closely related to the family that was playing such an overwhelming role in the Scranton community. William would have enjoyed some of the glow from even the more distant Connell relatives, such as the first cousins and uncles of his mother, and his mother and his Uncle Alex were making sure he was not left behind. Since the Scranton mayor and industrialist Alexander Connell never married and had no other close relatives in the next generation, the three

---

15 See especially pp. 62-63 in *Coal Dust on Your Feet* and other sources listed in the bibliography.

37

children of his sister Jemima were the closest he had to direct descendants. In *Sister Helen's Stories* we read that Uncle Alex paid for his only nephew, William, to go to a series of schools, apparently expensive private ones. And until she died in 1906, William's mother was clearly highly respected in the community.

An obvious question then is why did the standard of living within the family go down so much from one generation to the next, both for Elizabeth and for William? I think that if we read *Sister Helen's Stories* carefully, we get the sense that this is a question Helen pondered as well and had her own theories for the answers. In the case of her mother, Helen suggests to us at several points that pride was an overriding consideration for Elizabeth throughout her life and that she sometimes suffered financially because of it. In the case of her father, Helen's theory was a little different. She suggests that William was the typical spoiled wealthy boy who took few things seriously and assumed that everything he wanted should be easily accessible to him. It seems that his sense of carelessness left a generally bad impression with his uncle, among others. My perception is that working with machines was one of the few things William took seriously as a young man, and this led to the kind of career that could at least feed his family. But he had assumed that it should be easy to attain a higher position in life. The conclusion then is that the privilege that both Elizabeth and William experienced in their youth played against their successes and prosperity as adults raising their own family, not in their favor.

But there is probably an even more fundamental reason that the William and Elizabeth Davenport family struggled financially throughout the rest of their lives. William was only nineteen and Elizabeth was only twenty when they married. Contrast this with what was considered the norm in both their families. Elizabeth's father married at the age of twenty-four. Though we don't have exact marriage dates for her grandfathers, it is reasonable to assume her paternal grandfather married at about twenty-five and her maternal grandfather at about twenty-four. Elizabeth's various uncles married at twenty-three or twenty-four. For that matter, Williams's own father had first married at twenty-five. When Elizabeth's parents objected to her plan to marry William, two of their concerns would have been that he was a non-Catholic and had a wild nature, but certainly they were also concerned that he was far too young.

Inevitably my perspectives are influenced both by my years living in a very different culture and my interest in history. On this basis it strikes me that the early to mid-20th Century in all Western countries, and particularly in America, was an extraordinarily romantic era. It was a common assumption in earlier centuries, and it is still true in many non-Western cultures today, that people should marry only after they were financially secure enough to raise a family. Examining marriage records from colonial times up through the end of the 19th Century in both New England and the Hudson Valley Region, typical first marriage age for men was mid- to late twenties, sometimes early thirties, and the range for women was roughly from about twenty-two to twenty-eight. Often when people married earlier, it was in cases where the couple was already pregnant, which we know because the first child was born four to seven months later. Human nature being what it is, surely there were young people with romantic feelings toward one another at earlier ages, but even so, they must have assumed that they should forego marriage until they had resources sufficient for family life unless it was unavoidable due to a an out-of-wedlock pregnancy.

In Japan, especially when I first lived there in the 1970s, most marriages were arranged, called *miai-kekkon,* as opposed to the relatively rare *ren'ai-kekkon,* meaning romantic love marriages. And marriages were arranged only when the two people were at a point in their lives when it was most practical to marry. Romantic attachments between younger people, especially of high school age, were discouraged by Japanese society. The teens and early twenties are times to study, learn a way to make a living, and begin building a nest egg. Japanese think themselves happier that way in the long run. Certainly, it generally results in greater financial security and unquestionably in more stable marriages.

Contrast this with 20th Century America, most especially the middle part of the century. Popular culture; including music, movies, popular literature, etc.; and peer pressure taught people that marriage was an essential consequence of falling in love. Only stodgy old people suggested it a good idea to postpone marriage for practical reasons. Median age of first marriage statistics fell to their lowest level ever in the United States during the 1950s. Young marriage became much more the norm, and this often quickly led to a financial struggle for the couples concerned. The hard part is that a growing family that starts out that way is unlikely to completely overcome the financial difficulties for decades, if ever. It is not wrong to be a romantic, but it is a mistake not to count the costs. Clearly, the experiences of William and Elizabeth illustrate the point.[16]

Everyone who reads Jessie's narrative, and perhaps *Sister Helen's Stories* as well, will form his own perspective and opinions on how they represent their early lives and the lives of those around them. It might be best to avoid commenting at all about how I interpret their stories, but I find it difficult to restrain myself from stating a few general observations and views.

Obviously, major factors in the life of young Jessie and her siblings were their parents. One of the harder parts was that there was often significant strife in the marriage of William and Elizabeth. A second hard part to discuss was that William had a violent bad temper. We can each form our own views about the sources of the troubles. If your interpretation is that William was a miscreant with absolutely no redeeming qualities, and Elizabeth was a saint, you'll likely continue with that. But stories where the villains are pure evil and the heroes are pure virtue are not particularly interesting, and generally aren't true to life. More to the point, a careful reading of both Helen's and Jessie's narratives suggest they also didn't think it was quite that simple either.

To be sure, there is convincing evidence that William was a man of a seriously flawed character, but I'll try to be fair in judging him and in considering that he had good traits too. Concerning his violent temper, it is important to avoid presentism, as

---

16 On the other hand, we now live in an age of diminishing populations in developed countries, so some would advise that marrying early is a good thing for the country, even if you are not yet financially equipped to raise children.

defined as an excessive tendency to judge past events according to present-day value systems. A few generations ago, even quite extreme forms of corporal punishment of one's children were common in many, though certainly not all, families. What's more, parents administering such punishment often did so while in a state of scarcely controlled rage or righteous indignation. It might have been true that fathers or mothers who were particularly frustrated by financial difficulties or other troubles would be especially prone to that sort of anger and were unconsciously taking it out on the children. Parents often rationalized their behavior with the adage, *Spare the rod and spoil the child.* Thus, this aspect of William's behavior was not entirely out of step with the values of his time. On the other hand, both Helen and Jessie describe his habit of grabbing ahold of a child by the hair and smashing his or her head against the wall. Even by the standards of the time, that form of corporal punishment would have been seen as extreme and careless of the wellbeing of the children. So, while this aspect of William's behavior would not have seemed as beyond the pale then as it seems to us now, it was nonetheless excessive. It might well be that it was because he was a more frustrated man than most, and that is an explanation, but not an excuse.

Another pattern in William's actions betrays an unmitigated character flaw, and I don't think presentism buys him any leeway here. There seems to be sufficient evidence to conclude that he had at least two, and probably three, intimate relationships with other women while he was married to Elizabeth. Both Helen and Jessie wrote about this, and we find out about another case from his personnel records with the DL&W Railroad. What is more, it appears that at some points he lied to these other women by telling them that he was single and had no family to support. If Helen's description of the one case is accurate, there was a bizarrely naïve aspect to William's behavior in what was probably the first case. According to her, he expected Elizabeth to be happy for him having the experience of falling in love, even if it was with another woman. And he somehow thought that the way to make a start at sorting it all out was for the three of them to go to the movies together. For Elizabeth to have gone along with this plan also seems odd the way Helen describes it.

But taking the writings of Helen and Jessie on balance, it does seem to me that the marriage of their parents was not always entirely bad either. It is clear at times that they reconciled their differences. And when it comes down to it, third parties never understand the complete story on any marriage anyway. A wise man once described it this way: A marriage could be made in heaven, but if one of the parties were to describe to you what happened on the worst days over the years, you would conclude that it was made in hell. And similarly, if someone in a miserable marriage were to tell you what happened on all the best days, you would go away believing they were very happy all along. And if it is reasonable to conclude the marriage of William and Elizabeth was a difficult one, part of the stress might be explained by their circumstances. As already noted, they found themselves with debt and a lower standard of living than they grew up expecting would be their lot in life. They also differed on matters of faith. Elizabeth was raised a strong Catholic, and during the time they were married William was Protestant, to whatever degree he took it seriously.

Furthermore, in the spirit of walking a mile in his shoes, I would suggest that some aspects of William's life were quite unenviable, among these his work. From the start, he had been working hard to support his rapidly growing family, and in spite of it was resented by his in-laws living next door and was even stabbed by one of them. Concerning his years working for the railroad, some basic research into what it took to operate a steam locomotive, and in later years a diesel electric one, reveals that it is a much more complex and demanding job than most people would first imagine. For most of the early, and for some periods later on, he was a locomotive fireman. One of the demands of this job required shoveling many tons of coal in a day, which is why having a "high standard of physique" was one of the requirements of being hired.[17] I suspect that no one ever fully recovers from a near fatal stabbing, which makes it all the more impressive that William could work in this role for many years. We might also remember the injured toe. And the job was far from a mindless one of just using a shovel. The fireman was responsible for carefully maintaining both the proper boiler pressure and water level in the boiler, as well as serving as general co-pilot to the engineer. It was also a particularly dangerous occupation. According to statistics from around the time William started working for the DL&W, a locomotive fireman was nearly twice as likely to die as a man of the same age in an average occupation of the time, and in these days nearly all occupations were more deadly than they are now. Specifically, he was about nine times more likely than the average man to die due to an accident on the job, followed by locomotive engineers who were about eight times more likely. The probability of serious injuries was also much higher. Just the process of maintaining one's footing on a shifting, jolting surface while stoking coal from tender to firebox was enough to make many aspiring firemen lose their courage, especially when working after dark.

After being promoted to engineer, William's job was only a little less physically demanding and only slightly safer; and carried much heavier responsibilities. He did this for long, irregular hours and had to be on call even when he was able to be home. And though travel for one's work seems interesting at first, it quickly becomes very tiresome to be away from home so many nights after one has done it for a while. Some businessmen complain if their job takes them away from home a few dozen nights a year. William had to be away more nights than he was home. In spite of all this heavy labor, he never could get ahead enough to have the experience of owning his own home and was often in debt and aggressively pursued by creditors. He should not have taken it out on his family, but I, for one, will judge him a little less harshly when I think about how frustrated I might have been living a similar life, even assuming I could have measured up to it in the first place.

---

17 For statistics relating to this occupation, see the 1914 journal paper by Henry J. Harris. For more details on the life on the railroad, see especially the book *Set Up Running* by John W. Orr, as well as other railroad-related books listed in the bibliography. There is also a lot of interesting trivia to learn from these. For example, I assumed that the throttle was always what the locomotive engineer used to control speed, but Orr explains that under most conditions, it was more efficient to leave the throttle wide open and to adjust the valve gear using the Johnson bar to control the timing of the injection of steam into the cylinders.

One other aspect of the family dynamic is that the older siblings were in some periods called upon to take major responsibility. This is not uncommon in large families where the parents are often busy, and it still happens in families in later generations as well. Nonetheless, it is worth mentioning here. Not only was railroad engineer William typically gone for days at a time, but Elizabeth too sometimes needed to be away for other reasons, such as when a child was in the hospital or when she visited relatives. There are interesting stories about Helen being in charge, especially during the years the family lived in Scranton. Some years later in Binghamton, Jessie herself was apparently expected to take on a remarkably responsible role while still in her mid-teens. By that time, Helen and Mary were married, and Marge was away at college. Their mother was often being treated for her illnesses at a hospital back in Scranton, and at other times was away helping other families. If the way Jessie described it is accurate, it is shocking how much responsibility she was expected to take on at such a young age, not only for keeping the house functioning, but also for family finances. She wrote of struggling to keep the grocery bill down. Teenaged Jessie even seems to have felt guilty about Claire going to school wearing shoes with holes in the soles and soles that were coming loose from the uppers. As though if only Jessie had been better at balancing the family budget, she would have been able to buy her younger sister proper footwear. This is a lot of responsibility for Jessie as a girl about fifteen.

With their father away so much of the time, it is obvious that for many years, eldest brother, Bill, was frequently expected to be the man of the house, even a protector of the family. Every indication is that he took on this role ably and willingly, if perhaps a little too enthusiastically at times. Jessie resented and resisted his efforts to keep her from spending too much time with boys during the Ithaca years, but later continued to expect him to take on a protective role. There is the amusing incident, for example, of expecting him to go down in the basement to confront a growling beast. We'll later find that there was a period after their mother died when he was the main source of financial support for most of his younger siblings.

Having discussed these few generalities about her family circumstances, I will also indulge myself in making a few general comments about my own views on specifically Jessie's behavior. As you read the chapters, you can judge for yourself if I am on target or not. Some of what my grandmother wrote came as surprises when I first read it, but more often it confirmed traits I was already aware of.

One of the most obvious points about Jessie, and she frequently emphasized this about herself, is that she greatly enjoyed reading novels and short stories, and she was in the habit of reading continually throughout her life. It has long struck me that this has been true of many of the women in the family. It was a trait of many of her daughters and granddaughters, for example. Clearly, Helen was also an avid reader, and it was probably true of at least some of Jessie's other siblings as well. It is not surprising given the family's background. Jessie's mother was a schoolteacher, and apparently there were always many volumes of fiction in their home. Jessie's father aspired to become a successful writer, as did Jessie herself at some points, and her youngest brother, Dick, would eventually have some of his short stories published in prominent magazines.

What is almost as obvious is that throughout her life Jessie generally looked at the world in a wildly romantic and dramatic way. My suspicion is that this natural tendency of hers was enhanced by at least two factors. One is the Irish heritage in which she was raised, and the other was the habit of reading a great deal of fiction as just mentioned. At times her sense of melodrama is so extreme as to be ridiculous. Inspired by a novel she had read, she convinced herself that her older brother might murder her simply because she had neglected to put coal on the fire in the furnace. As in the novel, she decided to leave a note so that people would at least know who her murderer was. As if this scenario was not already absurdly overdramatized, she went on to feel guilty that if she had somehow died due to an accident, poor Bill would have been falsely accused and sent to prison or worse.

In reading how Jessie felt about many of her experiences, it strikes me that she was sometimes much more self-conscious than she was at other times. In most of her day-to-day social interactions, she comes across as a reasonably self-confident young person and feels quite comfortable about her own behavior. But in sharp contrast to that, formal situations, where high class rules of etiquette might apply, tended to make her painfully nervous, even panicky, and we feel for her when we read these parts.

The nature of the times might explain in part this tendency to feel much more awkward in formal situations. Views on class in American society have evolved over the past century. In the past, it was generally more common for people to feel at a distinct disadvantage when they were in the company of people with more money and more exposure to the social graces than they had. Even so, Jessie seems an extreme case of this. As already discussed, Jessie grew up in a family that had continual financial struggles and was certainly not well off, but on the other hand they were not the disastrously poor either. They were surely better off than some, and not worse off than many other, families in their time. And in terms of nonmonetary factors, if anything, Jessie came from a family background with more than average opportunities for higher education, being well read, and other refinements. Perhaps it is fair to say that Jessie's lack of self-confidence came in part from a sense that she was insecure about her own and her family's place in society. Another probable factor, particularly during her teenage years, was that Jessie felt that she wasn't measuring up against the high standards set by her slightly older sister, the very cultured Marge.

Thinking back to my own childhood, I can relate well to the kind of self-consciousness my grandmother experienced. Especially when I was a child, it seemed to me that embarrassing situations were even more painful for me than they were for most people. When I read of some of Jessie's experiences and how she felt about them, she seems to be like me, and I admire her honesty in writing about these feelings.

It is also admirable that Jessie tried to be very honest about her own behavior as a child, even mentioning in places that she was sometimes frustrated in trying to understand why she did the things she did. For instance, she wrote about wanting desperately to be liked by others, and then inexplicably taking precisely those actions that would surely make her disliked. My own best attempt at a partial explanation is that these patterns relate to birth order. Authorities on the subject tell us that being a middle child comes with its own set of challenges. And being the fifth of nine children is the ultimate in being in the middle. Jessie resented her older siblings at times for their seemingly greater privileges and autonomy, and at other times resented her younger siblings for their peskiness and for being held to less stringent standards with fewer responsibilities. A plausible explanation is that frustration over these feelings is what caused her to be a little irrational and misbehave on occasion against her own best interests.

I am amazed by how good my grandmother's memory was concerning matters of fashion and artistic endeavors. More than six decades later, she recalled in detail the colors, patterns, and cuts of various clothing items she or her sisters had. She could also describe in vivid detail some of the drawings she had made. To someone like me, who can rarely remember what color shirt I wore the day before or what color car a friend recently bought, this seems an incredible ability. Yes, it is true that this likely has something to do with the differences between women and men, but I suspect that many women would not remember as many details as Jessie did.

Most of us who knew my grandmother during her later adult years remember how much she treasured her collection of dolls. I have heard some relatives state that it seemed at times that she valued dolls over people—a rather harsh statement, but perhaps one that is justified. It is no surprise that this tendency relates to her memories of experiences from her childhood. In the Dalton chapter we learn that she still remembered the envy she felt for the many beautiful dolls her well-off friend had. Later, she described how Claire and Carmel had neglectfully damaged one of her dolls by leaving it outside on what turned out to be a rainy night. After they moved to Ithaca, Jessie was disappointed that her parents felt she had outgrown dolls, so they gave her more grown-up gifts for Christmas, while Santa still gave lovely dolls to the younger Claire and Carmel, which she clearly still envied. She remembered fondly the dolls the college girls dressed for the Ithaca Girls' Club and playing with paper dolls taken from her mother's magazines.

Perhaps what surprises me most in what Jessie wrote about her youth is just how much space she dedicates to the subject of boys and how numerous were the boys she discusses. Not just that, but her feelings about these experiences are complex, sometimes conflicting, and not always entirely honorable.

Of course, we all know that companionship with any member of the opposite sex other than a close family member is by its nature complex. Just how much of it is platonic friendship and how much of it is mixed with romantic feelings or sexual attraction? We also know that especially for adolescents, and even for small children, these questions are not straightforward. Even so, the pattern of Jessie's experiences and how conflicted she felt about them seem more extreme than most. At some points in her narrative, she wrote of not liking boys "in a mushy way" in one paragraph, and then about how much she enjoyed being kissed by a boy in the next. A few pages later, she was back again to never being mushy. But considering Jessie's nature and circumstances, maybe this sense of confusion isn't so surprising. On the one hand, we have noted that Jessie was by nature a romantic, and that this was exacerbated by all the story-reading she did. On the other hand, she was being raised in a strict Catholic environment and in a family that was concerned that she might at some point get herself into trouble.

Beyond the confusion, some other aspects of how Jessie described her connections to the boys she knew are a little disconcerting. There would be nothing wrong of course with being attracted to older boys, but Jessie's beaus are always older and sometimes much older. What is more, at least once she exaggerated an already large age difference. In the Ithaca chapter, she wrote about her relationship with Ralph's cousin, Earl, when she was fourteen, and she claimed Earl was "about twenty-two". I have found that, based on available records, the Earl in question certainly could not have been more then eighteen at the time. That already seems an elderly suitor for a girl of fourteen, so why in her memory is his age blown all the way up to twenty-two? A little more disturbing is that she viewed some of these relationships with boys in a particularly mercenary way. In some cases, she was happy to receive and even demand lavish gifts from boys for whom, by her own words, she had no real affection. Earl was also a good example of this point, and there were others as well.

On another point, Jessie clearly had a double standard when it came to fidelity. Near the end of the Ithaca chapter, she wrote about Mike, the Irish boy who worked in the barbershop. After already establishing that Mike was a boyfriend, she described how much she enjoyed playing kissing games with college boys on the night of her fifteenth birthday party. In her own words, "Mike took a backseat that night." She also wrote of how in the weeks after the party, she wished she would have opportunities to spend more time with those same college boys. Soon after, she described how outraged she was when she believed that Mike was going to do nothing more serious than take a classmate of hers to the movies. It is true that she ended the discussion by stating that she was ashamed, but this shame was only for making the mistake of believing the homely girl, not for the double standard itself. Perhaps all these points relate on some level to female ego.

During her adolescence, especially during the Ithaca years, Jessie's family was concerned about her interest in boys in general. Especially her mother and her older brother were working hard to protect her from making serious mistakes. The description of the exploits about town Jessie and her friend, Helen W. had trying to meet rich college boys while avoiding interference from Bill are particularly telling. They are interesting not only in terms of what clever extremes the two girls went to in avoiding detection, but also in terms of how much time Bill was spending shadowing them. He must have been very busy with other things, so only a deep sense of concern would have prompted him to follow Jessie and Helen around town every time they went to the library or to the movies.

I was raised in an environment that taught me to believe that I was in an era of hopelessly reckless, rebellious, and decadent youth as compared with the pure innocence of young people in the good old days. I eventually came to see this model of history as nonsense based on evidence like this. I was shy and had nothing close to the number of adventures with girls while growing up as my grandmother had with boys. In the Binghamton years, my grandmother smoked whenever she was out with boys and drank enough wine, liquor, *and* beer to make herself severely sick on the day of her parents' silver anniversary. At least in those ways, I come off as the naïve innocent, and she as the worldly sophisticate of the Roaring Twenties. My point is not to be sanctimonious. I certainly have my flaws, and it might have been shyness and timidity that most kept my behavior in check as an adolescent. The point is there are wayward youths in every era and my generation was far from the first.

As one final point, Jessie herself wanted us to understand that her experiences as a small child relating to death haunted her for the rest of her life. She remembered acutely the death of her little friend, Augie. Her memories of seeing so many black wreaths on the doors of neighbors' homes were likely due to the Spanish flu pandemic. For children to experience the death of someone they knew well was more common when medical science was less advanced than it is now, but the experiences seem to have been especially hard on Jessie. She wrote of having a phobia even of Christmas wreaths for the rest of her life.

Jessie's story represents a time earlier than that experienced by anyone alive today. As a setting, small cities of Pennsylvania and Upstate New York will not be equally familiar to everyone. And, most of all, Jessie was an individual. I hope you will find it as interesting as I do to read her story in her own words and see how much you might have in common with her.

Hal Lewis
Berkshire, New York
March 2023

Chapter 1—Scranton

The first thing I remember is the house in Scranton. I was born in that house. It seemed very big to me when I was a kid, but if I could see it now, it probably would seem very small. It was a twin house with three floors.[18] On the top floor there were three bedrooms and a bath. The middle floor had a big front room and a sitting room with stairs going up as well as down. It also had a small bedroom. Down in the basement we had a kitchen and a dining room. There was a big furnace in the dining room. I remember many a cold morning making toast on a long fork in that furnace. Around Christmas every year, we would burn our letters to Santa in the furnace. There was a smaller room where coal and wood were stored.

We lived on a street called South Hyde Park Avenue. It sounds ritzy, but it wasn't.[19] There was a big dump in back where people dumped ashes from their stoves in the winter. It didn't look too bad in the winter, but in the summer it was ugly. I was born in that house, the fifth of nine children. The four eldest had been born in

---

18 We know from various sources that the exact address of this house was 424 South Hyde Park Avenue, which is an address that no longer exists, and it seems clear that there must have been a slight adjustment in the numbering scheme in that neighborhood. We can still be sure it was on the northwestern side of South Hyde Park Avenue, between Luzerne and Rock Streets, but whether it was part of a building still there and just renumbered or a building no longer there, I can't be sure. It could be the duplex on the west corner with an alley called Oliver Place or one closer to Rock Street. All the streets near there are narrow. The topography of this part of Scranton is one with many small, but steep sided, knolls, meaning most of the streets have a steep grade, but the grade changes frequently as you go along. For example, South Hyde Park Avenue slopes up to the southwest, so that when family members walked out their front door and turned right, they would be walking up a steep slope for a few dozen yards.

19 It is indeed a less ritzy location than the fancy sounding street name might suggest. Even though there is no longer the ash pile, it is a rather dilapidated, though not necessarily unpleasant, neighborhood in the southwestern part of Scranton. One of the advantages of their location would have been convenience. In the days before the average urban family had an automobile, access to streetcar stops was a major factor, and their house was only a few minutes' walk to stops on two of the most important lines of the trolley system, then known just as the Scranton Railway. They were probably just a one-minute walk to a streetcar stop on the Luzerne Street line, and a three-minute walk to a stop on the Main Avenue line. For day-to -day shopping and diversions, they probably didn't even need to bother with the streetcars in some cases. As close as they were to Main Avenue, there must have been groceries, small movie houses, etc. within a five-minute walk of home. If you have ever lived in a country where car ownership is less common than in America, you can relate to this. For a family without a car, it must have seemed a wonderfully convenient location.

A few interesting points about the composition of the neighborhood show up in the 1920 census data. First, a surprisingly large proportion, well over half, of the adult male neighbors worked for the railroads. Second, a quite high percentage of the neighboring families were immigrants from Wales. There were also a few immigrants from other countries, including Germany, England, Austria, and Russia, but among the nearby neighbors born in other countries, an overwhelming percentage of them were Welsh. It was only later that I read this neighborhood of Scranton has long been thought of as little Wales.

Shamokin, Pennsylvania.[20]

I remember a few of the Christmases we had in that house. One Christmas, Helen and Mary, who were sleeping in the bedroom on the second floor, heard a noise. They were scared it might be rats. They took their shoes and threw them into the room where the Christmas tree was standing to try to scare them off. The noise would stop for a while and then start up again. Finally, they fell asleep. The next morning, they found out that the noise had been made by two big rabbits that were Bill's Christmas present. Christmas was always a happy time for us. We each got a pair of stockings that we hung over the banister for Santa to fill. We got dolls, books, and games to play, and with a crowd like ours, we always had someone to play with.

One time the ceiling in the back bedroom fell down and left a big hole. After several weeks, the ceiling was repaired, but it was still a vivid memory for us. One time when Claire was very sick, my mother put her to bed in that room. The window was open, but the shades were down, and Claire was lying there looking up at the ceiling. The breeze started to blow on the shade, causing the shadow cast on the ceiling to move. It made Claire think that the ceiling was falling on her. She screamed, and mother came running. She could only quiet her by taking her out of that room.

I remember when it seemed as though the whole family fell sick at the same time, with measles, for example, or similar ailments. Anyway, when we were sick, my mother would sit in a chair with a bottle of some vile tasting liquid and a spoon. She would make the sick ones march around her, and she would measure out the stuff. We would swallow it and go back to bed, and then three or four hours later the same process would start over again. My mother also dosed us regularly with some stuff called Mother Gray's Worm Powder. It was a dry powder that mixed with water and dished out to us. That one didn't taste bad, a little like licorice.[21]

Once Helen and I were sick with scarlet fever. We were in the front bedroom. Helen was very sick, but all I had was a sore throat. One afternoon, we were lying in bed. Outside the sun was shining. It was March, and the ice was melting from the roof. I hated to be kept in bed when outside I could hear the kids yelling and playing on the

---

20 Just as Jessie describes here, her four elder siblings; Helen (born 1904), Mary (1906), Bill (1907), and Marge (1909); had been born near Shamokin, and this was in a cottage owned by the Fitzpatrick grandparents and adjacent to their own large house. The records available seem to indicate that they moved from there to Scranton sometime in late 1910 or early 1911. For the first several months, they lived on the very western outskirts of the city, which Helen, in her memoir, describes as a particularly inconvenient location, a long walk uphill from the nearest streetcar stop. They moved to the new house on South Hyde Park Avenue only a few months before Jessie was born on the 24th of October 1911. Her four younger siblings; Claire (1913), Carmel (1915), Jim (1917), and Dick (1919); were also born there.

21 Mother Gray's Sweet Powders was an inexpensive and popular medicine at the time. It was advertised to cure many digestive ailments, and apparently was especially effective for eliminating worms. It contained enough sugar, anise, and licorice to be pleasant tasting. Unfortunately, some of the active ingredients were poisonous enough to cause long term harm if taken on a regular basis.

streets. Helen, of course, hated to share her bed with a younger sister who was not really very sick and therefore restless and always wanting to have a story told to her. Helen could have made a faster recovery if I had let her sleep. Finally, my mother fixed a chair for me by the window. She put pillows for my back and a light blanket over my legs. I could see the birds outside my window, so I was content for a while.

One time when my mother took some of us shopping, I had a dime for a surprise gift. These were little packages wrapped in red or white tissue paper and tied with cord. You could buy one for a dime, and until you opened it, you didn't know what was in it. That was, of course, the surprise. I picked out a package, and inside was a doll-house-sized stove. But what I remember most about that day was the ice cream my mother treated us to. We had it so seldom that it was a big treat.[22] I was eating mine very slowly to make it last as long as possible when my mother said we had to go, as the streetcar was coming. I had to leave my unfinished ice cream and run out to the streetcar. To this day I remember that unfinished ice cream with regret.

It was while we lived in Scranton that Claire became very ill. Jim was just a baby, and Carmel was a little over two. I would have been almost six, Marge would have been about eight, and Bill was ten. Mary would be eleven and a half and Helen, thirteen. My mother was in and out of the sick room all day, and she also had to nurse Jim. It finally got to be too much for her, and they had to take Claire to the hospital. Mother went to be with Claire and took Jim and Carmel with her. Mary had scarlet fever, so she went too. Father, as a railroad man, was away much of the time. That left Helen, Bill, Marge, and me at home. Helen was supposed to take care of us kids. That was a big responsibility for someone her age. Marge and I were supposed to do the dishes. We played around most of the time while Helen was upstairs making the beds. She would come downstairs and sit in the window reading a book while she made us do the dishes. Marge and I would tell the neighbors that Helen made us do all the work. As they could see her in the window with her head bent over a book, they believed us.

I remember one day in particular, Helen was upstairs, so Marge and I decided to play ladies and have our lunch on the back porch, which was enclosed. We called it a shanty. For a table, we took the ironing board and propped the ends on blocks of wood. We set the table with little dishes, and in the center of the table we had a pot of cooked beans. When Helen came downstairs, it was to find the sink full of dishes and her two "helpers" enjoying themselves on the back porch. She lost her temper and came running out. She lifted her foot and kicked the ironing board. Dishes flew all over, and the beans hit the wall like little bullets. Marge and I flew down the alley and over the fence. We sneaked into the house about an hour later. By this time, Helen was over her anger and was glad we had come home.

---

22 Based on other parts of the narrative, it seems that they regularly had homemade cakes, fudge, and other confections, but in the days before electric refrigerators and freezers were common, it must have been impractical to enjoy ice cream at home, and thus rare because they could have it only when they were eating out.

Helen put up with a lot from us kids. She had a way of making her nostrils flare whenever she wanted us to think she was angry, and we ridiculed her about this whenever we got mad at her. Helen didn't know much about cooking. She fixed hot dogs for supper every night. She could make good fudge and made some every day. She would give Marge and me each a piece and give some to Bill. Then she would sit in the window, reading her book and eating the rest of the fudge.

Though my father could not be home every night, on the nights he was home, he would clean up and go to the hospital. He used to bring baskets of fruit, and once he bought a huge Easter basket filled with candy and fruit to take to Claire in the hospital. Marge and I would stand there looking at these goodies with longing eyes and drooling mouths, but that was all we got, just a look. He took the basket to the hospital where Claire was at first too sick even to taste its contents. As she started to get well, she would take a nibble here and there, leaving those pieces contaminated. I don't think she ever ate one whole piece of that candy. As for the fruit, she might take a bite or two and then put the piece back in the basket. One night, my father brought a basket home with the partly eaten fruit and candy and told Helen to destroy the stuff and not to let us kids touch it in the meantime. Years later she told me that she had eaten some of the chocolates. She didn't get sick, so I guess her guardian angel was watching over her.

The house had to be fumigated to avoid the spread of the disease. They used sulfur candles in all the rooms except the kitchen and the bathroom. When we had to use the bathroom up on the third floor, we placed a rag over our noses and ran up the two flights of stairs. For fun, we just made a game of it. Bill was the only one who was allowed to leave the house during the quarantine, and I remember leaning out of the bathroom window and yelling at him as he was on the way to the store.[23]

Having a big brother as well as a younger one by then shouldn't have left me curious about boys' private parts. Marge, Bill, and I used to get up in the morning, and if we didn't hear Helen yelling at us to get downstairs, we would run around in our nightgowns and jump on the beds. Jumping on the beds was a lot of fun, and it was something we couldn't do when Mother was at home. Anyway, one of the things I liked to do was flip up Bill's nightshirt so his whole backside or front was exposed. We'd laugh ourselves silly over that. Bill would protest, but the next chance I got, up would go his nightshirt again.

I remember that every day, quarantine or not, Marge and I would sneak off with the two boys from up the street, Layton and Harvey Walker, who were six and eight

---

23 Though Jessie informs us that Mary had scarlet fever at this time (also that she and Helen had it another time), she doesn't specify why Claire was severely ill, which leaves us guessing a bit whether it was the same disease. In any case, scarlet fever is extremely contagious, and in the days before antibiotics it was a very serious disease. It would have justified the quarantine and fumigation as well as the fear of contamination from the candy and fruit. She Jessie takes pains to tell us her age and ages of her siblings when this episode happened, we know for certain that it was more than a year too early to have anything to do with the Spanish flu pandemic.

years old. We'd cross a big field and visit a lady named Marcella. She always had cookies or something good for us. We did this every day. Helen would threaten to tell our father, and we would promise not to do it again, but come the next day, away we would go again. I'm surprised that some of the neighbors didn't squeal on us, especially Mrs. K.[24] I know *she* didn't like me. Her daughter, Anna, was about my age, and we were always getting into fights.

One day, Anna, who had everything, had her doll carriage out, and I asked her if I could wheel it to the corner. As I reached the end of the street, I saw an ambulance coming. I dropped the carriage and ran as fast as I could back to my house. I knew it must be my mother and the kids coming home, and I was right. It was a happy day for all of us except Mrs. Kinsman, who had a screaming fit when she found Anna's doll carriage lying on its side at the end of the street. I mean she literally screamed. Of course, she tried to spoil the homecoming, but everyone was so happy to see each other that even a witch like Mrs. Kinsman couldn't ruin it.

I remember one time I was trying to do a good deed. All of us kids were chasing each other around a big field. Anna started to run after a beautiful butterfly, so I chased after her, screaming for her to leave the butterfly alone. I knew if she handled it in her hot hands, the butterfly would die. As I chased after her, I stepped on a broken bottle and got a terrible gash on my right foot. I hobbled home, leaving a trail of blood behind. It wasn't until my mother put my foot into cold water that I began to cry. I still have a scar on my foot to prove that the adage to *look before you leap* is a good rule. I did have the satisfaction of knowing that Anna didn't get her hands on that butterfly.

Another time, when we were playing by the church, I had another accident. There was a little fence around the sidewalk. I guess it was supposed to keep people off the grass. It was made of iron and was about three feet high.[25] We used to do tricks on it. If you sat on the fence and put your hands one way, you could go backwards, or if you put your hands a different way, you could go forward in almost like a somersault. One day, I forgot to position my hands correctly, and I went forward and fell to the concrete sidewalk on my nose. There was blood all over the place. I ran home crying, and for a few days all you could see was the big nose on my face. Sometimes I look in the mirror now and think it hasn't changed much over the years.

---

24 The Kinsman family lived either in the other side of the same duplex building, or the next building over. Anna was indeed about the same age, approximately one year younger than Jessie. Interestingly, Mr. Kinsman was also a fireman for the DL&W at the time, and his first name was also William. Apparently, the Walker family lived a little south of them on South Hyde Park Avenue.

25 Over time there have been many Roman Catholic churches in Scranton, and we can't be certain what church Jessie is discussing here. It seems likely though that the closest church then, as now, was St. Patrick's Church on Jackson Street, about a ten-minute walk to the north. Even now, there is an iron fence much like the one she describes surrounding the lawn of the rectory. This makes it quite likely that this is indeed the church that is the setting for the event Jessie is describing here. The current building was erected in 1883 and it is a beautiful church.

One time when my mother was talking over the fence to a neighbor, Carmel was digging in the dirt by the curb. She found a caterpillar and was busy scooping dirt to cover it. She would dump her spoonful of dirt on the caterpillar and run back to the curb for another spoonful. By the time she got back, the worm would have crawled out from under the dirt, but it kept her busy and happy until Father came along and stepped on the caterpillar. Poor Carmel burst into tears, screaming, "Oh, my cattie," as though she had lost her best friend.

We didn't always have toothbrushes. I can remember winding a piece of cloth around my finger and dipping it in wood ash from the furnace. It must have worked, because when I was fourteen, a dentist who came to the school to examine us for free said I had a perfect set of teeth. I also remember that when we didn't have toothbrushes, we would sometimes do the same thing except we dipped the cloth in baking soda.

I don't know whether I should write about one aspect of what might have happened when my father and mother separated for a time. I never saw this myself, and it was only told to me years later by my sister, Mary, and thus is third hand information to me.[26] The story was that one time my mother went to see my father. He was staying at the home of his sister and her husband. Mother and Father got into a terrible fight, and it is claimed that my Aunt Helen and her husband held my mother while my father

---

26 Everyone can decide for themselves what exactly to make of this part of the narrative, but it is sad in any case. Even if he is not guilty of everything he is accused, Jessie's father, William, certainly had a far less than perfect moral character. It is also sad that clearly there was a great deal of ongoing strife in the marriage of William and Elizabeth.

First, to clarify some of the background, the Aunt Helen here is William's younger sister, Helen C. *Davenport* Janes (1893-1964), his only surviving sibling at the time. She is therefore our Jessie's aunt, not to be confused with Jessie's eldest sister, Helen E. Davenport (later Hawley, 1904-1990). Much of the background information we have about this Aunt Helen (1893) comes from Chapter 3 of the *Sister Helen's Story* (the one born in 1904), where she tells us quite a bit about the adolescent years of the young aunt whose name she shared. I describe the difficult relationship the older Helen and Elizabeth in the introduction. The husband here is of course the Fred Janes (1891-1972) I mentioned there. It is hard to pin down an exact timeline of when William was staying with his sister and brother-in-law, but it may have been at times when Fred and Helen Janes were living quite close by, possibly at an apartment they rented for a time on North Rebecca Avenue.

People can believe what they like, but the one part I find difficult to believe is that Fred and Helen held Elizabeth while William hit her. The very image of a sane, grown woman in the early 20th Century, not known to be a criminal, and her husband holding their sister-in-law for another man to beat her just isn't credible. The younger Helen in her book indicates that Fred was a generally good, decent man. We can be sure that William did have a nasty temper, and that he did direct violence toward his children, but there is no other mention anywhere of him being physically violent with his wife, no matter how bitter their arguments sometimes were. In the manuscript that I am working from, Jessie made a marginal note suggesting that she wondered if the incident should be included at all given that it was hearsay, which could mean she doubted it herself.

On the other hand, the part about William having a young girlfriend is credible. We have evidence, including something that turns up in his personnel file with the railroad, that a series of affairs might have been a pattern for him, and that he might have had a habit of lying to some of these girlfriends by claiming that he did not already have a family.

hit her. My father had a young girlfriend. One night, my little brother, Dick, was very ill, and someone got in touch with my father and told him that Dick was not expected to live through the night. Apparently, he had told his girlfriend that he had a brother who had a large family, so that evening he told her he would have to leave early as his nephew was dying. *He never had a brother.*

I remember one time, when my mother was talking to her friend, Mrs. Walker. Mother said she was expecting a bill collector and explained that she hated to tell him she didn't have the money. Mrs. Walker told her to have one of the kids answer the door and say that Mother wasn't home. Mother said she wouldn't have one of her children lie for her, and Mrs. Walker said she would do it then. I don't think Mother thought that was quite honest, but she finally agreed to go along with the plan. When they saw the bill collector coming up the front steps, Mother went and sat on the steps to the upstairs, out of sight from the front door. Mrs. Walker answered the door, and I heard her say, "I'm sorry, but Mrs. Davenport isn't home. She went downtown."

I immediately yelled at the top of my lungs, "Oh no, she didn't. She's sitting right here on the steps." My mother never tried that again.

As far back as I can remember, I never saw my father drunk. He used to stop at the corner for a beer, but that was usually it. But one day, as my mother was talking to a neighbor, she saw Father staggering down the street. She was mortified and wanted to run and hide, but with the neighbors looking on, she straightened her back and held up her head. When my father got close, she could see the blood running down his face. She ran to him and helped him into the house. He had a gash in his forehead and couldn't speak very clearly. Mother washed the wound and bandaged his head. By this time, he had gained control enough to tell her that he had fallen and hit his head on the bar rail. She was relieved not that he had hit his head, but that he wasn't drunk. He used to bring beer home in his lunch pail, and if he was in a good mood, he would give us kids a little taste. All kids seem to like the taste of beer.[27]

I learned to read while we lived in Scranton. Sometimes I think it is a mistake to love reading so much, but at other times I feel sorry for people who don't like to read. I used to read all the fairy tale books, and as I got older, I would read romantic stories. We always had books around our house. One Christmas I got *The Red Book of Fairy Tales*.[28] Mother was an avid reader, and my father, when he wasn't dreaming up another

---

27 In his book *Digging Dusky Diamonds*, about life in Shamokin, John R. Lindermuth explains that it was a common custom for miners to stop at a bar on their way home from work each day to have their lunch pails filled with beer to take home. This might have been the case in many other working-class localities as well, and apparently it was where the term "a growler of beer" comes from. The idea of William bringing home beer in his lunch pail is therefore definitely not unusual. On the other hand, given that most people consider beer to be very much an acquired taste, Jessie's claim that all kids love the taste of it does seem surprising.

28 *The Red Book of Fairy Tales*, edited by the Scottish poet, novelist, and anthropologist, Andrew Lang was first published in 1890. Reprint editions are still available today.

invention, always had a book in front of him.

One summer Mother met a lady who was in Scranton visiting a friend. She and Mother became great friends, and when the lady had to return to her farm, she invited Mother and the whole family to visit her there. It was a really hot summer that year, and the lady kept writing to Mother and repeating her invitation to come to the farm where it would be cooler. My mother in desperation took her up on the invitation. We kids were so excited. At that point in our lives, we had never been to the countryside where they had real cows and chickens. We went by train. The lady's husband met us at the station with a horse and wagon. I remember that Marge and I wore pink sailor dresses, and the top of my dress had a little pocket. I had a nickel in the pocket (riches), but I lost the coin down between the keys of their piano. Of course, I put up a howl. The lady got the hired man, and he got the nickel out for me. It was all for nothing though, as I lost the nickel anyway when I was playing in the field. No amount of crying would bring it back. We had a wonderful week, running around all day in the good country air and eating fresh vegetables and fruits. I hated to go home at the end of the week, but I think the lady was glad to see us go.

One thing that happened at the farm concerned Helen, Mary, and Bill. They had a good time roaming through the fields and woods. One day they dressed up in some old clothes that the farm lady said they could play with. They went into the barn and got into some paint that was stored there in cans and streaked their faces with it until they looked like something from a horror movie. They were in the woods near the road when they heard voices. They peered out of the bushes and saw three small children walking hand in hand. These children were going to meet their father. They ranged in age from about eight down to the smallest one who was about two years old. I don't know what possessed my brother and sisters, but they jumped out of the bushes, screaming and yelling, and making horrible faces. The poor kids were so scared they ran as fast as they could down the road. The littlest one was pulled along so fast by her siblings that her feet didn't touch the ground. At that point Helen and her partners in crime began to worry about what they had done. They went hurriedly down to the creek and scrubbed the paint from their faces. They took off the costumes they were wearing and got into their regular clothes. It was a good thing that they did, because the father of the kids they had scared came to the farmhouse. But after seeing all of us kids looking like angels, he left with just a warning to the farmer to be on the lookout for the tramps that had scared his kids.

Today, when so many bad things are happening to children, I recall a story my mother told me about Mary. It happened before I was born. Mary and Helen were playing out in front of the house in Shamokin. Helen came into the house for a drink of water, and Mother asked her why Mary hadn't come into the house with her. "Oh," said Helen, "Some man came along and took Mary up the hill." My mother was frantic. She ran out of the house just in time to see Mary and a strange man at the top of the hill. She ran as fast as she could, calling to Mary to come to her. Mary was trying to get away from the man, but he had a tight grip on her. By this time, all the neighbors on the street were coming out of their houses to see what the commotion was all about. At the top of the hill was a field, and beyond that, a wooded area. Just as Mother and half a dozen of the neighbors reached the top, the man was about to enter the woods, still dragging Mary by one hand. She was screaming at the top of her lungs. She stumbled and fell, loosening the man's grip on her hand. He put on a burst of speed and disappeared into the woods. In the meantime, someone had called for the police, and they could be heard running up the hill.

Mother got to Mary and picked her up in her arms. Mary was crying and showing Mother where the bad man had hurt her hand. It was a very shaky mother who took her little girl home. For the rest of the summer, she was afraid to allow Helen and Mary to play outside without a grownup nearby. Although the police searched the woods, they never did find the man. By the time the next summer came, Mother had drilled into her children's heads never to go with a stranger or take anything from one.

Helen used to tell the neighbor kids some truly gruesome horror stories. One night, Bill was sitting next to a neighbor girl, who was so terrified that she fainted. Poor Bill didn't know what had happened when he felt her sag against him. He knew something was wrong, so he yelled for someone to turn on the lights.

We had no electricity.[29] My mother would light the gas jets in each room. Marge once had an unusual experience relating to that. One night she came up from the basement and quietly sat on the floor beside some of the rest of us kids. Helen must have been telling a fairy story because the lights were off. Marge sat for a while and then got up from the floor and started up the stairs. At first Mother thought Marge was going to the bathroom, but then she realized that the lights were off, and Marge, as much as the rest of us kids, was afraid to go upstairs in the dark. Mother followed Marge up the stairs and into our bedroom where she lit the gas jet. She asked Marge why she was acting so strangely, and Marge confessed she had an egg in her bloomers. Mother was very surprised and asked Marge what she was going to do with a raw egg. Marge had heard that if you put a hole in each end of a raw egg, you could suck out the contents. Mother decided to play along with the idea, so she took a needle and put a tiny hole in each end of the egg and told Marge to suck out the egg. I believe she thought Marge

---

29 Histories tell us that most urban homes in the United States were supplied with electricity by about 1910, though it was much later for most rural areas. And Scranton's nickname as the "Electric City", comes from its relatively early power grid and early adoption of electricity for lighting in public venues, for streetcars, and for other purposes. It does seem ironic then that the Davenport household did not have electricity when Jessie was a small child in the 1910s. Still, it was not altogether unusual to be using gas lighting then. Perhaps even in Scranton, it took a while for the grid to reach every neighborhood. Also, the universal adoption of a new technology tends to lag its availability by several years. Even after power came to a neighborhood, it might have been years before every house there had wiring, outlets, and lighting fixtures installed. And sometimes landlords are extra slow to install new technology in their rented buildings. Gas lighting was at least considered preferable to kerosene lamps.

would chicken out, but she took the egg and did indeed suck on it. She said it tasted wonderful. I never did find out if she really liked it or not. When I asked, she would only smile and say, "Why don't you try it and find out?" I couldn't do that. The thought of a slimy egg going down my throat was too much.

One time, on a dark and dreary afternoon, my mother told me to go down to the basement for something she needed. I looked down the dark stairway to the even darker area at the bottom of the stairs. I began to cry, saying I was scared that there were rats down there. Marge said she would go down. She ran down the stairs and as she stepped off the bottom step, she stepped right on a rat's tail. Mary went running down the steps to rush to her aid. They chased that rat around the room until they finally managed to hit it over the head with the broom. I had to admire their courage, but I was so glad I hadn't been the one to go down the stairs.

Back in those days, boys wore pants and girls wore dresses. My mother was ahead of her time and dressed her little girls in overalls. I loved them because I had always wanted to be a boy. One day I got the idea of using a carrot to emulate how a boy urinates. Claire was shocked at first, but I talked her into doing it too. I'll say one thing. We gave it a good try, but all we got was wet. If Marge had caught us, she would have told on us, and we would have been punished in no uncertain terms. I had talked Claire into going into the storage room to try it, even though it was dark in there, and we were both afraid of rats. But the desire to be a boy was too strong. I used to remind Claire that after our experiment, she decided to eat her carrot, but that I threw mine away. A lot of years passed before she saw the humor in that one.

I remember my first day at school.[30] I was so afraid to ask the teacher where the restroom was that I wet my pants and cried all the way home. My mother said when I was born, I had a big mouth, and it was always open. According to my sister, Helen, I cried when I got my way, and I cried when I didn't.

I don't remember the day Jimmy was born, but I do remember the night my baby brother, Dick, was. I was seven and a half years old at the time. He must have been born early in the evening, because all of us younger kids had been sent next door to the Kinsmans'. Helen and Mary were down in the kitchen boiling water. I didn't want to stay at the Kinsmans', so I sneaked out and went home. My Aunt Babe[31] was coming down the stairs with some sheets bundled up in her arms. As I came in the front door, she told me I had a new baby brother.

There is a story about the new baby and who he belonged to. It seems that Mary and I had been fighting over a doll for several months before Dick was born. Mother

---

30 It seems likely that she attended a public school, and the locations of the elementary schools in the Scranton School District does not seem to have changed much since that time. It is therefore a good guess that she went either to Charles Sumner Elementary, only a four-minute walk to the northwest, or to Frances Willard Elementary, about seven minutes to the south. She probably didn't have far to walk in any case.

31 Probably one of Elizabeth's sisters was nicknamed Babe, though I don't know which one.

said whoever gave up the doll could have the next baby. In those days, babies weren't talked about before they were born, so even Mary didn't know that Mother was expecting. In later years, Mary and I would argue over who gave up the doll. Neither of us could remember. I suspect it was Mary who did. At that age, a bird in the hand was better than something that might never happen. It didn't really matter as Dick became in effect everybody's baby. He was a perfect picture-book baby—big, blue eyes and long lashes that should have been on a girl. He had blonde hair and a sweet disposition.

I remember one day in particular. I was holding Dick's hands as he walked. There was this old lady visiting our house. We called her Old Lady Pryor. She loved to swear and get us kids all upset, and I think she went after me most of all. I guess it was because she could make me cry. My mother was downstairs, making tea for the old lady. I happened to walk Dick right by the woman's chair. For some reason, she grabbed my arm and said, "Do you know what that baby's name is?" Of course, I said, yes, that his name was Richard, but we called him Dick. She gave me a nasty look and then said, "His name is Shit-Pot-Piss-Pot." I was horrified. How could she call my beloved baby brother such ugly names? I grabbed him up in my arms and took him into the next room where I sat and cried, my tears wetting his golden head.

Another time Old Lady Pryor asked me to go to the store for her, which I did. My mother had taught us never to take money for helping other people. When I returned, the old lady offered me a nickel, but I refused it. She threw the nickel on the table and yelled at me, "Damn it! I said take it!"

That did it. I screamed back at her, "My mother doesn't swear at me, and you are not going to either." Then I went crying down the stairs. We all hated that old lady. She had a musty smell of moth balls. We could always tell which chair she had been sitting in, and none of us would sit there until we forgot about her being there.

I had an embarrassing moment in the little store on the corner by our house. We kids would play a game. We would stand in front of the candy counter and pretend we could have any candy bar we wanted. We would point a finger at the one we happened to want that day and say, "I'll have that one." Most of the time the owner of the store would be too busy to pay attention to what we kids were doing. But one day when I pointed my finger at the candy I wanted and said I'd have it, to my surprise and joy, he reached in and handed me the bar. I smiled at him and said a bashful "Thank you."

Then he asked, "Where's your nickel?" When I said I didn't have one, he reached over the counter and took the candy from my hand. I ran out of the store, and as usual, cried all the way home. I never forgot that embarrassing moment.

My mother and father separated for a while. I know they had a terrible fight. I don't remember much about that, and what little I do know was what Mary told me when I got older. Anyway, Father left. I must be honest. I didn't love my father or even like him. I was scared of him. One of his favorite things when he got angry at one of us was to grab that person by the hair and bang their head against the wall. I faintly remember him having Helen by her long hair and banging her head against the bathroom wall. Of the nine of us, he had two favorite kids—Jim, who was next to the youngest, and Marge, who was two years older than I.

Anyway, he and Mother separated, and Mother was left with nine kids, none old enough to work. My mother went out scrubbing floors. In those days this meant on her hands and knees with a scrub brush. I don't know what kind of soap they used then, but my poor mother's hands were red and cracked. I remember one Sunday she dressed Marge and me in our best clothes. We had new plaid capes that the neighbor lady had made for us. Mother had Helen take us to visit my father who was living with his sister. I remember how uncomfortable I was. I didn't like my Aunt Helen. I was very young, but I knew by what little I had heard that she had done something to my mother that wasn't very nice. Although things were later patched up, I never got over that feeling of dislike for her. I know I never trusted her.

I had to go to the store one day, and my father came in while I was waiting to get my purchases bagged. He asked about everyone. Then he bought me a bag of candy. In those days, a quarter bought a lot of candy. I was supposed to take the candy home and share it with the other kids. I went home thinking how wonderful my father was, and I cried when I handed the bag of candy to my mother and said how I wished my father would come home. *To be bought for a bag of candy!*

We were poor, and I mean really poor. I know Mother told me that before Marge was born, she was often hungry, and after being born, Marge didn't cry for three days. Whether it was because my mother was malnourished, I don't know. She must have gotten plenty to eat before I was born, because I came into the world squalling, and from what they say, I never shut up. My mother told me that my father had rich relatives, but my mother was too proud to ask for help. I think my father asked Uncle Alex for help at times, and he got it when he did.

We used to have a lot of fun on Halloween. In those days, you had to perform for your treats. We had to recite, sing, or even dance. We dressed in all kinds of costumes. We went as bums with burnt cork on our faces, or we dressed as pretty ladies, clowns, or witches. All our costumes were homemade from whatever we could throw together. We planned for weeks how we were going to dress and what we would perform to get a treat. One time my father's cousin, Jessie, who was very rich, promised Helen and Mary some really beautiful costumes—Marie Antoinette or something like that.[32] They were so excited when the package finally arrived that they almost had a fight over who was going to open it. Helen got the honor because she was the eldest. When they opened the box, all they found was little girls' clothes, no costumes. A mix up had happened, and a maid who worked for Cousin Jessie had given the box of costumes to another family. I

---

32 This Cousin Jessie is generally assumed to be Jessie Grant Connell (1865-1947, never married), though another possibility was Jessie *Connell* McAnulty (1862-1926). They were both of the wealthy and influential Connell family of Scranton, and both were first cousins of William's mother. Thus, either would have been first cousin twice removed (almost like a great-aunt) to little Helen and Mary, the intended recipients of the beautiful costumes.

guess my mother was glad to get little girls' clothes. I remember a very nice white dress that just fit me, and I proudly strutted up and down the street so Anna Kinsman could see me!

On our birthdays we got a penny for each year old we were, and Mother would bake us a cake. So, at the age of ten I received a dime, which was riches to me. Do you know how much candy you could buy for ten cents? We always shared with each other.

We all loved the ice man. He would drive his wagon down the street, and when he stopped and took a piece of ice on his shoulder to deliver to one of the houses, we would gather around the wagon and steal pieces of ice. I don't know what they packed the ice in, but we would brush off the dirt and run, sucking on the frozen water. We did a lot of crazy things. For instance, we loved to chew hot tar right out of the barrel. The workers would be repairing the street, and when they weren't looking, we would run to the barrel and grab some of the tar. Of course, we got burned some of the time, but if you were really careful and took tar from around the rim, it was usually only warm.

One thing I remember about Scranton was a night when Marge took a licking for me. We were all in one bed—Marge, Claire, and I. Claire and I had the giggles and were fooling around. My mother would call in for us to be quiet and go to sleep. We'd quiet down for a while, and then start giggling again. Mother would holler at us again to be quiet, and we would smother our giggles for a few minutes and then start in again. In the meantime, Marge had pulled the sheet over her head, so the night light wouldn't shine in her eyes and maybe she could go to sleep. My father was home that night, and after listening to my mother telling us to be quiet and not getting anywhere, he took matters into his own hands. I had just gotten out of bed to go to the bathroom when I heard him coming down the hall. I scooted under the bed. When he came into the room and saw Marge with her head under the covers, he thought she was hiding from him. He pulled down the covers and gave her a spanking.

While we were living in Scranton, Helen got a job at the park as a bathhouse attendant. Uncle Alex, who was mayor of Scranton got her the job.[33] She would take me to the park with her sometimes. She liked to have company, and I loved to go. I spent the day swimming. There was also a playground with slides and swings. I had a wonderful time, and I would sulk on the days when Helen took Marge instead of me. I

---

33 Alexander Thomas Connell (1861-1947) was listed as one of the "prominent men of Scranton". He was mayor of the city from 1903 to 1906, and again from 1918-1922. I discussed more details about him in the Introduction including his relationship to his only nephew, William.

Nay Aug Park, especially in those days, played a very significant role in the life of Scrantonians. At that time, it was a combination of zoo, amusement park, and general recreation area with wooded walking paths, a playground, and a swimming area in the lake. The park is about three miles to the east of where their house was, and they likely traveled there by streetcar. It might be true anywhere that political connections are useful in getting even mundane jobs working for a city, but it seems to have been especially true of Scranton. That is why Uncle Alex tried to help the Davenport household make ends meet by arranging a job for their eldest daughter, Helen, to work in the bathhouse for the swimming area at the lake.

remember the bathing suits we wore. They were made of some kind of stretchy material, and when they were wet, they hung almost to our ankles. The bathhouse smelled of wet suits and rubber, and adding to the odor, there were only inside privies. We even wore rubber slippers into the water. There was a man who worked for the park. He cleaned the cages of the zoo animals and did odd jobs. He liked me and every day he would have something for me, mostly peacock feathers. He was a nice man and very good to me. He was handicapped. Specifically, he was deaf and dumb. Like all young children, I could communicate with him. We understood each other.

We loved the movies. At that time, they were silent and only cost a nickel. My Aunt Helen used to play the piano at the movies. It was a tricky job, because she had to play all kinds of music and be ready to switch from one type to another as the mood of the story shifted. She played soft music when there was a love scene, and when a storm came up, the music would have to be loud and crashing. Saturday was the day that we were allowed to spend a nickel at the nickelodeon.[34] I suppose my mother was glad to have a few of her kids away for a few hours. The movie house was at the end of our block, so she felt it was safe for us.

Christmas was always a very exciting time for the family. We talked about Santa Claus for weeks before the big event. We would go upstairs the night before Christmas, all excited. Marge and I would be determined to stay awake until everyone had gone to bed, and then we would sneak downstairs and wait for Santa to come. Every so often we would wake up, and if we heard voices, we knew Santa hadn't come yet. There was a place between the bookcase and the sideboard that was just big enough for a couple of small bodies to hide in. Marge and I planned to hide there, but we never made it. We would get too sleepy waiting for the grown-ups to go to bed. We never saw the tree trimmed until Christmas morning. When we came downstairs in the morning, the tree would be all sparkly and beautiful. We thought Santa Claus had trimmed it.

One year when I was about eight years old, I was very bad. I had younger brothers and sisters, and I wasn't very nice to them. I pushed and shoved them whenever I got near them. All of this was behind my mother's back, of course. The kids finally had enough of the way I was treating them, so they told my mother what I had been doing. She scolded me and said that if I didn't stop, I would get coal in my stockings. I didn't believe her, and when her back was turned, I stuck my tongue out. Why did she have to treat me like my baby brother? By that time, I was pretty sure there wasn't any Santa Claus. I made faces at the other kids and in general acted like a spoiled brat. I wanted Christmas to come, and deep in my heart, I still really did believe in Santa Claus. It was as though I had to act so badly just to see if I would be punished.

A few days before Christmas, I began to worry. I was filled with doubts. What if I didn't get any presents? I wished I hadn't behaved so badly. I tried to make up for it by

---

34 Although "nickelodeon" later came to mean a jukebox sort of device, originally it meant the earliest type of movie theater, which charged five cents for admission. They were usually simple spaces, often set up in converted store fronts. Jessie seems to be referring to that meaning.

being very good. I was nice to the kids, and whenever Mother wanted me to do something, I ran to do it as fast as I could. I was hoping it was enough to make up for all the bad things I had done, just with those last few days of good behavior.

We always got a new pair of stockings, and we would pin the tops together and hang them over the banister. The next morning, they would be lumpy with all kinds of good things inside—nuts, oranges, apples, and of course, candy. The fruit was as special to us as the candy, as we didn't get fruit that often.

So, on this particular Christmas Eve, we hung up our stockings and went to bed where we whispered and giggled before dropping off to sleep. That was the one night in the year when we didn't have to be told more than once to go to bed. The next morning, it must have been before six o'clock that we kids were sneaking down the stairs to see what Santa had left for us. The first thing I did was grab my stockings and feel the lumpiness. Santa had not forgotten me I thought with relief. The other kids were looking at the piles of presents under the tree. Each little pile had a name tag on it, and as each kid found the tag with their name on it, they knew that pile was his or hers. Claire and Carmel were squealing over new dolls. Helen and Mary were already absorbed in new books. Marge was quietly wheeling a doll carriage.

I looked and looked for my name tag, but I couldn't find it. I was heartbroken. Why had I been so bad? I stood there as the tears rushed into my eyes, and there was a lump in my throat. I felt some relief when one of the kids hollered, "Hey Jess, here is your name tag." But when I looked at the tag lying on the bare white sheet, I realized there were no presents for me. I grabbed my stockings to my chest. At least I would have what Santa left in my stockings. I got an empty box and dumped out their contents. I started to remove the tissue paper that was wrapped around what I thought was an orange. To my horror, out fell a lump of black coal! I started to ball at the top of my lungs. I hated Santa Claus and the whole family. I had to blame someone.

Finally, my mother and father groggily came down the stairs asking what had happened. I sobbed brokenheartedly as I told them that I had not gotten any presents. My mother had a sad look on her face. She said, "Jessie, you deserved to be punished for the way you have been behaving, and I don't blame Santa for not leaving you anything." That didn't make me feel any better, and I cried harder. A few minutes of this, and I settled down to just sniffles. Then my mother said, "However, if you promise never to behave so badly again, especially at Christmas, I'll tell you what Santa did." I perked up my ears and looked at her as though I couldn't believe what she was saying. *Did Santa tell her he would bring me some presents after all?* She went on, "He left a note for me that said that if I thought you had been punished enough, to give you the gifts that are behind the tree." I ran and looked behind the tree, and there was a little pile of presents with my name on them. I was so happy. I suppose I did a lot of naughty things during the year, but after that experience, I was a model child for the month leading up to Christmas each year. I didn't want to go through that experience again.

My mother told me that the night I was born, the other kids came into her bedroom to see the new baby. I was lying in a basket. The kids would walk around the basket to see me, except Marge, who was only two, and she just wanted to get in bed with my mother. When it came time for Bill, who was four at the time, to take a peek at me, I made a little noise. Mother told Bill that I had said, "Oh, there is my big brother, Bill." He really believed that I had known who he was. I loved my brother Bill very much, and when I was too little to know better, I would tell everyone that I was going to marry him when I grew up. One time we were fooling around, and Bill was giving me a horsey-back ride. We were having so much fun that I forgot to answer nature's call, and poor Bill ended up with a wet back. Was he ever *mad*!

I am told that I was the only kid out of the nine who was born at night. I arrived at three o'clock in the morning. My father had been there when the older four had been born, but he didn't make it home from his work for the railroad when I was. I always felt like the odd one in our family. I was argumentative and would quarrel over the least little thing. Bill used to stick up for me. I remember one time when my parents went out and left Helen and Mary in charge. When it came time to go to bed, I got stubborn. I kept making a fuss, and finally they took me bodily and tried to make me go upstairs. I screamed and cried. Finally, Bill jumped in between us and told my sisters to leave me alone. They turned on him and began hitting him all over his body. When he sagged onto the steps with his head lolling to the side, I got scared and ran up the stairs and into bed. I thought Bill was dead. He wasn't hurt. He was just putting on an act so the girls would let go of him. It was a sad day for me when my mother told me I couldn't marry my own brother.

Marge was scratching herself one day, and Mother pulled up the girl's shirt to find three blisters on her side. She wasn't sure what they were, so she took Marge next door and showed the blisters to the lady who lived there. They looked like chicken pox, but as there were only three of them set in a triangle, neither my mother nor her friend was sure. After Marge and Mother came back inside, I was sitting on the couch. Mother noticed that I was rubbing my back up against the back of the couch. She pulled up my shirt and found that my back was covered with red blisters. No doubt about it—I had the chicken pox. Marge never had more than the three spots, but I was plastered.

I don't think dying was very real to me back then. I had a little friend named Augie. One day I heard that Augie had died. Some said it was from eating green peaches. I suppose that is the only way they could explain his death to a small child. The sad thing is that I only remember Augie because of his death. In those days, the funerals were held in the home, and one of the things I remember most was the black wreaths hung on the front doors. All that last summer in Scranton, wherever I went on almost every street, a black wreath was on at least one house. I would get the shivers whenever I passed a house with a wreath hung on the door. I hated those wreaths, and to this day, I will not have a Christmas wreath on my door.[35]

My mother got really upset with Mary when she went shopping with a girlfriend of hers. It was a rainy day, so they each carried an umbrella. They didn't have much money, so it was mostly just window shopping. They went into the five-and-ten store and sauntered around the aisles giggling as two girls always do. When they came out of the store, the rain was really coming down. Mary's friend asked Mary to open her umbrella, and when Mary did, the girl crowded under it with her. Mary asked her why she didn't open her own umbrella, but her friend just hurried her along until they were about two blocks from the five-and-dime store. Then the girl showed Mary why she hadn't opened her own umbrella. It was full of small items that the girl had stolen from the store. Mary couldn't wait to get on the streetcar and go home. When she told Mother what had happened, Mother said she was very lucky that the girl wasn't caught, because although Mary hadn't stolen anything, she would be blamed anyway. That was good-bye to Mary's girlfriend.

One time I was out on the front porch, where I was lying on my stomach, reading a book. Mother wheeled Dick out on the porch in his baby carriage and told me to wheel it back and forth until Dick went to sleep. Not wanting to give up my book, I turned on my side and started to wheel the carriage with my foot. Bad mistake! I came to an exciting place in the book, and forgetting about the baby in the carriage, I gave it a hard shove. The carriage rolled to the top of the porch and swayed there for a moment, and then bounced down the steps, dumping Dick out on the sidewalk. My eyes bugged out as my mother came running out to pick up a screaming baby. He wasn't hurt, just frightened. I do not remember how I was punished for that one, but I am sure I was.

One of the things I remember most about the house in Scranton was coming home from school on cold winter days. As I opened the door and stepped into the kitchen, the smell of homemade bread, hot from the oven, was the most wonderful aroma in the world. The loaves would be lined up on the counter while mother rubbed an oiled paper over the brown crusts. Hot cocoa and a slice of homemade bread were *Heavenly*!

---

35 The Spanish flu pandemic, one of the deadliest diseases in history, lasted from 1918 into 1920. It may be that the reason Jessie remembers so many deaths and so many black wreaths in the neighborhood is the result of that terrible disease. The high death rate must have been traumatic for a young child, and the lifelong dread of wreaths, even Christmas wreaths, is easy to understand.

Chapter 2—Dalton

I guess I was eight or nine when we moved to Dalton, a small town about twelve miles from Scranton.[36] The house we moved into was like a palace compared to the one we had left. We had a huge front lawn, and on the side, there were fruit trees toward the back and pine trees toward the front. The house had a wrap-around porch and big rooms. Adjoining the kitchen there was a pantry, which is where the sink was. We had a dining room and two living rooms, one with a sliding door. There was a path from the back door that went right down into the schoolyard. Upstairs we had four bedrooms and a bathroom. The bathroom had a sink and a bathtub with running water, but there was no toilet, which frequently caused a problem. There were both front and back stairways. The back one opened into the bedroom that was for us four younger girls. The front stairway opened into a hallway with the other three bedrooms off of that. The big front room was for Mother and Father, and the next room was for Helen and Mary. The third room was for the boys, but you had to go through that room to get to the bathroom,

---

36 The length of the Dalton chapter implies that this was a location of particularly rich memories for Jessie, and it seems that they were generally pleasant ones. She must have enjoyed living closer to nature than in the more urban homes, and toward the end of the chapter she mentions that the family had hoped they would eventually own the house and be its permanent residents. I cannot seem to find any other documentation about their time in Dalton, but perhaps that is OK since she describes it clearly enough without that. Documents show them living in Scranton in the summer of 1920, so it was likely either later that year or, as Jessie later suggests, early in 1921 that they moved to Dalton. She later recalls clearly that she was just about twelve and a half when they moved to Ithaca, which would have meant it was in the spring of 1924, making in total their time in Dalton around three or three and a half years.

Jessie describes the Dalton community well, and just adding a little more detail here, it is part of a collection of suburban municipalities northwest of Scranton informally known in the region as "the Abingtons". The Abingtons are said to include Clarks Summit along with several smaller surrounding boroughs and townships, and Dalton is a borough toward the northern end of these. In 1920 the population was about 800, and Dalton had a rapid burst in growth to over 1000 in the next decade. For those accustomed to driving past on I-81, we can think of it as closest to the exit labeled for Waverly. The Lackawanna Trail (US-11) goes right through Dalton, but I-81 passes some miles to the east of it.

There are enough clues here to indicate that they probably lived near the eastern or northeastern edge of the Dalton settlement, but not enough clues to give us an exact address. Jessie describes a school just down a slope from the house and a church just beyond that, but there is no longer a school in Dalton, and the only remaining churches close by probably don't quite fit her description. Several of the memories she records relate to Lily Lake. She describes the hike to the lake as crossing the railroad tracks, heading through a field containing a pond, and then passing through a short, wooded stretch to arrive at the lake shore. Assuming that the field might now be somewhat overgrown, this seems to fit exactly a cross-country hike of about three-quarters mile heading east from a northeastern part of Dalton. In any case, they could not have been too far from the center of the borough, which would have been convenient since it meant they were a short walk from a store, the streetcar station, and especially to the school.

When they first settled into the house in Dalton, depending on exactly what month that was, Helen might have been sixteen, Mary fourteen, Bill thirteen, Marge eleven, Jessie nine, Claire seven, Carmel five, Jim three, and Dick one.

which also connected to the room for us younger girls. Our room had two beds, one for Claire and Carmel, and the other one for Marge and me.

Like I said, having no toilet led to problems. The small children couldn't be expected to go out to the privy at night, so Mother said we could have a chamber pot, but we older girls would have to keep it clean. We were all supposed to use the privy in the daytime, but kids being kids, we would use whatever was nearest. We took care of the pot, but only when we remembered to. In the summer, when we were mostly out of doors, we used the pot only at night, and sometimes we forgot to clean the darn thing. My father hated that "thundermug" as we all called it. If he came home when we weren't expecting him, we would make a wild dash to the thundermug and hide it in the stairway that led up to the attic. He always found it anyway, and he would go to the window that looked out onto the backyard and heave it out.

One night Helen and her boyfriend at the time were walking down the path. The trees were in bloom and apple blossoms were perfuming the air. As they were strolling along, they heard my father yelling, and then the thundermug came bouncing down the path. Poor Helen, who was always so ladylike, almost died of embarrassment that night. Somehow the thundermug never broke. The next day we would go out, pick it up, and bring it back inside, while the whole time promising Mother to keep it clean. But, more often than not, we would forget again the next time. With all the times the thundermug made a bouncing trip down the garden path, it really is amazing it never broke.

One day Claire and I were fooling around in the parlor. The sliding doors were closed at the time. We'd pull down the shade and let it go. It would roll up to the top and make a snapping noise. My mother called into us to stop, but as usual we kept doing what we thought was funny. Finally, when my mother opened the doors to come into the room, Claire and I took off. We ran up the two flights of stairs to the attic, since we knew she wouldn't chase us up there. I was punished in a way that was worse than getting a spanking. We had been eating dill pickles at the time, and I still had a piece of one in my mouth. As I ran up the stairs, it became lodged behind my nose, where it burned for about an hour before I managed to get it out. I was very careful after that not to be eating dill pickles when I got into deviltry.

My eldest sister, Helen, took me to the library,[37] and I got my first library card. I can't tell you what joy I had taking out my first library book. The book was *Humpty Dumpty*, and I can still remember the first line: '"I hate eggs," said Meg.' I went to the library whenever I got the chance. We could only get to that library by car, as it was in a little town about twenty miles from where we lived.

Love of reading sometimes got me into trouble. Our teacher was reading a book

---

37 What town this library was in is unclear. It is confusing in any case that they would have needed to go twenty miles to a small-town library, when the big Scranton library was much closer than twenty miles and could be reached by streetcar when they didn't have access to a car.

to the class, the title of which was *Toby Tyler*.[38] I wanted to read that book so badly. One chapter per day was just teasing. As our house was just up the bank from the school, I asked the teacher if I could take the book home for the weekend. I told her I would bring it back on Monday. Understandably, she refused. She explained that the other kids wanted her to continue reading the book, and if I had already read it all, I would be bored. Well, I decided to take the book anyway. I thought I would read it over the weekend and return it on Monday morning before the teacher got to the school. No one would know I had taken it except my best friend, Marie. There was a side door into the classroom, so I thought it would be easy to sneak in and put the book back on the shelf early Monday morning.

I snitched the book and took it home, and sure enough I enjoyed reading it that weekend. On Monday, I woke up with a sore throat, and my mother wouldn't let me go to school. I was on pins and needles the whole day, waiting for Marie to come to the house and tell me what had happened when the teacher couldn't find the book. The hours dragged by until, at about three thirty, Marie came to the front door. I had been standing there watching to let her into the house without anyone hearing us. I was scared. Marie told me that when the teacher went to the shelf to get the book, she was surprised to find it missing, so she questioned the kids in the class. No one knew anything about why the book was missing except Marie, and she didn't tell. I thanked her for not telling on me, and I pleaded with her to continue to keep her mouth shut. She promised she would.

This went on for two more days. I was still staying home due to my claim of illness, and Marie came every day to tell me what was happening. About Thursday of that week, Marie broke down and confessed to the teacher that I had taken the book. The teacher apparently wasn't surprised, but when Marie told me, I didn't know what to do. I went upstairs, threw myself on the bed, and cried my heart out. I told God that if I got out of this mess, I'd never take another thing that didn't belong to me. Finally, my mother, who had come upstairs to put away the clean laundry, heard my sobs and came into the room to see what I was carrying on about. I sobbed as I told her what I had done. I told her she should send me to a home for bad girls. She didn't get upset. She just told me that I would have to return the book and tell the teacher how sorry I was, and I would have to do it the next morning.

As I walked down the bank that next morning, I felt as though I was going to my doom. I handed the book to the teacher and told her how sorry I was. She gave me a lecture, and I promised never to take anything again that didn't belong to me. She acted as though she believed me, but every time someone lost or misplaced something after that, the teacher looked at me as though she expected me to jump up and give it back.

My mother had been a teacher when she married my father. My dad was a year

---

38 The original *Toby Tyler* or *Ten Weeks with a Circus* by James Otis was first published in book form in 1881. It was an exceptionally popular novel for children. It had twenty chapters.

younger than my mother, and if I remember the story correctly, he was still in college.[39] It seems that he had taken my mother on a date, or whatever they called it in those days, and when they came home, he asked her for a kiss. She told him that she wouldn't kiss any man unless she was engaged to him. So, my dad proposed. I don't know how soon they were married, but I remember my mother telling me how much they wanted a baby and prayed every night that they would be blessed. I always thought they must have prayed too hard, because they had nine kids in quick succession.

Anyway, Mother didn't teach again until almost all the kids were in school or married. She got a teaching job in a one-room schoolhouse—all eight grades taught by one teacher. One day, Mother happened to meet Jim's teacher at the school we went to, and during the conversation, she told Mother that Jim had been absent from school one afternoon. When the teacher asked him why, he told her that he had to stay home to keep the cat off the table.

Isn't it funny how some things stay in your mind for the rest of your life? They have to be either very good or very bad to come into your mind at odd times. I remember one such experience. When I was about ten years old, I was invited to a girl's house for dinner, only we called it supper at our house. This girl was an only child, and I envied her for the pretty clothes she had. It was a lovely house, and she had her own bedroom. After looking at all the beautiful dolls she had, I thought of my little beat-up doll who had been left out in the rain. I can honestly say that although the dolls and toys that she had were in perfect condition, I still loved my old doll. Supper time came and I sat down to the table with their family. It certainly wasn't what I was used to. At each plate was a small dish with a roll on it and a knife. When the butter was passed to me, I picked up the knife and buttered my roll. Then I put the knife back on the butter dish. I watched the rest of the family and realized that I was supposed to help myself to the butter and place it on the side of my dish. I was so embarrassed that I couldn't enjoy the food that I was putting into my mouth. Everything tasted dry, and I was afraid they would hear me when I swallowed. I was glad to go home. I was never asked back.

My mother ordered our coats for the winter from catalogs. She ordered them so big that they reached to our ankles. Mother sewed in big hems, and all winter long, whenever the coats got wet, they weighed a ton. They were always big and bulky banging around our knees. By the time we grew into them, they were all worn out, which means we never had coats that actually fit us. Once in a while Mother would take us into Scranton to buy shoes. We kids were so nervous about getting shoes, we said the first pair we tried on fit us just fine, even if they were so tight they pinched. We were just that afraid that we wouldn't get any shoes at all if we complained about the first pair

---

39 Whether or not William went to college is unclear. In her memoir, *Sister Helen's Stories,* Jessie's eldest sister claims that their father's formal education came to an end the day he was kicked out of Valley Forge Military Academy for the pranks he did, and in those days that institution did not offer post-secondary courses. Still, it is possible that he had some later technical training more or less at the college level.

hurting. We always started out winter with a bunch of mittens, but they didn't last long. We were always losing them. We didn't have galoshes either. Instead, we would put heavy socks on over our shoes. They kept our feet dry for a while. At times we did have rubber overshoes, but we often broke our fingernails from struggling to put the darn things on over our shoes.

The kids in our school were mostly farm kids, and they lived far enough away that they had to bring their lunches rather than going home for lunch. I wished I could be like them and take my lunch, but as we lived next door to the school, that was out of the question. Somehow, I thought taking your lunch to school was a big deal, but I was afraid I might never have that pleasure. Then one day when we got up in the morning, the snow was about three feet deep. My mother needed some things from the store, and she asked us kids who would volunteer for the job. I was chosen, and my mother bundled me up. I asked her if I could take my lunch to school that day, and she agreed. She told me to buy some pimento cheese and a dozen oranges, and when I got back from the store, she would make me a lunch to take. I was happy both when I went to the store and when I went to school. That was the only day I stayed at school for lunch. I never took my lunch again, but I always remembered how good my pimento cheese sandwich and my orange tasted.

People can be so cruel to kids. Marie's father had a farm outside of Dalton, and one Saturday I had permission to spend the afternoon with Marie at the farm. I walked two miles to the farm only to find out that Marie couldn't play, as her father needed her help to harvest the potato crop. He would turn the earth, and the kids' role was to pick up the potatoes and put them in sacks. All of his kids had to help. I thought I might as well help as well. I thought it might be fun, and it might mean Marie could finish earlier and still have time to play. I didn't know much about picking potatoes. It was hard work, and I was glad when we were done that day. Marie's father was all smiles as he looked over the sacks of potatoes. He told the kids to line up, and he handed each one, except me, a nickel. There I stood, covered in mud and sweat, and tired to the bone. I had worked just as hard as the other kids, and I got nothing except a two-mile walk home that day.

Except for Marge, we kids were careless with our clothes. Marge was always the neat one. We used to pile our coats on a chair or the banister. If a few slipped onto the floor, we just ignored them and left them there. On one unhappy day, I was in a hurry and grabbed my coat from the floor. I ran down the bank and into the school. I hurriedly hung my coat on a hook in the cloakroom and took my seat. Then I began to notice a horrible smell. I looked around to see which of the farm kids had brought something that smelled on his boots. They were all looking at me, so I looked down at my dress and didn't see anything wrong. But then one of the kids, who was sitting behind me, leaned over and said in a loud whisper, "Hey Jess, you've got cat shit on the back of your dress." I jumped up, ran into the cloakroom, and got my coat. Sure enough, there was cat poop all over the lining. I ran out the door and raced home to change my clothes. I don't remember saying anything to the teacher, but I'm sure she didn't mind me leaving. I never really liked cats after that.

I remember stories my mother told me about her days teaching school back in Shamokin before she was married. They had a little performance every Friday afternoon when the pupils would either recite a poem or sing a song. On the coldest winter days when the mines were closed, some of the boys who worked in the mines would return to school. Some of these boys were really young men almost as old as my mother. On one particular Friday, after a few other kids had performed, a little girl came to my mother and said she wanted to sing a song her father had taught her. This is what she sang.

Yankee Doodle went to town.
Behind a load of peaches.
He left a fart behind the cart.
And blowed it all to pieces.

At that point, my mother was terribly embarrassed in front of the young men from the mines. They must have really liked their pretty, young teacher, because not a one of them even laughed. Mother still held the little shows every Friday, but she would find out in advance what each child planned to recite or sing.

Good Fairies—that was what Claire and I sometimes were. When my mother took the younger kids upstairs after supper, she would tell us we could wait a while before coming up. Once in a while, Claire and I would be on such a cleaning streak that we would use those times to go into the kitchen, clean all the cupboards, shine the stove, and really give the floor a good sweeping. If we really felt like working, we would get a bucket and take turns mopping the floor. The next morning, we would wait for Mother to come and see what we had done. She never failed us. She would come into the kitchen, and in a tone of wonder, she would say, "The good fairies have been here and cleaned up my kitchen." Of course, she knew that Claire and I had done it. It was fun to surprise her.

One summer a new girl moved from the big city to our small town. We were in the same grade in school. She was a very pretty girl. Her name was Elizabeth, and everyone called her Beth. We became pretty good friends. I'll always remember my first visit to her house. Her only sibling was a brother, and that is the closest thing to being an only child. Her mother was very nice. What really stunned me was when I first followed Beth into her bedroom. I almost flipped at the bookcase filled with so many books. I asked Beth if I could borrow some to take home to read. She asked her mother, who at first refused. She explained that Beth had loaned out some of her books before, and they were either not returned at all or returned in such a bad condition that they had to throw them out. I had already picked out in my mind two of the books that I really wanted to borrow. One was from the *Little Prudy* series, and the other was *At the*

Back of the North Wind.[40] I could imagine myself hurrying home across a little bridge over a creek in the twilight as I clutched the books to my chest. I was so disappointed when Beth's mother first refused that I could feel the tears about to fall from my eyes. What a relief it was when she relented! "Promise to be very careful with them," she said to me. I was willing to promise anything.

When I got home, I told my mother about this nice family I had met. She said I was very lucky to have friends like that, and that I must be very careful with the books. She showed me how to make book covers from brown wrapping paper to protect them. Everything went fine for a while. I handled those books as though they were made of gold. When I returned them to Beth, her mother smiled and told Beth she could lend me some of the other books.

I think I borrowed a total of six books, continuing to be very careful, but in the end, disaster struck. One day, while I was reading *The Birds' Christmas Carol*,[41] my mother called me and told me she needed me to run an errand to the store. Usually, when I had to put one of the books down, I would carefully place it on a shelf where my younger brothers couldn't reach it. But this day, I was in such a hurry to get to the store and back that I just left the book on the little table by my bed. I could hear Jim and Dick playing in their room, so with them occupied in that way, I thought the book would be safe until I got back from the store. It was a rainy day, and I loved walking in the rain so much that, in spite of my plan to hurry, I began to walk slowly and to daydream as I went along. When I got home, I had the task of setting the table for supper. Jim and Dick began showing us some paper airplanes they had made from some small sheets of paper.   Mother finally told them to stop playing and eat their suppers. Jimmy had to launch one more airplane, and it happened to float down onto my plate. As I picked it up, I began to read what was printed on the paper. I startled everyone with my loud yell as I ran up the stairs to my room. I was afraid to look, but I had to. About half of the pages in the book were missing. The boys had torn them out page by page to make their airplanes. I sat and cried. Mother said she would pay for the books, but Beth's mother would not lend me any more books to take home. In fact, it was weeks before Beth would even speak to me. I lost my chance to read the rest of her books, and I lost a friend, all due to being careless.

One incidental remark by my eldest sister stuck in my mind for a long time. I was nine or ten at the time. One Sunday I was very bored, so I decided to make my doll some new clothes. There was an abundance of discarded clothing in the attic, so I picked out what I thought would be material for making a pretty dress for my doll. I ran downstairs and asked Helen, who was babysitting us that day, for a needle and some

---

40 The several volumes of the *Little Prudy* series were first published from 1864 up through about 1900 by an American author known as Sophie May. *At the Back of the North Wind* was first published in 1871 by Scottish author George MacDonald.

41 First published in 1888. Written by the American educator, Kate Douglas Wiggin, who is best known for a later book, *Rebecca of Sunnybrook Farm*

thread. She looked at me for a moment and then said, "If you sew on Sunday, then when you die, God will make you take out all the stitches with your nose." For days I went around wondering if God would be attaching a hook to the end of my nose, because how else would it be possible to pull out stitches with my nose? Well, I didn't sew on that Sunday, or on any Sunday for years afterwards. I finally concluded that Helen had told me a made-up story. I started sewing on Sundays after that, but always with a slight twinge of fear that maybe Helen had been right after all. It is likely that Helen told me that story just to avoid the bother of looking for a needle and thread, and to think that I had so much fear just due to that minor remark.

Like most kids, Claire and I had our list of bad words. We didn't hear them at home. My mother hardly ever even said "damn", and my father didn't do much swearing either. Some of the worst words I heard were the ones written on the railroad underpass. Claire and I would sit either in the closet or under the dining room table and go down the list of all the vulgar words we knew, and we would giggle if either one of us came up with a new one.

One Saturday, we had washed our hair, and my mother had put it up in rags, so we could go to church the next day with curly hair. We thought we had found the perfect place to practice our cuss words—the privy. Usually if someone came down the path to use the privy while we were in it, we could hear them coming. But one day, Claire and I were sitting on the two-holer, and I was telling her a new word I had heard. It was "bastard", and we thought it was a good one to add to our list. We were giggling over some of the other words too when the privy door flew open, and there stood Marge. "I heard what you were saying," she stormed, "And I'm going to tell Mother on you." She ran back up the path toward the house, and Claire and I were scared. There was only one thing to do—*run,* and run we did. We ran across the field behind the privy, tearing out the rag curlers as we went along. All afternoon we hid in the bushes. As the hours went by, we got so hungry that we decided we had to go home. We snuck into the yard and picked up all the sticks we could find in the hopes that Mother wouldn't find one to spank us with. Finally, we decided to go into the house for supper. All Mother did was give us a lecture on using bad language and made us promise not to do it again. We went to church the next day with straight hair.

Unfortunately, it didn't end there. A few days later, Claire and I were walking by where Mother was talking to a neighbor. We thought we heard Mrs. Cain tell Mother she was taking a medicine called "Bastard" for her tired blood. We concluded that must not really be a bad word after all. Another few days after that, we saw Mrs. Cain showing a visiting friend of hers a rose bush that she had planted in her front yard. As we passed, Claire, trying to be polite, shouted over, "How is your Bastard working today, Mrs. Cain?" I won't go into detail about what happened when Claire and I got home from the store, but I can tell you I didn't sit down in comfort for a few days. When Mother finally calmed down enough, we explained what we thought the word meant and that we thought it was a word Mrs. Cain had used. Mother did see the funny side of it.

The church that was located at the bottom of the hill behind the schoolhouse sometimes had hot meals for sale. For a special treat, one time Mother said we could have them for our midday meal if I would go and pick them up. Marge was busy making fudge, so I had to go alone. It was a hot day in spring, and I made four trips up and down that hill carrying hot plates. The last trip had me dripping with sweat. As it was getting late, and I had to go back to school, I had to hurry to eat my dinner. Marge gave me two pieces of fudge. Between eating too fast and the heat that day, I was far from feeling well that afternoon. For years after that, I couldn't stand the smell of peanut butter fudge. It made me nauseous.

I believe everyone has pipe dreams and fantasies. When I was nine or ten, my dream was to find out that I had been adopted and my real parents would someday find me. They would be rich, of course, and I would have everything I ever wanted. I usually indulged in such daydreaming while I walked to the store. I dreamed I would also suddenly find I had beautiful curls.

My mother wouldn't let the younger kids have long hair. She said that we could let our hair grow out once we were old enough to do for ourselves all the washing and brushing that went into having long hair. But in my case, by the time she considered me old enough, the boyish bob hairstyle had become popular for girls, and therefore I was never to have long hair.

Mother didn't mind if we played with tree toads or other crawly creatures so long as we kept them out of the house. One day I found a tiny tree toad and without letting anyone see me, I snuck it into the house and up to my bedroom. I found a pan up in the attic and filled it with water. I left a stone in the middle so my little toad could choose to sit on the rock or swim, whichever he preferred. Much of the time, he seemed content just to stay on the rock. After watching him for about a half hour, I heard my mother call me to dinner. I didn't want to leave the toad in my room, because I was afraid he would jump out of the pan. If he did, I would never be able to find him again. I decided then to place the pan, with him in it, in the middle of the bathtub, reasoning that he would not be able to jump high enough to get out of the tub even if he did escape the pan. I figured I could come back and continue watching him after I ate. After I washed the dishes, the kids wanted to play kick-the-stick, and I forgot all about my little toad in the excitement of the game. That was, until I heard my mother scream. I knew she had discovered the toad. I ran up the stairs to try to resolve the situation. Mother was very annoyed with me and demanded that I get that frog out of the house.

I picked up the pan and carried it downstairs. I looked at my little toad and knew that I didn't want to get rid of him just yet, so I slipped him into my shirt pocket. That evening Mother had just placed a bowl of mashed potatoes on the supper table, when Toady, whom I had half forgotten, decided to come out of hiding. He jumped out of my shirt pocket and right into the bowl of mashed potatoes. What an uproar! The kids were all screaming, and my father was yelling about how I had brought that damned toad into the house. Mother calmly lifted the little toad out of the potatoes and placed him outside the kitchen door. I hope Toady found his way back to his toad family. Mother scooped out the part of the potatoes where he had landed, and without a word, she served the rest of the meal. I cannot recall what punishment was handed out to me for that event. I only know I never ended up touching a toad after that.

I once told my little sister, Carmel, who was about six or seven at the time, that if she found a big toad and kissed it, a beautiful little fairy would appear and give her lots of toys. One day my mother was horrified to see Carmel holding a very large toad. She was just about to kiss it when Mother screamed at her to drop the toad. Carmel burst into tears as she placed the toad on the ground. When Mother found out that I had told Carmel to kiss the toad, she was very upset with me. Punished again.

Often on quiet days, we would just sit around playing jacks or a card game. Helen and Mary would be reading books up in their room since they felt they were obviously too old to be playing childish games with little kids. So, most of the time it would be Bill, Marge, Claire, and I involved in the games. Jim and Dick [Carmel too?] always pestered us, as they wanted to play with us, but we told them they were just too young. We had this one thing we used to do. Heaven help the one who broke wind. All the other kids would jump on the guilty party and pound him or her, while the guilty one had to recite a jingle, which to the best I can remember went like this:

Haily, baily, bundle of straw
Farting is against the law
Hit me now, hit me then
Hit me when I fart again

Then the victim had to say, "Air slips, no plugs," and then whistle. Most of the time, it was just in fun, but sometimes when four or five kids jumped on you, you might end up a little black and blue. We were always on the lookout for someone to slip up, and then we would jump him. As mother cooked a lot of beans, we were forever jumping and pounding on someone.

If there was anything I hated to do more than anything else, it was washing the dishes. The water always seemed to be lukewarm. Of course, we couldn't have the water so hot that it would burn our hands, so we'd have to add some cold water, but always it was too much, and by the time we started to put the dishes in, the water was chilled. We used regular soap back then, and we generally used the Ivory brand, because it floated. If we tried using any other brand, we'd soon be complaining that we couldn't find the bar of it among the dishes. It was good that the Ivory soap floated, but so did all the grease to coat it. The smell of greasy dishwater stuck to our hands for hours afterwards. The one who washed the dishes was also expected to wipe off the table and the stove and would have to deal with washing all the pans too. The one who dried the dishes also had to clear off the table and sweep the floor.

It seemed to me that I was the one washing the dishes far too often. When I was old enough to help, I ended up washing, because Marge, being older, claimed that her seniority gave her the right to choose which job she wanted. But then when Claire was old enough to help, I was expected to be the washer out of kindness toward a younger sister. I just couldn't win. No wonder I hated doing dishes.

Before Mary and Helen got jobs at the telephone company, we all did a lot of hiking. We kids loved the outdoors. We dressed in old pants, and the younger kids wore bib overalls. This led to us being the subject of gossip. *Those wild Davenport girls going around dressed like boys.* It was great not to have to wear dresses, and in the summer, we ran around barefoot. We had a lot of fun on our hikes, and it didn't take long for us to find Lily Lake. We had to go up over the railroad tracks and across a big field that had a pond at one end. People called it Bunnel's Pond. Most of the time it was stagnant, but in season it had the most beautiful water lilies. There must have been snakes and other crawly things lurking in there. But we didn't worry about such things back then. As I got older, I would have been scared to death to walk anywhere near that pond. After we crossed the field, we would come to a wooded area. Following a path through that, we came out on a sandy beach by the lake.

One time all of us, including my parents, were having a picnic at the lake. My father was in the lake with some of us kids. When I doggy-paddled near him, my father grabbed a part of my bathing suit and pushed me out a little further into the lake. That prompted me to try to touch bottom, and since the water was too deep for that, I sank. I don't remember swallowing water, but maybe I did. My eyes were open, and the water was green. Bill said later that the only part of me to float to the top was my hair. He soon realized that something was wrong, so he grabbed me by the hair and dragged me out.

We loved the water, though I never became an expert swimmer, and there were a few things about the lake that were uncomfortable. There were leaches in there. I never had one attach to me, but when a light summer rain came down, the leaches would come up to the shore. When swimming through the water, they were almost a foot long, but if one fastened onto you, it would compress itself to a fat inch. I hated them.

My sister, Mary, eloped when I was eleven. She and her boyfriend, Ralph, went to Scranton, supposedly to see a movie. Instead, they got married by the Justice of the Peace.[42] I guess in those times they didn't require blood tests, and Mary must have lied about her age, because she was only seventeen at the time. At first, the only one who knew they had married was Helen, and she was sworn to secrecy. But Helen kept the secret only over the weekend before she broke down and told our mother. Our father was in Buffalo at the time, so Mother contacted him there by telephone. He said there would be no point in trying to get the marriage annulled. Mary would soon be eighteen and would be able to get married without parental consent anyway.

---

42 Mary married Ralph Clark in Scranton on June 6, 1923. Ralph had a small farm too, but his main job for most of his career was working for a feed mill. They eventually had eight children. Mary would turn eighteen in February of 1924.

I think Mary and Ralph were happy, but there was a problem. They had no place to live. Ralph was still staying with his family and Mary with ours. After a week of that arrangement, my mother decided to take a trip to Shamokin to visit with her relatives. Mary and her husband could spend the weekend sleeping in Mother's room. I was shocked to learn that Mary was going to sleep with a man, and even more shocked later. The bathroom opened off of our room, so when Mary was getting ready for bed, she was standing in front of the mirror brushing her hair with the door open. I could see she was wearing a sheer nightgown. I was startled and asked if she was going to bed like that. When she answered, "Of course," I was so indignant that I stood there sputtering about what I would tell Mother when she got home. Marge was thirteen and knew more about such matters than I did, so she tried to shut me up.

It was late that summer when I started to learn more about where babies come from. I don't think before that I even noticed when a woman was pregnant. If I noticed at all, I just supposed the woman was getting fat. My friend, Marie, and I were playing at my house one day. My parents had gone on one of their frequent trips, and Mary was looking after the house and us kids. Marie noticed that Mary's tummy was getting bigger and asked me if Mary was going to have a baby. I was surprised and said that I supposed so when the stork found out that she was married. Marie started to laugh and said, "Don't you know where babies come from?"[43]

"Of course," I said. "The stork brings them and sometimes he leaves them with the doctor, who then brings them in his little black bag."

Marie shook her head. "You are so dumb. Don't you know that Mary's husband puts his thing in her thing and tinkles, and that is how a baby gets inside its mother."

I was shocked and told Marie to go home. I told her I didn't like her anymore, as I ran into the house, crying as I so often did. When Mary asked what had happened, I blurted out what Marie had told me. To her credit, Mary didn't laugh in front of me. She just patted my back and said that when Mother came back, I should tell her what Marie had said. A few days later Mother came home, but by that time I had convinced myself that Marie was a liar, and I wasn't going to tell Mother what she had said. I was afraid Mother wouldn't allow me to play with Marie anymore. I never did ask my mother how babies were started. I was about fifteen before I knew the whole story, and that was only because I listened to the older girls at school. To tell you the truth, I thought the whole thing was disgusting.

One day Claire, Carmel, and I were at the lake when Claire decided to build a diving board. She and Carmel found a plank and piled rocks on one end to anchor it. The water was not very deep, so when Claire bounced high off her makeshift diving board and plunged into the water head-first, her head got stuck in the sand and mud on the bottom. There she was, upside down, with her feet sticking up in the air, and she

---

43 As Jessie explained earlier in the chapter, her friend Marie was a farm girl. That is probably why she would have been better informed about reproduction and had a more natural view than Jessie did at the same age.

couldn't get loose. Carmel and I had to pull her out. Carmel and I laughed so hard we were in tears, but Claire didn't see the humor in it. Her hair was all muddy, her face was beet red. She was mad. She yelled at us for laughing and took off for home at a dead run.

Claire was a thin little girl with long legs, and she was very flexible. She could contort her body into shapes that were unimaginable for me. I was more the stocky type. One day she put first one leg and then the other behind her head such that she had her left foot on her right shoulder and her right foot on the left shoulder. She balanced like that on her hands and buttocks and gloated that neither Carmel nor I could do the same thing. But then it turned out that Claire couldn't manage to unhook her legs from that position on her own. Carmel and I had to pull her legs back around toward their normal position. After that mishap, Claire never boasted again about being able to do tricks that we couldn't.

One day when Mother packed a picnic lunch and the whole family went to the lake together, there was a bit of an accident. Most of us kids were swimming in the lake, but Bill and my father were fishing. There were bullheads in that lake, and I suspect those were what they hoped to catch. I guess everything went fine for a while, but after lunch, when we kids were quietly resting before going back into the water, we watched Bill and my father fishing a little way along the shore from where we were. Father was standing near some trees untangling his fishing line. Bill was standing knee-deep in the water. He flipped his line back in preparation for casting out into the lake. He couldn't bring the line back forward, so, thinking it was snagged on the tree, he pulled harder. He heard a yell behind him and was horrified when he turned around to see his hook embedded in our father's lip. I don't know how they got the hook out, but my father went around for several days with a very fat lip. I don't think he and Bill ever went fishing together after that.

I learned the "f-word" from graffiti written in the railroad underpass. I had no idea what it meant at the time, but I liked the sound of the word. All day I went around singing the word under my breath. I didn't think anyone paid attention to this, but I was wrong on that point. After supper, when Mother was giving Dick a bath, he began singing out the word just the way he had heard me. I was in big trouble again. I hated that word after that.

My tastes in reading evolved over time. When I was about thirteen, I was crazy about books that told of knights and their deeds of daring-do, but that developed later. Back when I was about ten, I read every book I could get my hands on about Tarzan and the apes. My imagination went in a wild direction, so rather than imagining myself as Jane, as most girls would have, I pretended to be the female ape that Tarzan grew up with. I used to try to swing in the trees, but I never quite got up the courage to go from branch to branch, and I never got higher than about two feet off the ground. I could always find boys willing to play Tarzan. They would climb high up in the trees above me and thump their chests while shouting out a Tarzan yell. I would climb on a tree branch too but would only chatter like a monkey.

One summer Mother's sister, Aunt Hattie, and her husband, Uncle John, came from Shamokin to visit us for a few days. They brought my cousin, Joe, with them.[44] He was about seventeen years old at the time. We always had a wonderful time when Uncle John was at our house. He and my father would play the piano and sing together. One song in particular sticks in my memory. There was a lot of laughing in it, and as Uncle John was a short, fat man, whenever he sang this song, his belly would jump up and down. To hear him sing this song got all of us laughing, and the more he sang, the harder we laughed.

My mother had bought cotton knickers for us younger girls. They were the kind of pants that came to just below the knee and buckled there. They were made of a pink and blue plaid material. Mother got them for us to have something nice to wear while our relatives were there, but at the end of the first afternoon, I had already ruined mine. I tore them while climbing down from the apple tree where I could watch my older sisters and brothers play ball with our cousin. To my twelve-year-old eyes, Cousin Joe was handsome. He was not very tall, and his eyes and hair were dark. This was the summer when I put aside the Tarzan books and started reading books about knights in shining armor. From the moment I first saw Joe, I imagined him to be my secret knight. I could stare at him to my heart's content from up in the apple tree, where no one would notice me staring. Marge made quite a hit with him, but that didn't bother me. In my heart, I knew he really liked me the best. Finally though, it was getting dark and it was time to come down from the tree. That is when I got into trouble. As I slid down the trunk I caught on a sharp broken branch and ripped the seat right out of my knickers. As I ran into the house, I heard Cousin Joe laughing just as hard as everyone else, and I suddenly hated him for it. The day they left, I didn't even go down to the car to say good-bye. I was just glad to see him go.

I often made silly mistakes as a child. In one case, I ran the risk of giving Dick, my beloved baby brother, pneumonia. Shortly after we moved to Dalton, I was nine, and Dick was just one year old. We had moved in the early spring. This event was on

---

44 Aunt Hattie (Harriet) was two years younger than Elizabeth, the closest sister in age, and they likely had a close bond. Harriet had married a coal miner named John Joseph Neibauer, and they continued to live in Shamokin. They named their first child, born in 1905, John Joseph, Jr., and the family must have fallen into the habit of calling him by his middle name to distinguish him from John Sr. The couple had altogether nine children, so it seems that all the younger ones must have been left back in Shamokin in the care of other relatives during this visit.

Jessie doesn't mention it here but her cousin, Joe, would die tragically only about three years later at the age of twenty. He was working as a laborer for the Pennsylvania Railroad. The cause of death is listed as a skull fracture due to a railroad accident in a town called Riverside on the Susquehanna River about fifteen miles north of Shamokin.

This Uncle John (a brother-in-law to Elizabeth) should not be confused with Elizabeth's brother, the notorious John Frances Fitzpatrick, the one who had stabbed William in Shamokin several years earlier.

one of the days when my mother went to Scranton. I don't remember who was supposed to be babysitting us, but they weren't watching us very closely. I got the idea of taking the baby bathtub out on the back porch and filling it with water. It was a very warm day for spring, so I thought I would give Dick a bath outside. I undressed him and put him into the water. The bath water was warm enough, but a cold wind started to blow. Dick still seemed to be enjoying the bath. My mother arrived home, and as she came around the corner of the house, she saw Dick in the tub. She let out a scream that must have been heard all over town. In less time than it takes to tell the story, she whisked Dick out of the tub and into the warm house. I was so scared that I ran and hid in the old hen house until dark. I think, if I hadn't gotten hungry, I could have stayed there all night, even though I was afraid of the dark. I could hear the other kids calling my name as they looked for me all over the yard. Finally, I needed to go to the privy, and the kids caught me as I tried to sneak over to it. I had no choice but to go in and face my mother. Sometimes mothers are gentler than we expect, and this time mine very patiently explained why I shouldn't have tried to give Dick a bath outside even though it might have seemed warm enough. I didn't get the spanking I expected, but I still cried.

One day when I was somewhat older, we had quite a scare. Mother and Marge had gone to Scranton to do some shopping, and Helen and Mary were working, so I was the oldest one at home at the time. I was in my room reading. Claire and Carmel were outside playing jump rope, and Jim and Dick were supposed to be playing in their room. I suddenly heard the two boys yelling, "Fire! Fire!" I jumped off the bed and ran down the stairs. I ran outside to look up at the house and locate the fire. By this time Jim and Dick were outside, hopping around, and pointing up at the window of Helen's room. Sure enough, I could see some flames. I ran upstairs and found the fly netting on the bedroom window was burning. I knocked out what was left of the netting with the broom I was holding. Luckily the flames had not yet spread to anything else. The boys had been playing with matches. For a change, there was something to tell Mother when she got home that I wouldn't be the one to be blamed for.

I am sure I did more stupid things when I was growing up than I can remember. I am just as glad I can't recall them all, because there were plenty enough I do remember. One morning I woke up with a sore throat. My mother was teaching school at the time, so she wouldn't be home for the day. She told me just to stay home from school, but if I felt better by afternoon, I could peel some potatoes or do anything else that might help with supper. I was feeling much better by afternoon, and with all the other kids at school, I was quite bored. After peeling the potatoes, I got the bright idea of making a pie. We had plenty of apples in the house. I had watched my mother and older sisters make pie dough, so I was sure I could do it too. I mixed up a gooey mess of flour, lard, and a little water and salt. I couldn't roll this dough as it was just too sticky, so I just plopped it into the pie tin and spread it around the best I could with my fingers. I then peeled some apples and sliced them into the pie tin and sprinkled on plenty of cinnamon and sugar. It at least smelled good. I tried to make a top crust, but it ended up just in sticky lumps. I thought that when it baked it would probably smooth itself out and come out looking better. I placed this pie in the oven and added a few shovelfuls of coal to the fire. Feeling very proud of myself, I waited for the kids to come home, thinking that the pie should be done about then. But just before they arrived, I looked into the oven and noticed the pie still looked pretty much as it had when I put it in. When the kids came in, we immediately got involved in a board game, and I forgot about my pie.

When Mother arrived home, she shook down the fire in the kitchen stove and started to prepare supper. She cooked chops, and along with the potatoes and some vegetables, that was supper. We all had good appetites in our house, so you can be sure that when we sat down to the table, no one had to be coaxed to eat. We were just finishing the meal when our conversation was interrupted by a sharp noise from the kitchen. "What was that noise?" asked Mother. "It sounded like a firecracker." We sat listening and soon heard another popping noise.

It was at that point that I remembered the pie. I jumped up from the table, ran into the kitchen, and yanked open the oven door. What a sight met my eyes! The messy pie I had put into the oven had turned a golden brown, and there was the delicious smell of the apples and cinnamon. Mother acted very surprised as I brought the pie into the dining room. "Did you do all this by yourself?" she asked as she cut into the flaky crust. I was so proud I almost burst. Everyone enjoyed the pie and praised it heartily.

It wasn't until a few weeks later when I asked my mother if I could make another pie that she told me the truth. When she was cooking supper that night, she noticed the pie I had placed in the oven, and without telling anyone, she replaced it with a pie she had prepared the day before. The popping sounds had been the result of pieces of the dough I had made that had fallen off and were exploding in the bottom of the oven. She didn't want me to be embarrassed, so she let everyone think I had been the one who made the nice pie. I eventually did learn how to make fairly good apple pies, but I never forgot that sloppy first attempt I made.

We picked berries as an extra food source—any kind of wild berry that was in season. The field on the way to Lily Lake was a great place for wild strawberries. We'd pick baskets full of them and come home all sweaty and sticky from the juice. My mother made jams and jellies from the wild fruits. After I was grown and bought jam in the stores, it never tasted as good. We could get a taste of summer all winter long when we ate the jams and jellies from the various berries we had picked. We picked wild blackberries, raspberries, and my favorite, huckleberries.

We picked wild produce for purposes other than making jam too. My father was forever trying to make wine. In the spring we picked dandelions for that purpose, and later in the year we picked elderberries. One time my father experimented by putting a peeled banana in a Mason jar filled with some kind of clear fluid. We kids looked at the jar from time to time, and after a while the banana had filmy particles hanging from it. It looked terrible!

Once again, I have to say that it seems like I was always getting into trouble. I often wonder how my sister Helen and I ever managed to stay on friendly terms. I know that at times I must have embarrassed her to distraction. Whenever she had a boyfriend over to the house, weather permitting, they would sit in the swing on the front porch. As soon as it started getting dark, Mother would tell me to go out and sit on the swing next to them. I enjoyed this. I could never keep my mouth shut, and for a courting couple, having the girl's kid sister sitting with them could not have been fun. It was enjoyable for me though, and Helen couldn't complain to Mother that I was annoying them, since in effect that is what Mother wanted to happen. To give an example of what I mean by having a big mouth, one evening the boyfriend asked me what we called Helen as a nickname. I told him it wasn't something very nice, but since he had asked, I would tell him. As a teenager with a sweet tooth, Helen was going through a phase when acne was an issue, and I told her boyfriend that we called her "Pimple Face." I feel so guilty now when I remember that. But Helen did forgive me, and as I got older, we had a close sisterly bond.

Easter was another exciting day of the year for us. Each of us always got a big chocolate rabbit in our basket along with a chocolate egg with either a coconut or fruit filling. I particularly remember once getting a solid chocolate pig. It seems to me now that Easter always fell on a warm spring day when we could enjoy running around outside without our coats. Many times, as the day went on, we would dump everything out of our baskets and then put everything back into them again. We had to make sure there were no jellybeans hiding in the grass in the bottom. Every Easter at least one of us kids got sick from gorging too much on candy.

Helen was about eighteen when she met her future husband, Jack. For some reason, I didn't like Jack at first. There was a lot of wall space in our kitchen. One day I went around the kitchen and behind each chair wrote on the wall, "I like Ralph, but I don't like Jack."[45] Whenever Helen was with Jack in our kitchen, she liked to sit on his lap, so that night she could easily see what I had written. I don't know why I acted the way I did. I wanted people to like me, but I had an impulse always to do exactly what would make them dislike me instead. Helen was furious. The next day was a Saturday, and I had to spend that whole morning washing those kitchen walls.

Here's a mean song we made up just to torment Helen.[46]

My sister's fellow comes to see her every night,
I wonder why, I wonder why,

---

45 I don't have an exact date, but it does indeed seem likely that Ernest J. (Jack) Hawley and Helen first met in 1923 when Helen was eighteen, and that they married in 1924. Jessie is contrasting Jack here to Ralph who was Mary's boyfriend and future husband.

46 This would appear to be a parody of the song "You're Just in Love" composed by Irving Berlin, except the time is not right. That song was not published until 1950. Perhaps there was an earlier similar song.

They go in the parlor and turn down the lights,
I wonder why, I wonder why.
I peeked through the keyhole, and I heard our Helen say,
"Now, Jackie, don't be naughty, and take your arm away,
And then she giggled like a girl that's getting gay,
I wonder why, I wonder why.

Helen tells me now that back in the early days of her marriage, whenever we kids visited her, she was always glad to see us and enjoyed our company. She and Jack lived only a few miles from Dalton, and we hiked up there quite often. Her house was always immaculate. I still remember the gray enameled stove they had, because it was the first cooking stove I had seen that was not black. She was always fussy about having everything just right in their house. It seems like it would have been a pain for her to have three or four of us kids showing up unexpected and asking for something to eat, but she didn't complain.

One summer night, Claire and I could hear loud voices coming from inside the kitchen, and we thought it meant our parents were having a big fight. One drawback from reading so many stories is that we had overly vivid imaginations. This led us to worry that Mother might be harmed. I'm pretty sure it was just our melodramatic imaginations that led us to think that way, because, as far as I know, Father had never hit Mother. Nonetheless, with the idea in our heads, we decided we had to do something about it. We snuck out of the house and ran up the bank to the neighbors' house. We knew they had a phone and would be able to call for help. Claire and I walked up to the front door and timidly knocked. When the lady of the house opened the door, we started to cry, and we told her to call the police, since our father was beating up our mother. Thank goodness, they had more sense than we did, and they just walked us back home. Both of our parents were furious when they heard what Claire and I had done. They actually weren't having a real fight. I'm just as glad I don't remember what punishment Claire and I got for that one.

One year, Mother decided we should keep pigs. She bought some piglets from a nearby farmer. Bill built a pen for them down in the backyard. We had to mix bran to feed them along with greens. Those pigs were so cute when they were little. But as they grew, they would get out of their pen every so often, and we would have to chase them all over the fields. Between the smell and the troubles catching them, they weren't so cute anymore. In the fall, Mother had the pigs butchered. The farmer who did the job got one of them as payment. I might not have liked the pigs, but I sure did like the pork.

Obviously, we didn't love the pigs the way we loved our pets. We had a big dog named Silver. He sort of came with the house. He had been left with us by the previous residents, and when we finally moved out, we left him with the new owners. I hope they loved him as much as we did.

Fortunately, fireworks weren't banned back then. It seems like every year the

Fourth of July would be a particularly hot and sticky day. We celebrated the holiday with firecrackers and the kind of fireworks they used to call red devils. At night my father and Bill would set off Roman candles and skyrockets. Our front lawn was lit up with sparklers. As we danced around in our bare feet, many a small foot had burns from the still hot sparklers we had dropped in the grass.

I think the last doll I received as a child came while we lived in Dalton. It was a big doll dressed in blue rompers.[47]   Claire had a similar one that was smaller, and Carmel's was smaller still. The chicken coop had a flat roof, and we could take chairs and a small table up there and play house. One evening after Claire and Carmel had been playing up on that roof, they forgot to bring back my doll when they came inside to get ready for bed. The doll was left out all night and was soaked in the pouring rain that came that night. The doll's head was made of a composite material, and the body had cotton stuffing. I tried to dry the doll out, but the head peeled and cracked, and the body became moldy and sour smelling. I don't remember having another doll as a child after that one, though it is possible I received one on a later Christmas and just forgot it.

One day, on the way back from the lake, two of the neighbor kids ended up embarrassing themselves. Sarah was the girl who lived next door and was about my age, and Todd was a neighbor boy she knew. Everyone else had gone home before us, so it was just the three of us walking back from the lake together. Sarah got all giggly and then told Todd to walk ahead of us as she wanted to tell me something. As requested, Todd walked several feet ahead of us, and Sarah whispered to me that she thought it would be fun to see Todd tinkle in front of us. I thought she was cuckoo. With three brothers, I wasn't particularly curious about boys' privates. I told Sarah she was crazy, but she only giggled harder. She called Todd back to us and told him that if he would tinkle in front of us, we would return the favor by tinkling in front of him. She turned to me and asked, "Isn't that right, Jess?" I nodded my head, because even though I didn't particularly care to see them tinkle, I still wanted to see how far they would go in making fools of themselves. Todd agreed and did as Sarah requested. Next Sarah tinkled as well. Then they both looked at me, waiting for me to do the same. I just laughed and ran home like the devil was after me. Every time I saw Todd after that, I'd start to laugh. He would turn red and turn his back on me. Sarah wouldn't speak to me for a long time after that day. We never were close friends after that.

We were forbidden to touch matches except under adult supervision, but children are often tempted by such things. I had seen someone light a wooden match with his thumbnail. It seemed like quite a skill, and I wanted to see if I could do the same. So, one quiet afternoon I snuck a match out of a box in the kitchen. I hid it in my pocket waiting for a good chance to try it. When I thought no one would notice, I went back into the kitchen and tried without success to light the match with my thumbnail. I tried a second time, but again I had no luck. Just then Marge walked into the kitchen. When

---

47 According to Dictionary.com, "rompers" (always used as a plural) are "a loose, one-pieced garment combining a shirt or blouse and short, bloomerlike pants, worn by young children."

she saw that I had a match in my hand, she tried to take it away from me. I put my hand behind my back to keep the match away from her, and in the process accidentally brushed my thumbnail in such a way that it burst into flames. I couldn't react quickly enough, and by the time I dropped the match, it had already burnt the top of my thumb. It was a long time before I tried being tricky with matches again.

There were no movies shown in Dalton. Since we didn't have a car, usually the only way to see a movie was to take a streetcar all the way into Scranton.[48] We didn't get to see too many movies during our time in Dalton. One day, some friends of my mother's were going shopping in Scranton. They happened to have a girl who was about my age. They asked Mother to let me go to Scranton with them, and while they were shopping, we girls could see a movie. After they finished shopping, they would then meet us in front of the movie house and bring me home. I hadn't been to the movies since we left Scranton, so I was thrilled when Mother agreed to the plan. When we got to the movie house, the adults bought tickets for us two girls and told us to go in and enjoy the movie. Unfortunately, at the time we went in, the movie had already started,

---

48 (For railroad history buffs): The mention here of taking a streetcar from Dalton all the way into Scranton relates to an interesting development in American transportation systems during the first decades of the 20th Century. Early streetcar systems (first as horsecars and later as electrified trolleys) were usually just for ease of travel within an urban area, often with lines just a few miles long. The actual railroads, on the other hand, were focused mainly on travel over long distances. They might have had some local passenger trains that stopped at stations every five to ten miles, but their main emphasis in terms of passenger traffic was on taking travelers on long journeys. Around the turn of the century, the idea developed that there was a demand to fill the gap between those two systems and provide for medium-distance travel. This was really how the modern concept of the suburb began—people could live many miles from the city center and still commute to a job in the city. Also, people living in more-or-less rural areas might have the chance to travel into the city occasionally for shopping, seeing movies, and so on. These lines could also increase the potential for city-dwelling families to get out to enjoy the country air on weekends and holidays, in some cases to resort areas designed by the railways for that purpose. Thus, the idea was to start railway companies with electrified train lines running for a few dozen miles in various directions out from the main city with stops every few miles. Stations every two miles or so meant that many people would live within a healthy walking distance of a station, or better still, a short bicycle or buggy ride away. It may be a slightly confusing term, but in America at that time, railway companies of this type were referred to as "the interurbans". They often ran about halfway to the next metropolitan area, or in some cases all the way. They compare roughly to the private railway companies serving metro areas in Japan today.

The way Jessie and her family were getting into Scranton for watching movies, for going to the hospital, for shopping, etc. was an interurban known as the Scranton, Montrose and Binghamton Railroad. Another name for the same enterprise was the Northern Electric Railway Company. Service from central Scranton to Dalton started in 1907 and gradually extended north from there. By 1915 the system had reached Montrose. Unfortunately, their progress stopped there, and despite the name, they never made it any closer to Binghamton than that.

so I thought this just meant we were too late to see the first part. Now once the movie finished, they would be starting it again a few minutes later. And the custom at that time was that, if you missed the beginning of a film, you could stay and watch it the next time, either for just the part you missed or even all the way to the end again if you wanted to. But we didn't know any of that at the time, so when the picture ended, we walked out. We ended up standing in front of the movie house for at least an hour before the adults finished their shopping and came back to pick us up. When I found out later that we could have stayed and seen the first part of the movie, I was angry at my ignorance. I never made that mistake again.

As already mentioned, we kids loved to hike. One day, Bill, Jim, and Dick went for a walk. Dick was four at the time, Jim was six, and Bill would have been in his mid-teens. It was supposed to be a boys' hike. They didn't want any girls to tag along, so we heard about what happened later. They planned to climb the big rocks on the embankment alongside of the railroad tracks. They were going over a particularly large boulder there when Dick looked over the edge and froze. Bill looked over the edge too, and then very quickly he snatched up Dick in his arms, grabbed Jim by the hand, and almost flew down the rocks they had just climbed. It turned out that just the other side of that boulder there were two big rattlers sunning themselves.

One other time, I took my four younger siblings—Claire, Carmel, Jim, and Dick—for a long walk. I don't know why I thought it made sense to take the two little boys along, because they were still too young for as long a hike as I was planning. To make matters worse, this time we hadn't even bothered to tell Mother that we were bringing them along. We walked even farther than I originally intended, and Dick started begging to go home. At one point, he strayed off the side of the road and stepped on a piece of broken glass. I didn't know what to do. I tried to carry him, but it was just not possible for me to carry him all the way home. Luckily, a truck came by at that time. Helen's husband, Jack, was working on the town road crew at the time, and this was a town truck that he happened to be driving that day. Jack stopped, got us all aboard, and drove us home to a very frightened mother, who was frantically worried about where her little boys were. She tended to Dick's foot, and then dealt with my punishment!

Jim had to have his tonsils out, so Mother took him by streetcar to Moses Taylor Hospital in Scranton. Jim had to stay in overnight, so Mother had to come home and go back to pick him up the next day. When she arrived back at the hospital, Jim wasn't in his room, and the nurses couldn't find him. Mother was frantic because no one knew how to find little Jim. One nurse explained that she had gotten him dressed and told him his mother would be coming by streetcar soon to take him home. Finally, an orderly who had been searching the hospital grounds, came back in and said that a little boy was sitting on the curb in front of the hospital entrance. Mother rushed out, and sure enough, it was Jim. He said he wanted to be ready to meet her when she got off the streetcar.

One night, Claire, Carmel, and I were sleeping together as usual in our room. The bed was wobbly because one leg needed to be fixed, and we just thought it would be fun to sleep on the floor for a change anyway. It was a terribly hot night, and little Carmel was going to sleep stark naked. She was crawling between Claire and me, and just as she was lying down on the floor with us, she let out a loud scream. Claire thought the devil had ahold of her, and I just assumed Carmel might have sat on a needle. Poor Carmel went screaming through the boys' room and into Mother's. It turned out she had sat on a wasp, and it stung her. I'll never forget the sight of that little girl running for her mother while holding her bare bottom.

I don't have as many memories of Carmel in those long-ago days as I do for some of my other siblings. She was the youngest girl in the family, and after our eldest sister, Helen, got married, she would often take Carmel to her place for the weekend. When Carmel came home from these visits, she always had something new to wear or play with. To tell the truth, Claire and I were a little jealous of our kid sister.

One summer night the church down the hill from our house was having some kind of fair, and we kids wanted to go. Mother gave her permission since my big brother, Bill, would be with us. We were getting together whatever pennies, nickels, and dimes we had accumulated in recent weeks. I happened to have all of sixty or seventy cents, and that was only because I had half-forgotten I had it to spend. Marge wanted to borrow some, but I refused. I was an easier touch with Bill though, so when he asked, I loaned him all except ten cents. This made Marge angry. She didn't stay with the rest of us that evening, and every time she saw me from a distance, she gave me a dirty look. It didn't bother me. She was still mad when we got home. She had gone back ahead of us, so when I got home, she was already upstairs, getting ready for bed. I said my prayers and climbed into the bed I shared with her, where I fell asleep almost immediately.

Sometime during that night, I woke with a start as Marge tugged at my arm and said, "There are snakes in the bed." I immediately drew my knees up to my chest. Marge crawled out of bed and turned on the light. I scrambled out of bed and onto the other bed in the room with Claire and Carmel. I watched Marge as she gingerly lifted the blankets and looked under the sheets. There were no snakes! Marge explained that, while walking back home in the dark from the church fair, she was startled when a few sticks she had stepped on moved in such a way that she thought they were snakes. She guessed that fright left snakes so much on her mind that she must have dreamed that some were in the bed. That cleared up, Marge and I then crawled back into our bed, but I still kept my knees up to my chest in the fetal position.

I finally dozed off again, but then Marge let out a groan loud enough to wake me a second time. She said, "Oh! It got into my tooth."

I gasped, "What got into your tooth."

"Oh, it was just my tongue," she said sharply, and asked, "Did you think I meant it was a snake?" We finally got back to sleep, but after those frights and that strange conversation, it was several months before I felt comfortable enough to sleep with my legs stretched out as normal.

In the fourth grade, I got great marks in reading and composition, but in math I failed. I just couldn't grasp fractions. My mother tried to help me with this, but even though she was a teacher, it didn't really help, probably because the way she knew how to do fractions was different from the way our class was being taught. I struggled, but every report card day, which was once a month in those days, I went home with an "F" or a "D" in arithmetic. I just hated bringing home the report card, but obviously, I had to. A parent had to sign it before I could take it back, and anyway, my mother would have noticed if the other kids brought theirs home and I didn't. I was in despair.

Then one day, we had a substitute teacher. After the math lesson, he asked me to stay after school. I worried all afternoon that he was really going to tell me how stupid I was. School was over at three o'clock, and when the bell rang, I stayed in my seat. Once all the other students had left, Mr. Cramer called me up to his desk. He sat looking at me for a moment that felt to me like an hour but was probably only really a matter of seconds, and then he said, "Jessie, you're not a stupid girl. I'm sure with a little help, you could bring up your mark. Now I am going to work with you for the few days that I am here, and we'll see what happens." I stayed after school every day that week, and wonder of wonders, everything seemed to fall into place. I finally understood how to do fractions. Mr. Cramer left at the end of that week. The next report card came out, and I was so happy to find a "C+" for arithmetic on mine. I wasn't ashamed to take my report card home that day!

Returning to an earlier point, I may have not known much about how babies are conceived, but by the time I was twelve, I knew at least a little about the subject of childbirth. Not knowing much about the conception part didn't bother me too much, since as a child of that age, I had plenty of other things on my mind. I knew, for example, that Mary was going to have a baby, but at the time that seemed like all I needed to know. The friend I mentioned earlier, Marie, at one time told me that after I became a woman, not to let a boy kiss me, because it could result in me having a baby. I reminded her that previously she had told me something about a different process than that, but she just said there are multiple ways to conceive a child. I didn't want to kiss boys anyway, but my intuition told me that Marie didn't know as much about the matter as she thought she did.

Mary came to stay with us as the time for the birth of her baby drew near. One night, a Girl Scout meeting I was attending ended about nine o'clock, and one of the girls and her mother walked me home. As I entered the front hall of our house and started up the stairs, my mother came into the hall from the kitchen and told me not to go into the room where Mary was staying. I asked why, but before she could answer, I heard Mary scream and plead for Mother to help her. I ran back down the stairs and into the kitchen, closing the doors behind me. I sat at the kitchen table with my hands over my ears so I wouldn't hear Mary screaming. It was horrible! I tried to read a book to keep my mind off of it, but later realized that I had read the whole book and couldn't remember a word of what was in it. Mary's husband, Ralph, came down the stairs with a pan full of instruments. He put them on the stove to boil and sterilize them, but seeing those instruments scared me even more. Bill came home about eleven o'clock and asked why I wasn't in bed. Mother explained to him that I would hear it all the more clearly if I was upstairs.

I sat there until five minutes after midnight when my nephew was born. I finally went upstairs and went to bed at that point. Since the next day was a Saturday, not a school day, Mother told all the kids we could get up and go see Mary's baby if we wanted to. But I refused to go. The next afternoon about one o'clock, Marie came over to play with me, but Mother said I couldn't go out to play until I went in to see the baby. I grudgingly agreed to go in and take a quick look, but Mother had a different idea. She made me sit down and hold the baby while she attended to Mary. As hesitant as I was at first to be around a baby, by the time Mary went home two weeks later, I had fallen in love with the little baby, Buddy Clark.[49]

It was just about when I was twelve and a half years old that we moved to Ithaca, New York. We all had thought we could go on living in Dalton until we kids grew up and left the nest, but alas, it was not to be. A wealthy relative had originally told my parents that they could live in the house on a rent-to-own basis. But that relative died, and the arrangement had never been officially put into writing, so in the end we had to move out. It broke our hearts as we really loved the place.

It would take a week or so for my parents to set up the new living arrangements in Ithaca, so they made plans for what would happen to us younger kids during that time. I can't remember what arrangement they made for Jim and Dick. I guess Helen and Mary took care of Claire and Carmel. I was farmed out with a family named Purdy. Mr. Purdy was a ticket agent at the train station. They were a young couple and had a three-year-old daughter named Eileen. I was being treated for ringworm on my arm at the time, and I had a scab the size of a nickel. The first thing Eileen tried to do is bite off that scab. I hated that kid. She was a bigger pest than all four of my younger siblings combined. I stayed at the Purdy house for a week. I guess they assumed I would be a big help around the house. I did indeed do the dishes and made the beds, but every afternoon, when Eileen was taking her nap, I would sneak off with Dick C. and some of the other kids in the neighborhood to play in the barn down the road.

I thought of Dick C. as my first boyfriend. He spent every summer with his grandmother in Dalton. One day back when I was eleven, a group of us neighbor kids had been swimming in the lake. After all the other kids had left, Dick and I sat on a log, skipping stones in the water. Dick put his arm around me and tried to kiss me. I turned my head just in time, so the kiss landed on my cheek instead of my mouth. I jumped up and gave him a shove that knocked him backwards off the log. I was so mad, I was yelling at him, "What were you trying to do? Don't you know I could have a baby if you kissed me?" Dick just laughed. He was fourteen and knew a little more about the facts

---

49 The first child of Mary and Ralph Clark was born in Dalton on March 29, 1924. They named him Ralph, Jr., and apparently the family called him Buddy. It was the first time Jessie became an aunt.

of life than I did. I ran home through the woods as fast as I could. I wouldn't have anything to do with him for a few days after that. Eventually we became friends again, but it was a long time before he tried to kiss me after that. While living with the Purdys, I saw Dick every day. We promised to write to each other after I moved, and we did for a while. I did see Dick once again when I was sixteen, but after that we lost track of each other. I often wonder what happened to Dick C. I wonder if he joined the military during the wars that followed.[50]

I can imagine the Purdys were glad to see me go at the end of the week. Mr. Purdy put me on the train that would take me to Ithaca. The trip was uneventful, except I got a cinder in my eye and was miserable until I got to our new home and my father could remove it.

---

50 Richard Francis C. was born in Dalton on November 7, 1910 and was therefore a little less than a year older than Jessie and certainly no older than thirteen. He grew up mainly in Scranton, where his father held a variety of jobs. In 1929 he married Louise Jean N., the daughter of an Italian immigrant coal miner. Richard and Louise had one child named Harold in 1929 and divorced in the 1930s. Early in his career, Richard worked in a bakery and later in a tire store. He did indeed serve in World War II as an army PFC. He died in Philadelphia in 1965 at the age of fifty-four.

Chapter 3—Ithaca

When I got off the train in Ithaca, my brother Bill was waiting for me at the station ready to show me the way to our new home.[51] We crossed the railroad tracks and came to a small bridge that went over what we called an inlet. There were several other small bridges in the neighborhood. After we crossed that bridge, we came to a little side street, and next there was a gas station, and then a funny looking building that was pointed at one end. That was our new home. There was a grocery store on the first floor, and we had to go up two flights of stairs to reach our apartment on the third floor. The top of the stairs led directly into our kitchen. We had three bedrooms—one for Marge and me, one for my parents, and the third for the boys. Claire and Carmel used the folding couch in the living room. The bathroom was opposite my parents' room.

A few days after moving in, we met some kids while we were playing in front of the grocery store. They came from a large family like ours. The oldest was named Barb

---

51 It is clear that Jessie's first impression of Ithaca is that it was a delightfully exotic place—bridges crossing inlets everywhere and an apartment in a strangely shaped building. She seems to think almost that she was moving into a fairy tale. The train station was so close to the apartment that Bill had only a two- or three-minute walk each way to meet his sister there. The brick building that was once the station is still there and now houses a bank branch. The building where they lived is on a small triangular shaped city block formed by the intersection of two major streets and one branch of the Cayuga inlet. The gas station next door is now a sort of drive-thru can-and-bottle redemption center. The building where the Davenports lived is still there, though it may be modified in several ways. The grocery store that was on the first floor is replaced by the headquarters of a nonprofit organization. The second and third floors might still be used as apartments.

Jessie was arriving in Ithaca in the summer of 1924, when she would have been still a few months shy of her thirteenth birthday. She mentions that the older family members had arrived a few weeks earlier, perhaps in the late spring, and they were already settling in by the time she arrived. At the time they moved to Ithaca, her parents were just past forty. Bill would turn seventeen that summer and seems to have been an exceptionally responsible young man, or perhaps a little overbearing in his sense of responsibility. Marge would soon be fifteen, and seems to have been excelling academically and socially, and though they shared a bedroom, she and Jessie were clearly growing apart. Claire, soon to be eleven, on the other hand, was becoming more and more Jessie's sidekick. Jessie spends less time in this chapter discussing the youngest three sibling: Carmel, who was turning nine; Jim turning seven, and Dick already five. The family remained in Ithaca until sometime in early 1927, so obviously we can add up to a little less than three years to these ages for how old they each might have been during the events described in this chapter. At the time that the rest of the family moved to Ithaca, Helen was nineteen, and living with her husband Jack in Factoryville, Pennsylvania. However, the young couple moved to Ithaca sometime within the next year. Mary was eighteen and living with her husband Ralph near Scott, Pennsylvania.

Ithaca was the terminal of a branch line of the DL&W Railroad that connected to the main line at Owego. Some of the records show William assigned to work in the engine house there, in fact as the foreman. But some parts of Jessie's narrative in this chapter seem to suggest that her father was still away from home for days at a time. These likely refer to periods after December 1926 when his personnel file indicates he was returned to service as an engineer in the Scranton Division of the railroad. There are also records showing both William's son, Bill, and son-in-law, Jack, as employees of the DL&W at one point, but likely they were employees only for the short term. They may have been working in engine house under William, who may not have been the easiest boss to have.

and was about my age, and she had little sisters who were the same ages as Claire and Carmel. Barb was in the seventh grade. I was only in the sixth, but I lied and claimed I was in the seventh grade too. I had been kept back a grade at some point. Marge was never held back, so I guess that means I wasn't as smart as I wanted to be.

As the summer passed, we kids did a lot of exploring. We found where the elementary school was. It was a lovely brick building with a yard shaded by trees. We also found the high school where I was going in the fall if I could pass myself off as a seventh grader. But the best thing of all that we found was Cayuga Lake. It was wonderful. I loved just to sit on a rock and watch the waves crashing on shore.[52]

The first day we went swimming in the lake was the first time I encountered prejudice. I met a little girl about my age, and we were having a wonderful time together. We could walk out quite far into the lake and the water would still only come up to our waists. As we came out of the water onto the beach, the girl's mother waved to us, and the girl took me over to meet her. The woman seemed very nice, but she asked a lot of questions. She asked how old I was and about my brothers and sisters. Then she asked me what church I went to. I told her that we hadn't been to church yet since arriving in Ithaca, but that we were Catholic. She changed her tone so fast, and I didn't know what I had done. She said she didn't want me to play with her daughter. She didn't say so in so many words, but even as a young kid, I could easily sense that she no longer liked me. My mother later explained to me that some people just don't like Catholics.

Fall came, and I had to go back to school. I was still going to try to bluff my way into the seventh grade, but I lost my nerve and went back to the elementary school and into the sixth grade.[53] I really enjoyed that first term in the public school, but then my mother decided to send us to Catholic school for the second term.[54] Most of the kids

---

52 The elementary school she describes is probably the one called Beverly Martin, which is still one of the schools in the Ithaca City School District. It would have been about a twelve-minute walk to the east. Ithaca High School at that time was housed in what is now the DeWitt Mall, near downtown Ithaca, about fifteen-minute walk east of where they lived. How far they went to swim in the lake depends in part on whether she is talking about swimming in the lake proper or in part of the inlet system. It might have been over a mile-and-a-half hike to the north assuming they walked the whole way. It sounds like she would have been more than happy to walk that far.

53 It seems that in the 1920s, most American school districts still packaged primary/secondary education according to the 8-4 system (8-year elementary school, followed, for some, by four years of high school). The concept of the junior high was only invented in 1908, and spread slowly until the 1930s, when the 6-3-3 system (6-year elementary, 3-year junior high, and 3-year high school) started to become more common, but even then, mainly just in urban areas. No doubt, Ithaca thought of itself as a progressive town to be an early adopter of junior high school and the 6-3-3 model.

54 I have not been able to determine where the Catholic school might have been located. As far as I can tell, there are currently no Catholic schools in or near Ithaca at either the primary or secondary levels, nor have there been for some time. These days, there is a system for the long-distance bussing of students to Catholic schools in Elmira or other localities, but surely Jessie was attending a school right in Ithaca.

who went there had parents who taught at the college and were real snobs. The situation was miserable for me. I didn't like those kids, and I didn't like the nun who was my teacher. In fact, by the end of the term I hated her. She showed her dislike for me right from the start. Her name was Sister Margaret, and she was a very fat nun. Her face was always at least a dark shade of red, and when she was angry with me, it turned purple. She must have had a hard time when she went to confession and had to tell the priest how much she hated me. No matter what others might have claimed to the contrary, I know she always toadied to the rich kids.

Sister Margaret seemed to take a special delight in embarrassing me. One of the boys in my grade wrote me a note expressing how much he liked me. I put the note in my history book and forgot about it. For some reason, during history class Sister Margaret strode to the back of the room and just happened to stop by my desk. She lifted up my history book and found the note. She told me to report to her after school. I supposed she wanted me for something else. Actually, I had forgotten about the note, so it came as a surprise when she started out by accusing me of flirting with boys. I didn't know what to say. Taking my stammering as an admission of guilt, she told me I would have to stay after school every day for a week. I accepted the punishment, resigned to the idea that I was getting blamed for something I had no control over. She never said a word to the boy who had written the note. So, while I stayed after school for the week, I had to listen to the evils that could happen to someone like me if I wasn't careful about how I behaved.

The Sister never missed an opportunity to humiliate me in front of the class. I never forgot one day in particular. My menstrual period came while I was in class, and since I had come to school unprepared for that, I was afraid I would have signs on my skirt. I went up to her desk and asked if I could go home. She asked why and when I explained, she said, "What?" I repeated myself, but again she said, "What?" Before it was over, she had made me repeat myself three times, each time louder. By that time, the whole class knew I had my period. I was so humiliated.

I came to hate Catholic school so much that I used to pray that I would break a leg or an arm just so I wouldn't have to go to school. I even tried to stumble over the curbs with the hope of falling and breaking a bone, but I never managed to fall hard enough. I read in a magazine that prison inmates would sometimes place wads of chewing tobacco under their armpits to make themselves sick. After reading that, I took some of Bill's tobacco, wet it in the bathroom sink, and placed it under my armpits. It was sticky and therefore not too comfortable, but the worst part is that it didn't work. I didn't get sick.

Sister Margaret would take us out on warm spring afternoons, and we would sit on the grass and do test papers from past years. When it was time to return to our classroom, she would tell us to pick up all the papers. After picking up the papers, instead of returning to the classroom, I would carry the papers to the top of the stairs and leave them in a neat pile on the top step. Then I would run like crazy out of the school.

I would do that every time we spent the afternoon outside, but Sister Margaret never said anything the next day. I guess she didn't think I was worth bothering with. The times she kept me after school I guess were just to get even.

As bad as that term of Catholic school was, the next year I found that junior high was very different and in a bad way. The kids who went to that school were just like the kids in Catholic school or maybe worse. It seemed like all of them had parents who taught in the college or the high school, and all of them had money. There were few kids there as poor as we were. With Helen and Mary married, the number of us kids still at home was down to seven, but we still didn't have enough money to have the things the other kids had.

Marge and I were in the same gym class. Marge, as always, took care of her things. I didn't care if I wore the same blouse and skirt every day. I'd wash the blouse and press the skirt, but I never had the neat look that Marge had. One day in gym class, one of the girls in my grade said to me, "How come Marge has such nice clothes and you don't? Doesn't your mother care about you?" I was very hurt. When I went home for lunch, I told my mother what the kids were saying, and right then Marge and her girlfriend, Barbara, who was there at the time, got the bright idea to fix me up for the afternoon. I know they meant well, but I look back at it now and wonder who the worst dumbbell was. Nothing matched, and I came out looking like a clown. The sweater and blouse didn't match, and the skirt was too big. The worst parts were the stockings with silver steaks and the velvet slippers with rhinestone buckles.

But at the time I felt I must look beautiful, and I marched proudly into school. During the first class that afternoon, I sent a note to the girl who had made the remark about my clothes in gym class. I wrote in the note, "Now will you still criticize my mother?" She quickly wrote back an apology saying how nice I looked, but I suppose now she was being sarcastic.

When I look back on those days, I realize we were rich in other ways than having money. We had brothers and sisters, and although we had our differences, we grew up caring about each other. I think now those days were really very happy ones.

I fell in love the summer after my thirteenth birthday. He was eighteen and my older brother's best friend. I can't remember now what he looked like, but back then I had a real crush on him. His name was Ray. All my family liked him very much, and my mother treated him like a member of the family. He was interested in photography and even set up a dark room in the closet off of our living room. I had never liked boys in a mushy way, more like in the way a tomboy does. I liked to play games like kick-the-stick, and I loved to climb trees, and so I often enjoyed being around boys for that reason. But the kind of crush I had on Ray was a whole new experience for me. Ray must have known I had a thing for him, but I was just Bill's little sister to him.

One day Ray stopped at the house and asked me if I would like a ride in his new car to go to Buttermilk Falls. I jumped at the chance. The other kids wanted to come too, and after getting Mother's permission, we all piled into Ray's car.[55] Once we parked at the base of the trail, we all got out of the car and started up toward the top. Along the way, there were these little benches where you could sit and rest. It was while we were sitting on one of those benches that Ray leaned over and kissed my cheek. I know my face must have turned as red as a beet, and I could not look at anyone. I was scared that my little brothers might tell Mother that I had let Ray kiss me. They were teasing me all the way home. I thought that if they told Mother, she might never let me go out in Ray's car again. I have to admit though that I was thrilled that Ray had kissed me.

That evening Claire and I were on pins and needles, waiting for the boys to open their mouths. As I look back now, I realize that they had thought almost nothing of the incident and would almost have forgotten it by the time we got home. If I had left well enough alone, nothing would have come of it. But no, I had to pester Jim and Dick with threats about what I would do if they told Mother. This just gave them the idea that they had something they could threaten Claire and me with. Claire was of course innocent of it all, but as we were growing up, Claire and I stuck together in times of trouble. Since I was almost always in trouble, this meant most of the time.

The next morning, thinking something awkward might come of the situation, Claire and I snuck out of the house. I don't know what we thought that would accomplish as we had to go home some time. We finally got hungry and went home. When Mother asked us where we had been, we just told her we went for a walk. After breakfast, we were in the bathroom when Jim came pounding on the door. We yelled at him to go away. He yelled back at the top of his lungs that he would tell Mother that Ray had been kissing me at the falls. The fat was in the fire. Claire and I walked slowly into the kitchen and began to clear off the table.

My mother didn't say anything until we were doing the dishes. She started out by asking me questions about what else I had done besides kissing. I was in tears as I protested that I hadn't been a bad girl. She said that any girl who let a boy kiss her at my age could get herself into big trouble. Then she told me that Mary was going to have another baby, and I would have to spend the summer with her as soon as school was out. Furthermore, she said I would have to stay in the room when Mary had her baby so I would see firsthand what kind of trouble I could get into. That was a terrible thing to threaten me with. After the screaming I had heard the year before when Mary had her first child, it scared me half to death. I can't believe that Mother really meant it. What was said to Ray I never found out. He seemed to remain in my mother's good graces. He might have laughed it all off, but he didn't know what nightmares I would have before vacation came.

I think I was the kind of kid that everybody assumed would go bad. I don't know why. Much later I found out from one of my sisters that they all assumed I had slept

---

55 Most of us in the region think of Buttermilk Falls as one of the most beautiful sites in Ithaca. It is about a two-and-a-half-mile drive south from where their apartment was.

with boys, but it just wasn't so. I never did anything like that, but I guess there was something about the way I acted that gave the other kids that impression.

At the end of the school term, I did get shipped off to Mary's.[56] I loved being there with her, and she loved having me. I not only helped her with the housework, but we also had a lot of fun. Mary was always ready to have a good laugh, and she made me feel that whatever I had to say to her was important to her. I loved Mary very much. She assured me that the doctor wouldn't even have let me stay in the room when the baby came, so I didn't have to worry about that. She explained that Mother worried about me and had only told me that I must see the baby born in order to make me stop and think whenever I felt mushy about a boy. So, with that worry off my mind, I settled down to enjoy the summer.

On the Fourth of July, Peggy and Ann, two girls who lived just down the road from Mary, asked her if I could go with them to see the fireworks. Their older brother had a car, and he would drive us there. Living in a remote area like Mary did, you couldn't go much of anywhere without a car. Mary said I could go, but that I must be home no later than ten. The brother stopped and picked up another boy. We saw the fireworks, and I could have been home by ten if they had taken me straight back after that. But the boys wanted to stop in a small town where they were having a dance that night. Peggy and Ann were allowed to stay out late as long as they were with their brother, so it wasn't a problem for them. I kept insisting that I had to go home, but I was still stuck with them there until they decided to leave. I have to admit though that I was enjoying myself with the music, the bright lights, and all the people laughing. I was thinking of Mary being worried about me, but I forgot that thought after a while. Sometime during the dance, it started to rain. By the time we left the dance hall it was a regular downpour. I was beginning to feel frightened. It was already two in the morning, and I didn't know how I was going to face Mary. I made matters worse by deciding I might as well stay the rest of the night and go home in the morning. I thought I would just tell Mary that it was raining too hard for me to come home.

The next morning was bright with sunshine, and I started walking up the hill toward home. I was trying to put on a bold face as I knew I had done something very wrong. Here was my beloved sister who was going to have a baby, and I had done something to worry her half to death. Then I saw Mary's husband Ralph's car coming down the hill. He stopped the car and, leaning out the window, he said, "Where the hell have you been?"

I thought my only choice was to bluff my way out of the mess I was in. Smiling

---

56 Mary and Ralph lived in the part of Scott Township known as Justus. (Think of getting off I-81 at Exit 197 "Waverly", passing over to the eastern side of 81 and driving a few miles south from there.) It would have been somewhere around seven miles southeast of where the family had previously lived in Dalton. It was far from any public transportation. When Jessie was sent there for the summer, if she had traveled from Ithaca by train, Ralph must have met her by car at one of the train stations, probably Clarks Summit.

brightly, I answered, "Oh, it was raining so hard that I stayed with the girls," though actually I was shaking in my boots. I didn't know exactly what time the rain started falling the night before. If it wasn't until after ten, they would know my excuse was just a flimsy lie.

Ralph started the engine again and growled, "Get yourself home. Mary had a baby boy this morning." I felt both scared and guilty, but above that, I felt a tremendous sense of relief. If the baby was born already, then there was no way I would possibly have to watch the birth. The baby was Richard, who turned out to be one of my favorite nephews.[57] Mary later told me that Mother had planned to be there for the delivery, but that the baby had been born early. Mary also said that as her pains got bad, she was too busy dealing with the delivery process to worry about me, so I didn't have to feel guilty about not being there. I also heard that the doctor didn't get there until after the baby was born. Mary never told my mother that I had stayed out all night. I had come close to being in trouble with everyone. Mary knew something about me that no one else did, and she never told on me.

One of the boys I made friends with that summer was named Bill James. For a while I entertained the idea that, if I ended up marrying him, I would be Mrs. Jessie James, almost like the famed outlaw. But that romance was short lived. One night Bill, along with our neighborhood friends Peggy and Ann, wanted me to go for a walk with them. I went without saying a word to Mary or my mother, who was staying there at the time. Two other boys walked along with us too. Bill James and I walked ahead of the rest. Every time we heard a car coming, we would hide among the trees near the road. I had an uneasy feeling that it would be my brother or Ralph coming to look for me. We just fooled along until we came to an open stretch where the only trees were far back from the road. We were laughing and talking like most teenagers do when we heard a car coming. This time there was no place to hide. It turned out that in the car were my mother and my older brother, Bill. I was embarrassed when they ordered me into the car without giving me a chance to say good-bye to the girls or Bill James.

Mary was a wonderful person. Her house was small and had no bath or running water. The drinking water had to come in a bucket from the neighbor's well next door. Mary had seven children in that house. She was the kind of person who always found the courage to face things as they came and could always find something to laugh about. I went to stay with Mary whenever she needed me. No matter what the intention was for sending me there, it certainly wasn't a punishment for me. I enjoyed being with her there as often as I could, during Christmas and Easter breaks, and when I was no longer in school. She would do needlework all summer, and then she would sell it just before Christmas to have the money to buy gifts.

It was during one of those visits that I met a cousin of Ralph's. Earl was about

---

57 Richard Harry Clark, second child of Ralph and Mary, was born July 5th, 1925.

twenty-two and worked as a mailman.[58] He had a crush on me, but I didn't have any romantic feelings for him. Earl would come to the house in the evenings, and he, Mary, and I would sit around the kitchen table. The table was covered with oilcloth, and I always doodled on it if there was a pencil handy. We sat in such a way that Mary could see the pictures I was drawing on the table, but Earl couldn't. I would let my artistic imagination run wild. I drew pictures of both sexes in all kinds of positions. Mary and I would be choking with laughter, but Earl would look at us as though he thought we were losing our minds. I always had a wet washcloth handy, so I could wipe off the drawings before anyone else saw them. Poor Earl never understood us. He was my constant suitor for a year or more. When I went home to Ithaca, he would write me every day. He also sent me gifts. I received from him a pen-and-pencil set, a camera, and several boxes of candy. I was not a very nice person, because I took all these gifts from him, and never gave anything in return. I let him kiss me once on the cheek. Some Sundays, Earl would stop at Mary's and take me for ice cream, along with all the kids. He was very thoughtful.

I did a terrible thing to Earl when I was fourteen. I received a letter from him asking me what I wanted for Christmas. He said he knew that I wanted ice skates, and he would like to get them for me if that was all right with me. I was in heaven thinking of owning a pair of skates of my own. My mother was going by train to Scranton to shop and visit friends. I was going with her as far as Clarks Summit to stay with Mary. I showed Mother the letter on the train and waited for her reaction. I was only fourteen, and she didn't think it was proper for me to receive expensive gifts like that. As I expected she might, Mother refused to give her permission. I went into a sulk there on the train. Mother sat looking out the train window for a while, and then finally relented, saying that I could receive the skates with the justification that I wouldn't be able to afford them any other way. She said that if she hadn't known Earl, or if he hadn't been Ralph's cousin, it would have been out of the question. I was in seventh heaven for the rest of the trip.

Christmas was getting close, and I hadn't yet received the skates. On the day before Christmas, a package finally arrived, but I could tell by the weight that there were no skates inside. I took the package up to my room so that I could be alone when I opened it. Inside was a pair of pink bedroom slippers. I was very angry and gave the slippers to Marge. I then sat down and wrote a nasty letter to Earl, telling him what I thought of getting slippers when I was expecting skates. I straightaway took it to the post office and mailed it. The day after Christmas I received a letter from Earl. Our letters had crossed in the mail. In his letter he explained that he was sending me slippers

58 This has to be Ralph's first cousin Earl Clarence W. (1908-1981). He would have been at most eighteen at the time, not even close to her estimate of twenty-two, which would have been pretty creepy anyway for a man courting a fourteen-year-old girl so ardently. Earl spent most of his life in or around Scott, Pennsylvania and worked at a variety of jobs. He married Emma "Dolly" V. (1919-1984) in 1937 when he was twenty-eight and she nineteen. They appear to have been Pentecostals. They had at least three children.

because the skates would be late getting there, and he wanted me to have something from him to open on Christmas Day. I felt so guilty that when the skates arrived a few days later, I could take no pleasure in them the way I would have if I only had not sent that terrible letter. The skates were lined in red plaid and were really nice. For a few days I pretended I was queen of the ice rink. Then Dick started sneaking off with the skates and trying to use them. They were too big for him, so he ended up skating on their sides, and soon the leather was scraped and torn. I could have killed him, but deep in my heart, I felt as though I was just getting what I deserved for hurting Earl.

Ithaca is surrounded by hills. No matter what direction you went, you would almost certainly be soon crossing a bridge and then climbing a hill. Every winter the police would rope off one of the streets so kids could go sled riding. One night Claire, I, and our friend Dorothy decided to take sleds and haul them up one of the hills not far from where we lived.[59] It was a very dangerous thing to do as the hill wasn't roped off at the time, and there would be car traffic. We went up the hill and came speeding down about four times, fortunately without mishap. On the fifth run, Dorothy and Claire had ridden ahead of me. As I approached an intersection, I saw Claire on her sled zipping right through the legs of a policeman. I decided to make a panic stop, so I turned my sled and slammed it into the curb. Someone had called the police and complained that some kids were sledding on an unprotected hill. The police confiscated our sleds and said they were going to keep them. Dorothy was using her own sled, but Claire and I were using Jim's and Dick's. If we didn't bring them back home, we would be in very hot water. We pleaded, begged, and shed a few tears. We explained that the sleds belonged to our brothers. After letting us sweat a little longer, the police officers gave us back the sleds with a stern warning about what terrible things would happen if they ever caught us again. They never would, because we were so scared of going to jail that we never rode those sleds on unprotected hills again.

One summer Marge heard about a farm where they needed cherry pickers, and she passed this information to us younger sisters. The workers would live on the farm until cherry season was over. The owners paid so much per basket but deducted the costs of the meals each week. It sounded to us like an easy way to earn money, and since Claire and I were anxious to buy our own bicycles, we decided to go work there. Our friend, Dorothy, decided to go too. The cherry farm was beautiful. The owners had a large house, but where we girls who were hired for picking the cherries slept was in the hayloft of a huge barn. It was clean and comfortable, and we had plenty of pillows and blankets. The meals were good. We lined up for breakfast, lunch, and supper. After breakfast we went to the orchard and were given either boxes or pails to pick into. After work was finished for the day, we could go swimming in the lake that was on the farm.

---

59 Perhaps in the incidents she describes both here and later with the bobsled, they were sledding on the steep part of East Buffalo Street coming down the hill from the Collegetown District of Ithaca. That would fit her description particularly well, but there are certainly several other steeply sloping streets in Ithaca they could have been using.

As I recall it, Claire, Dorothy, and I worked only one full day. The second day after lunch we slipped away to the lake, and we continued spending most of the day at the lake from then on. We were always back in time for supper though. The owners sent us home at the end of the week, but we had no pay coming. In fact, we actually owed them money.

There was a beautiful clubhouse in Ithaca in those days. It was sort of a Boys' Club and Girls' Club combined. We had so much fun there. We could take sewing or cooking lessons. Women from the college would come to the clubhouse to teach. One of them took a liking to me, and when she went home for Easter break, she sent me a pair of roller skates that she had used back when she was a kid. They were very nice skates, and I loved them. Of course, Jim and Dick loved them too and lost one of the skates. The college women dressed dolls for us at Christmas. Mine was dressed in lavender. At Christmas time we would put on a play, and one year I had the roles of both Santa Claus and the father in the play. But one night, I had a mishap there. Several of us kids were playing outdoors, and one of the other kids was chasing me. I ran behind the clubhouse and almost got killed. For some reason, someone had strung a wire from the clubhouse to a nearby pole, and I ran into that wire in the dark. I was knocked to the ground and was seeing stars.

In the winter Bill and some of his friends would get a bobsled, and several of us kids, my age and older, would pile on it and fly down a hill. We were young and didn't think about dangers, including running into traffic. We would come flying down the hill through an intersection of five roadways. It was a wonder we never got hurt.

Dick had his own way of saying good-bye to Mother before he went to the club in the evening. He'd stand in the doorway and sing:

> Pack up all my cares and woes,
> Here I go, singing low,
> Bye, Bye, Blackbird.[60]

It has quite a few verses. My mother would get the biggest kick out of the way he would stand there and sing. Dick was the baby of the family, and he had a strong bond with Mother. Jim, on the other hand, was my father's son. Jim could get away with things that my father would have had a fit about if one of us other kids pulled the same stunt. Jim and Dick had a song they would sing while marching around the kitchen table.

> Tramp, Tramp, Tramp,
> The boys are marching,
> All the bangle, bangle boo.

---

60 These are lyrics from the song "Bye, Bye, Blackbird" first published in 1926. It would have been a brand new pop song at the time.

For to buy a stick of candy
at one cent apiece
All the bangle, bangle boo.

One day as we were walking home from school, for some reason, some of us girls were discussing how we could get away with sneaking out of our houses at night if we wanted to. I said I would sneak down the fire escape. Another girl said she could just walk out the front door as her parents slept in the back of the house. We thought of all sorts of ways. Dorothy came up with the idea of staying the night at my house, with the idea that we would then sneak down the fire escape and meet up with her boyfriend. To think it was to do it. We decided on doing it that very night, because my mother was visiting relatives in Shamokin and had just left Bill and Marge in charge.[61] Part of the attraction in the plan for me was that I was becoming more curious about what went on between boys and girls and was anxious to learn more about sex. Dorothy's boyfriend worked at the gas station next door to our apartment. When she told him about our plan to sneak out at night, he said he would get one of his friends to come along too.

According to our plan, Claire, Dorothy, and I would sleep on the foldaway bed in the living room. That would make it easy to slip out the window to the fire escape. We went to bed at the usual time, but we stayed away talking and giggling. Claire said she wished she could sneak out too, along with Dorothy and me. Ten o'clock came, and Dorothy and I snuck quietly down the fire escape, leaving Claire behind. Dorothy's boyfriend wasn't quite finished at the gas station, so Dorothy and I just wandered along the side street. By chance, we met a boy we knew and started joking about our little escapade. He said he would like to go with us too if there was another girl in our party. We therefore hurried back to the house, and I climbed back up the fire escape. I called Claire to the window and told her she could come along after all because we had another boy joining us. She hurried into her clothes and came down to join us.

We all joined up at the gas station, and I met the boy who was to be my date. He was at least eighteen years old and very good looking. We walked up to the schoolyard playground and tried out the swings. As we walked a little way from there, I asked my date something I had been dying to know more about. I had read in a magazine about a "soul kiss" and asked him what that was. I think the question surprised him, but he explained very nicely that I should wait until I was a little older before I tried a kiss of that kind. My thought was that if it was something more extreme than a regular kiss, I wasn't sure I wanted to try it anyway. Once a boy had kissed me on the mouth, and I scrubbed my mouth for days afterwards. In any case, I went home just as ignorant about soul kissing as I had been from the start. And I was very disappointed after all that this

---

61 Assuming this incident happened around 1925, Marge would have been about sixteen and Bill about eighteen, presumably old enough to look after their wayward younger siblings. Jessie might have been fourteen, and Claire maybe only twelve, which seems very young for any plan involving meeting older boys at night.

99

boy didn't kiss me that night.

We girls didn't really stay out very long before slipping back up the fire escape and going back to bed. We had to lie there spoon fashion as the foldaway bed was too small for three people. We were giggling about our little adventure. Finally, I asked Dorothy, "What is a soul kiss?" Before she had time to answer, a voice came out of the darkness and then the light went on.

There stood Marge, looking like an avenging angel, holding a walking stick in one hand. She said, "I'll tell you what a soul kiss is," as she started whacking the feather comforter that we had over us with the stick. She was very angry and was yelling that when Mother came home the next day, she was going to tell her what we had been up to. It seems that little Carmel had tried to come into the living room while we were out, but since we had wedged a chair against the door, she couldn't get in. She went back and told Marge about this, and of course Marge had to check out the situation. She forced the door open and found our bed empty. This made her furious and at the same time worried that we might be in trouble. Bill wasn't home yet at that point. After she put Carmel back to bed, Marge waited in the living room until she heard us coming up the fire escape. When she heard us giggling back in bed, she knew we were safe, but she was still very angry. To make matters worse, she happened to come back into the room just as I was asking Dorothy about soul kissing. She began bringing the cane down really hard. We started to cry and after a few more whacks Marge stopped. The thick feather comforter cushioned the blows so much that they didn't actually hurt us, but we were frightened by Marge's fury.

The next day when my mother came home, I had to confess to her what we had done, but I was relieved that she didn't get too upset. She said I was growing up and it was natural to have new friends, but I should have them to the house rather than sneaking out to meet them at night. I guess I took her too much at her word about that, because I started inviting kids over to the house every day after school until Mother finally put a stop to that. She then limited me to having friends over only on the weekends and other times when there was no school.

I remember many a warm Sunday morning when we would sit around enjoying the comic strips in the Sunday paper. My father got first crack at the paper, and we kids would wait impatiently to get the funnies. We all liked *The Katzenjammer Kids* and admired all the tricks they played. *Happy Hooligan* and *Maggie and Jiggs* [aka *Bringing Up Father*] were two of our other favorites. We always had our big meal at noon, and on lazy summer afternoons nobody wanted to do the dishes. Mother would mention several times that the dishes were waiting, but we'd just whine, "Do we have to?" But then when Father lowered his paper, glowered at us, and said, "Girls, Get into the kitchen!" we moved. Mother could tell us something five or six times, but my father only had to speak once for us to fly to our chores.

We enjoyed the several magazines my mother got each month. *Ladies' Home Journal* was one of them. We looked forward to these magazines mainly for the paper dolls. We'd spend many a happy hour cutting them out, being careful in how we cut around the tabs for the clothing and the little slits in the hats. If we didn't have enough clothing to suit us, we cut out clothing pictures from the fashion sections of the magazines and fit them to our paper dolls. My favorite doll was called Dolly Dimples. Kids today don't even know how to play paper dolls. Today, a girl the age I was then would think we were off our heads to play with such things as that. Times do change.

During the year that we went to Catholic school we became particularly familiar with all the holy days and saints' days. One year on Good Friday, Claire and I decided to keep silent for the three hours that Jesus suffered on the cross. We had heard that if you did this, you would get a special dispensation. I didn't know what that was, but Claire and I still decided not to speak a word for three hours. At exactly twelve noon we buttoned our lips and walked silently around the house doing whatever tasks we were supposed to be doing then. I was feeling very holy and was sure God would be looking down on me and thinking what a good girl I was. My father was home that day, and of course, not being Catholic, he had no idea what was going on. He noticed that Claire and I were walking around silently, with our eyes downcast and solemn looks on our faces. Mother tried to explain to him why we were doing what we were.

It all went fine for about an hour and a half, but then I guess my father got bored with watching his little angels walking back and forth so quietly, and he decided to stir things up. One time, as I was walking past him, he grabbed me by the wrist and asked me what time it was. I mutely shook my head and tried to pull away. He hung onto my wrist and started to ask me silly questions. I knew he wanted me to break my silence, and when he saw that I wouldn't, he started to yell at me. At that point I began to cry, and I answered his questions.

That was the last time I kept my mouth shut for that long. To this day, I am never silent, and find myself talking out loud even when I am alone. I don't remember how long Claire remained silent. I hope she made it to the end of the three hours and got her special dispensation.

My father was a man with many dreams. He could do many things very well, but, as the saying goes, he had actually mastered none. He was forever trying to come up with an invention that was going to make us rich. And his biggest ambition was to have his writings published, but that never happened to the extent he wanted. He did have a few short stories published in the railroad magazines, but never in any major publications as he would have liked. At one time he had a radio program, but that venture failed too. I sometimes think he must have been a particularly frustrated man. For one thing, he and my mother had nine kids within a relatively short time, and the first three were not even two years apart.

One of the many things my father tried his hand at was hypnotism. One day, when I was about fourteen, he tried practicing it on me. He sat me in a chair and dangled a watch in front of my eyes. I wanted to go to sleep like he told me to, but I just couldn't. He got very angry over not being able to put me under. I honestly wish I could have done it for him. I often think that if my father had only made a big success of one of the things he tried, he would have been a different man—one who was less angry.

My first pair of high heels were a pretty shade of gray. Whether I somehow convinced my mother to buy them for me or got them some other way, I don't remember now. Most likely I just cried and coaxed until my mother finally gave in and bought them. I was so proud of those shoes. I wore them to school, and sadly one day when I was rushing down the stairs to the girls' room, one of the heels caught on a step and came right off the shoe. That was the end of high heels for that year.

I'll also never forget my first pair of glasses. No one was free to go with me, so I had to go to the eye doctor by myself. The doctor examined my eyes and then told me that if I wore my glasses for two years, my eyes would correct themselves well enough that I would never have to wear glasses again after that. During part of the process, he put drops in my eyes, so when I left the office, I couldn't see very well. I was afraid to cross the street. Fortunately, a girl I knew from school came along and kindly walked me home. A few days later I got the glasses, and I was thrilled. To me it seemed that any kid would love to wear glasses. But after a few weeks they started to seem like a pain in the neck, even if they did help me see better. For one thing, it was troublesome to have to be so careful about putting them down in a place where they couldn't be knocked around and broken. One day in gym class I put my glasses on a bench next to my books while I played volleyball. When I came back, I couldn't find them. Someone must have stolen them. It would be two years before I got another pair, and apparently my eyes didn't get better in the meantime.

One February day some of my siblings and I were sitting around the kitchen table cutting out homemade Valentine cards. Just in the way it often works for Valentine's Day at school, each kid had a Valentine box, and you had to leave a Valentine in the box of each of your classmates whether you liked the person or not. In our house we couldn't afford store-bought Valentines, so we had to make our own. I was having trouble thinking up verses for each of these, and when it came to the card that I was making for one of the boys in the class, I thought of using a poem that I had heard somewhere. It went like this.

> I love you so much,
> I love you so mighty.
> I wish your pajamas,
> Were next to my nightie.
> Now don't get excited,
> And don't be misled.
> I mean on the clothesline,
> And not on the bed!

I just thought it was cute, but Marge happened to pick up this card, and she had a fit. She asked Mother if she was going to let me give such a Valentine to a boy. We had a big fight over it, and in the end, I had to tear up the card. I really didn't think the poem was that bad.

Another time that I got into trouble, it was over a riddle rather than another poem. A girl in my class asked me: *Why does the ocean roar?* The answer was *You would roar too if you had crabs in your bottom.* The innocent picture in my mind was of a person coming out of the water with a big crab hanging from the seat of his bathing suit. That evening, Bill's friend, Ray, had stopped by the house. While the riddle was fresh in my mind, I thought I would impress Ray by asking him, "Why does the ocean roar?" He didn't know the answer, so I told him. I was disappointed that he didn't even smile.

He waited until Bill came into the room and then told me to ask Bill the same riddle. I went through it again, and when I said the punch line, Bill hit the ceiling. He ran into the kitchen, and I heard him yelling to Mother in a loud voice, "You have to do something about that kid." I was confused. I didn't understand what I had done wrong. No one explained it to me, so it wasn't until years later that I figured out the real meaning of the riddle. At the time, I was just told never to repeat it again.

One evening I wandered quite a few blocks from our house with some of the neighborhood kids I played with. We were having a good time, and though it was the time of year it got dark early, I didn't have to be home until nine. In all the fun. The time went by quickly, and when I realized it was getting late, I headed for home. I knew my father was home that night rather than away for the railroad, so I would be in hot water if I came home late. I began almost running, and just then I thought I heard a noise behind me. Looking over my left shoulder, I saw the moon, and it seemed to me a very bad omen, so I began to think I was in big trouble. A little further on, I saw a black cat, and although I tried to avoid it, the cat ran right in front of me, so I was scared all the more for my bad luck. My mind ran in circles trying to think of excuses for being late coming home. I couldn't think of a thing. Sure enough, my father met me about half a block from our house, and all he said was, "Get yourself home!" I got there as fast as my legs would carry me. When I reached my bedroom, my mother was standing there, and she let me have it right across my legs. She was using the same cane Marge had swung down on the feather comforter, but this time there were no feathers to cushion the blows. It really stung, and I screamed my head off. All the same, I was glad it was my mother rather than my father wielding the cane.

Whenever my mother made one of her trips to Shamokin to visit relatives, she could travel by train without expense, even when some of us kids went along with her. We had a railroad pass, since my father worked for the DL&W Railroad.[62] Even when

---

62 The DL&W did not have a line to Shamokin, so when Jessie is referring to her mother being able to get passes on another railroad, she probably means she got a pass to transfer to the Pennsylvania Railroad, which did have a station in Shamokin. Perhaps Elizabeth changed trains from the Lackawanna to the "Pennsy" at Wilkes-Barre. The PRR was a much larger operation even than the DL&W and had very extensive routes. At one point in the late 19th Century, it had been the largest corporation in the world.

my mother had to transfer to another railroad, it was still free, because there was a system whereby families of employees of one railroad could get passes when needed to ride on another. When she made one of these trips in summer, she sometimes took one or two of us kids with her. But on one summer visit, she left for Shamokin alone, and when she came back, she brought her niece Agnes with her. Agnes was my age, and it didn't take Claire and me very long to get to hate Agnes.[63] (We called her "Aganess".) She had gorgeous, long, brown, naturally curly hair. Every day, while Claire and I did the dishes, my mother would brush Aganess's hair. It made me jealous to see those beautiful curls, because they were just what I wanted all my life. She never had to help with the dishes or make the beds. Claire and I couldn't understand why. We always had to help when we went for a visit to relatives in Shamokin.

One day my parents took Agnes, along with our three younger siblings—Carmel, Jim, and Dick—on a day trip to see our married sister, Helen, who lived in Factoryville, Pennsylvania. They couldn't take Claire and me, because there wouldn't be enough room in the car.[64] They left us home with some money, which we promptly squandered on candy. After that, we just got pickles and olives from the grocery store downstairs and put them on our parents' bill. We were having a really good time by ourselves until later that afternoon. Claire was in the bathroom, and I was in the kitchen when a loud explosion sounded. I ran to the hallway and clutched at Claire, who had just come flying out of the bathroom with her underwear still down around her ankles. She was afraid that the world had come to an end. I am not sure what I thought, but we were two scared kids. It turned out that a small gas tank had exploded at the gas station next door.

The plan was to go to the movies that night with our friend, Dorothy, but we didn't have any money left after having spent it all on candy. We were pretty downhearted about the situation when Bill came home for supper. We poured out our tales of woe to him. Not only had we been denied the chance to go to Helen's with the family, but we couldn't even go to the movies either, because we didn't have any money, us poor pitiful girls. Bill gave us enough for the movie and a little extra for candy and popcorn.

When Dorothy showed up at our house, she was wearing a raincoat, because it was raining hard outside. Neither Claire nor I had raincoats, but Agnes had left hers hanging in the closet. Claire decided to borrow that one. I borrowed one from Mrs. McCabe[65] who lived on the second floor, and we cheerfully set off for the movie.

---

63 Jessie and Claire's cousin, Agnes, was daughter of their Aunt Hattie and Uncle John Neibauer, which means she was a younger sister of the Cousin Joe who died in the railroad accident in 1925. Agnes was born in 1912 so she would have been about halfway between Jessie and Claire in age.

64 One of the places Helen and Jack lived early in their marriage was Factoryville, about three or four miles north of where the family had previously lived in Dalton. The DL&W might still have had a station at nearby La Plume at that time, but Jessie seems to suggest that the whole trip was made by car in this case.

65 Maud McCabe lived on the second floor. Her husband, Charles, was a printer. Clearly the two families must have been friendly neighbors if they were doing things like borrowing raincoats.

Knowing that Agnes always had a fit if we touched anything of hers, we hoped to be back in time to hang her raincoat back in the closet before everyone got home. Well, we were out of luck on that one. As we came up the stairs and into the kitchen, we could see my mother and Agnes waiting there for us. Agnes was in tears, because her terrible cousins were using the precious raincoat that her mother had bought her. Needless to say, Claire and I were punished for that one, . . . as usual.

Agnes walked around the next day looking very smug, but that wasn't going to last. A few days later, some of us went to the lake together. It was supposed to be a farewell swim with Agnes because she would be leaving us soon after that. The McCabe family on the second floor had a son named Bob, who was about fifteen at the time, and he came along with us. One of the things I liked about Bob was that he couldn't stand Aganess any more than Claire and I could. After the swim, Bob, Claire, and I started fooling around, but Agnes just sat quietly on a rock nearby. She had brought along her raincoat, apparently thinking it might start raining on the walk home, but she had half forgotten that it was lying on the sand a few feet from where she sat. I snatched up the coat and started dancing around waving it like a matador would wave his cape. Bob caught on right away and took the role of the bull, repeatedly charging at the bright red raincoat. Agnes was in tears. She started for home ahead of us, screaming that she was going to tell her Aunt Elizabeth on us. When we reached home, it was no surprise to see her crying her eyes out to Mother because we had been so mean to her. Claire and I were punished again. It was a happy day for us when Mother took Agnes by train back to Shamokin. Claire and I cheered when the train pulled out of Ithaca Station with Agnes aboard.

I'll always remember one of the happy experiences I had in the eighth grade. We were studying Greek mythology at the time. One day the teacher told us that we were going to have a sort of contest and divided the class into three groups. The group I was in chose me to be the one to draw a picture based on the stories we were reading. I was both surprised and flattered by this honor. My drawing was to be of Hope rising from Pandora's box. In my drawing, the box was clad in gold, and based on a suggestion from Marge, it had pleated satin inside. Hope had golden blond hair with blue ribbons tied in the back. Her wings were light blue, and her gown was a darker shade of blue with golden ribbons. I thought I was creating a beautiful picture. Bill's friend, Ray, had paints he used to colorize the black-and-white photographs he took, and he let me borrow those to use for my drawing. That worked out really nicely. This was all done on a cream-colored background, and it was fastened to the front cover [of a booklet our group made of the story] with blue and gold cords, those being the school colors. Of the three pictures drawn, mine was judged the best, and though I don't remember getting an actual prize for that, I was still happy for the honor of coming in first!

One time Marge made two dresses of flannel, one for herself and one for me. Hers was red, and mine was blue. The dresses were cut out straight from the shoulders to the hem, and they had short sleeves. They were really pretty with white cuffs and collars. I was five foot six inches tall, and I think I looked great in that style. Marge made us hats out of felt to go with the dresses. Mine was of pink felt with a curling feather along one side. I thought I looked beautiful.

One Sunday at church, I just decided I didn't want to take Communion, though I am not sure why I didn't. I usually tried to get out of going to Confession, but I had already gone the day before, so that was not the issue. Anyway, skipping Communion meant that I was leaving church early and heading for home. When I came in, Mother wanted to know why I was home so early and where the other kids were. I told her that they were still in church, but that I had felt I was going to faint, so I came home. There was some doubt showing in her face as she looked at me, but she told me that if I still felt faint after changing out of my Sunday dress, I should just lie down until I felt better. After lying down for only about ten minutes, I got back up again and said I felt fine.

That next Sunday I went to High Mass instead of the eight o'clock Mass as I was supposed to. It was an unusually hot day. My hair had started to grow out from the boyish haircut I had in those days and was just at the scraggly looking stage. In order to have my hat look right under these circumstances, I would part my hair in the middle and comb the long parts to come down beside my cheeks in a slight curl, and I would pull down my hat hard enough to cover the short part of my hair.

After sitting through most of the Mass that day, I began to feel dizzy every time I had to stand up. I was scared since I didn't know what was happening to me. I had never felt this dizzy before. I managed to hang in there until Mass was over, but by then I was desperate to get outside for some fresh air. I had to push my way through the crowd to make my way to the exit, but then I came up behind a woman who refused to be pushed. When I tried to pass her, she poked her elbow out so I couldn't get by. My forehead broke out in a cold sweat, and I couldn't even see well. I was sure that if I didn't get some fresh air soon, I would pass out. Finally, in complete desperation, I grabbed the woman's arm and gasped out, "Please help me. I think I'm going to faint." She was with her brother, and he picked me up and carried me outside, where I collapsed. Then they took off my hat. Oh, vanity of vanities, even only half conscious, I thought how awful my hair must look and tried to raise my arm to brush it back. These nice people first took me to the priest's house for a little taste of wine, and then walked me home. When I got there and explained to Mother about my real fainting spell, I knew by the way she looked at me that she hadn't quite believed the pretend spell the week before. I felt that God had just punished me for lying to her then.

There was at least one time that I got Marge almost angry enough to kill me. I don't remember exactly what I had done that time to get her that mad, but it probably had something to do with swiping some of her clothes and either tearing them or getting them dirty. Anyway, we were really going at it on that day. There was a box I had that had once held a two-pound Easter egg, and I was using it to store my collection of junky knick-knacks. In those days, all cars had hood ornaments, and I had made a habit of collecting all of these I found, and I kept them in this box. Most of them were actually broken. That day I had left the box on a table in the living room, which was where Marge and I were having our big fight. She was so enraged that she picked up the box and threw it at me. I didn't duck fast enough, and the box, heavy with all the junk metal inside, hit me in the head. I screamed bloody murder. It wasn't common for Marge to be angry enough to throw something like that, so it must have been something extra bad I had done to make her so extremely upset. My head was cut, and to this day I still have a scar.[66] Marge was very sorry and scared about hurting me, but a few days later the two of us were fighting again.

For a variety of reasons, starting junior high school was a woeful experience for me. In every previous school I had attended, all my classes for the day were held in the same room, so the junior high system of moving from room to room felt alien to me. We did have our English lesson in the same room that was our homeroom, but then for the rest of the day, each of our other subjects was in a different classroom. How I longed for the familiar way things were done in the sixth grade!

I think it might have been a little easier for me to adjust to it all if it had not been for sewing class. Sewing had always been extra challenging for me. My mother could sew beautifully, and she was, for example, planning to make a lot of clothes for Marge when she graduated. Despite the fun classes at the Girls' Club, I really didn't know how to sew a straight seam. I think I might have liked sewing if only my mother had had enough time to teach me, but she didn't. The first project in junior high sewing class was to make an apron. My mother had to buy a yard of cotton fabric for me to use for this. The apron pattern was a relatively simple one. It just involved a waistband that was to be tied in a bow in the back and a skirt part attached to it, but the skirt part was to be sewed on with a gather. I didn't have any trouble cutting out the pattern, but after that I became confused. I tried to gather the skirt part properly as I basted it onto the waistband part. But before I could take it to the sewing machines for attaching securely, the teacher wanted to inspect what I had done so far. She came over to the sewing table where I was sitting and held up my apron. Her mouth fell open, and for several seconds she just stared without saying anything. Near one end of the waist band, I had gathered the whole skirt so much that it took up only six inches on the band, which left an extra-long streamer as the other end. It would have been the most lopsided apron imaginable, with a skirt that was only six inches wide. Of course, she made me start over again.

One summer my parents rented a cottage on the lake, and that was wonderful. While it was true that we could always walk to Cayuga Lake from our apartment, there was something special about staying right there on its shore. I think my mother also enjoyed the break from all the cooking and cleaning, since at the lake there were always

---

66 Without diminishing entirely the severity of the various injuries she discusses throughout her accounts; we should consider it possible that Jessie might exaggerate a little how much scarring took place. People who knew Jessie and her siblings as adults don't remember ever noticing some of the scars she describes as lasting the rest of their lives.

enough people around to help with the chores. Mother had a friend visiting her and staying with us at the cottage. Marge invited her friend, Barbara, along, and Claire and I had Dorothy. Some of us kids slept on the floor, because there weren't enough beds for everyone, but we were having so much fun we didn't mind that at all. We were in and out of the water all day long, so by nighttime we were tired to enough to sleep so soundly we barely moved. As for meals, as long as we had our Campbell's pork and beans and a spread called Olive-naise, we were content. I suppose my mother did do some cooking too, but we kids were fine with just our sandwiches of those ingredients.[67]

I've already mentioned that Marge had always been in the habit of taking good care of her clothes. She just had a natural inclination to be neat, and I did not. I'd often try to borrow something of hers without her knowing, but in the end, I would always be caught doing it. If I borrowed a pair of her stockings, for example, I'd be sure to get a run in them. She often would be looking for a slip of hers to put on and would discover that I was already wearing it. One time when she wasn't home, I took one of her dresses and wore it downstairs out in front of the house. I didn't mean to play in it, but when I saw the other kids playing tag, I just couldn't resist joining them. It all went fine until one of the kids saw Marge coming down the street. I ran up the fire escape, and when I climbed through the window at the top, I caught the dress on the windowsill and tore a big slit in it. I scooted into the bedroom, and the dress was off and on a hanger in the closet before Marge got up the stairs. By the time she walked into the bedroom, I was lying across the bed with my nose in a book. It wasn't until several days later, when Marge wanted to wear that dress, that she found the tear. I was in trouble again.

I think that whenever anything went wrong, everyone would just assume from the start that Jess was to blame for it, and I have to admit that they were usually right. The few times they weren't, I'd walk around looking wounded for days, playing the role of the abused victim.

In the early evenings, we kids gathered outside in front of the grocery store. Even in the fall months when the sun set early, the store would be brightly lit, so we were allowed to stay out there until nine o'clock as long as we stayed close. Just to the right of the door for the stairs leading up to our apartment, there was another door for a small apartment next to the store on the ground floor. An old man lived in that apartment who was usually drunk, and he sometimes sang loudly enough that we could hear him through the walls. One particular evening, he was sitting on the stoop by his door, obviously drunk as usual. Carmel was standing not far away, and the man asked her if she wanted to earn a quarter. She naturally said she would. But when he said he wanted her to go into the hallway and pull down her pants, of course she got scared and ran

---

67 In the early 20th Century, there was a product known as Mrs. Sclorer's Olive-naise. It was a gourmet mayonnaise mixed with a relish of minced olives and pimentos with spices. If it isn't entirely clear from her description, Jessie is describing a strange sort of sandwich. The main ingredient was cold Campbell's pork and beans scooped directly out of the can onto bread spread with Olive-naise. She continued this practice into adulthood. Some of her children still remember her serving them "bean sandwiches" that were made in exactly that way.

upstairs to our apartment. Our father happened to be home that day. When he heard what the old drunk had said to Carmel, he ran down the stairs and grabbed the old man by the front of his shirt. He punched him in the head and face. He then banged the man's head against the concrete pillars at the gas station next door, and when he finally let go, the old man collapsed on the ground. There was blood all over the place. The people in the store came running out when they heard all the ruckus. After they heard what the old man had wanted Carmel to do, they were yelling to my father that he should kill the man. The man was just lying on the ground crying, and at one point he was so still I was afraid my father had killed him. My father made us kids go upstairs. The next morning when we came downstairs on our way to school, we could hear the old man sitting down by the inlet singing at the top of his lungs. What a relief it was to know my father hadn't actually killed him.

At Christmas time the year I turned fourteen, I got a job in the local Woolworth's five-and-dime store. Marge already had a job there, and I guess she put in a good word for me. I was to work there until Christmas, every weekday afternoon and all day on Saturdays. I was thrilled to have a paying job even though I would have to turn over all I earned to my mother. That was the way it worked at our house. When we were old enough to have a job, we turned our pay over to our mother, and she would use it where it was most needed. But I wasn't thinking about money anyway my first day working at the store. I was just hoping I could avoid making any stupid mistakes. I was assigned to work at the hosiery counter, but, in a rather odd combination, at one end of the counter there was the glass case with the hard candies in it. There was a brass scale to weigh out the candy, but I didn't know how to use it. When I asked one of the girls to help me, she showed me how to shovel up the hard candy and how to read the scales, but she didn't explain how to balance the pan while I was doing it. The first customer I served must have gotten at least double the amount of candy she paid for. I couldn't figure out how to keep the pan balanced when there was candy in it, so I would just hold a paper bag under the pan and let the candy go straight into the bag. I'd just wait until I thought there was at least a pound in the bag before closing it up and handing it to the customer. They all really got full measure when I was working at the candy counter.

That Christmas Eve, I went to midnight Mass with Marge and some of her friends. The snow was falling softly when we came out of the church, and it was just a beautiful Christmas scene. But the thing was, now that I was contributing to the family finances, I would be playing a more grown-up sort of role in the family Christmas, and I had mixed feelings about that. It was good in a way to be treated as someone mature enough to stay up and help trim the tree. But when I saw the lovely dolls Claire and Carmel would be getting from Santa Claus, I wished I was still young enough to get a new doll too.[68]

---

68 People who knew Jessie as an adult often speak of her lifelong obsession with dolls, sometimes complaining that she seemed at times to care more about dolls than she did about her kids. It is probably that this tendency goes back to various situations she describes of being doll-deprived in her youth.

And Christmas mornings would no longer hold those thrilling surprises for me.

As a girl considered too old to get a doll, I was given a purse instead with a fifty-cent piece inside. I was rich! I could use ten cents to go to the movies, and then buy a love-story magazine for fifteen cents. That would leave a whole quarter to spend on candy or whatever else I wanted. But when I handed the fifty-cent piece to the girl at the movie ticket window, instead of one ticket and my change, she shoved out five tickets at me. I just took them since I was too embarrassed to tell her that I only needed one ticket. I didn't really enjoy the movie, because I was thinking the whole time about the candy I didn't have. I went home feeling down in the dumps. I had four tickets I didn't need, but not the love-story magazine I wanted. Helen and Jack were at our house that night.[69] They must have felt sorry for me, and they gave me fifteen cents for two of the tickets. I gave the other two to Claire and Carmel, and then went out to use the fifteen cents for my love-story magazine. But all in all, some of the magic had gone out of Christmas for me.

Whenever Claire and I were sent to pick up some groceries, it was obviously a quick errand during the Ithaca days, since the store was in the same building. Grocery stores in those days still sold certain items straight out of the barrel. In this store, there was a small barrel of smoked herring near the door. I'll never forget that on one particular day, as we were leaving the store with our groceries in hand, when we walked past that barrel, Claire reached in and took out a piece of herring, and then quickly put her hand into her pocket. It wouldn't do to holler at Claire right there, so I just took a tighter grip on the bag of groceries I knew our mother was waiting for upstairs and hurried out the door. I was afraid that the grocer might have seen her take it and would be yelling after us to stop, but we made it safely as far as the hallway. I stopped and looked at Claire. I pointed a finger at her and said, "Claire if you eat that fish, you'll go straight to Hell when you die."

Claire just took the herring out her pocket, looked at it, and then took a big bite that consumed half the fish. I looked at her in horror, thinking of the hellfire that surely awaited her. Claire just chewed slowly, and after she finally swallowed her mouthful, she said, "If I do go to Hell for this, it will be because I swiped it, not because I ate it. It tastes terrible." She threw the other half into the garbage can that stood in the hallway.

Winter weather sometimes brought suffering to the family. One January night, the wind was whipping around the corner of the house, and the snow was swirling around in little cyclones. These were not big fat snowflakes, but hard, small, icy ones. Bill was working a late shift in his job at the time as a dispatcher for a taxi company, and, as was

---

69 This apparently would have been shortly after the Christmas of 1925, and by that time eldest sister, Helen, and her husband, Jack, had moved from Factoryville to Ithaca. Jack had taken a job with the DL&W Railroad, likely due in part to help from the influence of his father-in-law. The young couple lived only a little to the east on West State Street, only a few minutes' walk away, so they likely visited the Davenport household often during this period.

usually the case, my father was away for his job with the railroad. The rest of us were all at home, asleep in bed. A noise awakened Mother about two o'clock in the morning. She sat up in bed and strained her eyes to see what it was that had made the noise that woke her. As her eyes gradually adjusted to the dark, she began to make out the image of a black figure with a white face approaching the bed. Even when she reached over to the lamp and turned on the light, she still wasn't sure who the figure was, because the face was all covered with bandages. Only after hearing his voice did she know it was Bill. He had been in a traffic accident and was taken to the hospital. His face had been cut up badly, and for the rest of his life he had a long scar down the left side of his face. He had been coming home in one of the company cabs when the car skidded on the icy road and hit a building. Bill went through the windshield. The cab company claimed that since he was sitting up front with the driver rather than in the back seat, they didn't have to pay for the damages. They were skunks.

I had a girlfriend named Josie. She was Italian. She lived on a farm outside of town, so she had to bring her lunch to school. Sometimes she would go over to a little grocery store that belonged to one of her relatives and have her lunch there. One day she asked if I would like to have lunch with her. She suggested that we could go to that store to get some cupcakes and bismarks and eat them by the inlet. It used to be more common back then to use the term "bismark" for the kind of squarish donuts with jelly or cream fillings. Of course, with my sweet tooth, I immediately agreed to Josie's idea, but I explained to her that I would have to go home first. My mother wouldn't let me leave the house until I ate my lunch. She had made tomato soup. I gulped down the hot soup and ran back down the stairs to where Josie was waiting for me in front of the house. We walked over to her aunt's store. There were strings of garlic hanging from the ceiling and round cheeses in that store. It smelled good and spicy. Josie bought six cupcakes and six bismarks.

We went down to the inlet and sat on the grass. Because we didn't have much time before we had to get back to school, we had to eat in a hurry. The first cupcake and the first bismark went down fast. The second ones went down a little slower. By the third cupcake and third bismark for each of us, we could just barely lift them to our mouths, but we ate them anyway. We slowly dragged ourselves back to school. I had a heavy head and an even heavier stomach. All afternoon, I fought back the nausea. Finally, the long afternoon came to an end, and I could go home. I didn't feel very well as I dragged myself up the stairs to the kitchen. Mother was sitting at the table all smiles as she lifted up a white cloth to show me what she had spent the afternoon making. There were rows of dark chocolate cupcakes topped with thick chocolate icing. I covered my mouth with one hand and ran to the bathroom. Because of my gluttony earlier in the day, I missed out on enjoying my mother's cupcakes, which were the best.

It is never a good idea to lie to your mother, because it will always come back to bite you in the end. One Friday I told my mother that I didn't want to go to school because it was the start of my menstrual cycle. I lied. This was still when I was going to the Catholic school, and I hated it so much I used every excuse I could to get out of going. Mother knew I always felt particularly bad the first day, so she allowed me to stay home. It was obvious that I felt fine the whole weekend. When Monday came, my period did actually start, and I really did feel terrible. I tried to tell Mother that I was still feeling badly. She said I had acted fine the whole weekend, so surely, I was well enough to go to school. I cried and carried on until my mother lost her temper. She had had enough, and she started toward me with the frying pan in her hand. I was afraid she was going to hit me with it. I flew down the stairs, and as bad as I felt, I rushed on my way to school. I knew I had pushed my mother too far, so I stopped at church on the way and did a little praying.

I had a few really close friends at school. Helen W. was one, and another was Ruby B. We decided to try our hands at writing stories. We thought our work was wonderful. We would each take turns writing chapters. The story was about three girls and their three boyfriends. The characters were older than we were, and most importantly, they all had money. At fourteen, we were still pretty naïve about sexual matters. What little we did know came from books, and it wasn't much. The love-story magazines focused mainly on the more platonic aspects of male-female romance. In our story, all three girls marry their boyfriends. On their wedding nights, they go to their bedrooms, kiss their new husbands good-night, and go to sleep.

It was during this period, when I thought I was well on my way to becoming a famous author, that I just missed getting mixed up in a fiasco at school. A filthy poem was making the rounds at school, and all the kids were making copies. I didn't understand what most of it actually meant, and I don't think most of the other kids did either. I made a copy only because all the other kids were, and we liked to giggle over the poem even without understanding it. I had a manila folder for keeping my story manuscripts. I had one in there that I had written and one written by Marge. For lack of a better place to keep it, I put my copy of the disgusting poem in the same folder.

That Friday night I came home from school, dropped my books on a table in the living room, and went into another room. Helen was staying with us for the weekend, and she was looking for a sheet of paper to write a letter to send to her husband.[70] She asked if I had any paper, and without thinking about the poem, I told her to take a sheet out of my folder in the living room. What a shock she got when she saw that poem. My mother was standing beside her, and when Helen gasped, Mother asked her what was wrong. Helen had no choice but to hand her my copy of that terrible poem. Mother didn't say a word after she read it. She just walked into the kitchen and burned it. I was in another part of the house while this was happening, so I didn't know about this until later. In the meantime, Helen had finished her letter, and read my story. She wrote her own ending to my story and returned it to my folder.

---

70 This might be when Helen and Jack were still living in Factoryville, in which case Jessie would actually have been younger than fourteen. Another possibility is that Jack, like his father-in-law, also had to be away for days at a time for his job with the railroad.

When Monday morning came, and I was about to leave for school, Mother told me she had read the poem and about how disappointed she was that I had such a disgusting thing in my possession. I cried as usual, and she continued to look at me as though I had committed a crime. It finally came time that I had to leave for school. I hated having Mother disappointed in me, which was a punishment enough in itself.

And the events of the weekend turned out to be fortunate for me in their own way. At noontime that day, when we were having lunch, the teachers searched all of our desks, so I was thankful that my mother had disposed of my copy. Even though they didn't find the poem in the folder or anywhere else in my desk, for some reason they took the folder with my stories anyway. I asked the teacher where my folder was. She told me that the principal had taken it, and I could go ask her if I had the nerve to do it. I had the nerve all right, but it didn't do me much good. The principal refused to return it. From the sound of the teacher's voice, I knew they were all disgusted with me, but I couldn't figure out why. I found out later that her own kid, who also went to our school, had the poem hidden in his history book, and it made her angry that she couldn't find anything to blame on me so that I would look just as dirty as her son was. Helen W. was lucky too as she had torn up her copy. Ruby wasn't so fortunate. They found her copy, so the principal sent for her parents, and Ruby ended up being grounded for a month.

I often wonder what my life would have been like had my family continued to live in Ithaca. Being the kind of rich boys' college town that it was, a girl couldn't walk down the street without a car stopping and the boys poking their heads out to ask her if she wanted to go for a ride. Helen W. and I did take a few rides like this, and when I think about it now, we were lucky that we didn't get into trouble. I would ask my mother if I could go to the library with Helen, and when I did, I would find my brother Bill standing on the corner watching us. Helen and I would go into the library, and when we came out, we would casually walk past Bill and saunter on down the street. If a car came along and asked us if we would like to go for a ride, we would tell them to go around the corner. We'd look back to see if Bill was watching, and when his back was turned, we'd scoot around the corner and meet the guys with the car.

Helen and I did meet a couple of very nice boys. They were good kids, and Helen and I started seeing them whenever we could get a chance. I sometimes stayed over at Helen's house. Her cousin would come to take us to the movies. He was a very generous guy, and we took advantage of him shamelessly. He would take us to the movies, and after the picture started, Helen and I would sneak out the side door of the theater. We had arranged to meet our two guys. We would go for a ride and be back in time to come out of the movie with Helen's cousin. If Bill saw us go into the movie and then come out the front door later, he would never know we hadn't really been watching the movie at all. So, yes, it really was a good thing we moved away from that town when we did, or I probably would have eventually gotten myself into real trouble.

There had once been a time when I was interested in boys only as someone to play Tarzan with, but by the age of fourteen or fifteen, it started to go well beyond that. This

113

is not to say I was thinking of anything overtly sexual in nature, but I was thinking in a romantic way and sought close connections with male friends. I met an Irish boy named Mike. He had dark curly hair and dark blue eyes. He was sixteen at the time and worked in a barber shop. The boyish bob cut was in style then, and I needed a trim for mine quite often, so it was an extra benefit that I could get it done for free by going to the barber shop where Mike worked. I don't think we ever went on what we thought of as a real date. Mother would have had a fit if we did. Mike would come to our house often and play cards and board games with the other kids. But there was absolutely no mushy stuff. I don't think he even tried to kiss me, and no other boys did either until the night of the surprise party for my fifteenth birthday.

Of course, the party wasn't a true surprise for me. I had hints all day, and had to pretend I didn't know what was going on. For one thing, Marge had a boyfriend in college, and I overheard her talking to him on the phone, so I knew he was coming. When he showed up, he had a very handsome friend with him. I was thrilled. They brought me a box of candy. Poor Mike took a back seat in my mind that night. About ten o'clock the party broke up. We had been playing kissing games, and I have to admit I rather enjoyed getting kissed by the college boys, so I guess I was growing up and getting interested in the mushy stuff after all. Bill was going to walk his girlfriend home, and Marge and the two college guys decided to go along with them. I had already gotten into bed when Marge came rushing into our bedroom. She said, "The boys wanted me to come and get you to come along with us. Well, too bad, you are already in bed. See you later." Then she rushed off before I had a chance to say I could get dressed again in no time. That was one time I really wanted to strangle Marge. She easily could have waited for me. For weeks after that, whenever Marge's boyfriend came to see her, I hoped he would bring his friend along, but he never did.

Mike had given me a silver dollar on a chain, and I wore it as a necklace. I told him that if I ever got mad at him, I would give him back his dollar. One of the ritzy girls at school liked Mike, and one day she said she needed to talk to me when we had study hall. She was a very homely girl, but with beautiful hair, lovely clothes, and plenty of spending money. During study hall, she came over to my desk and dropped her bombshell. She said that Mike was taking her to the movies Saturday night. I was so stunned that I couldn't say anything. I felt hurt, but most of all, angry. Instead of asking Mike if she was telling the truth, I pretended that nothing was wrong. I went to the barber shop to have my usual trim. After the haircut was complete, I took the silver dollar and chain off my neck and handed them to Mike. I said, "Here is your pay for the haircut," and walked out of the shop, leaving Mike with a surprised look on his face. Later I found out that the girl had been lying, but I was too ashamed to go back and tell Mike I was sorry.

I can't remember too much more from our days in Ithaca, but one incident that happened to poor Dick comes to mind. One day he was standing on a corner not far from our house. School had just been let out, and Dick stopped to watch a kid practicing his marksmanship. The boy was using a rubber band to shoot a folded piece of tin foil at a tin can. He turned to say something to Dick and accidentally let go of the rubber band. The foil just happened to take a trajectory such that it struck Dick right in the eye. There was a lot of worry in our house, and Dick had to lie in a dark room for six weeks while his eye healed. He was very lucky not to lose sight in that eye, but it did leave a black mark on his iris for the rest of his life. It was a warning to us kids not to play shooting games around other kids.

One time my father received free passes for the Wild West show that was coming to Ithaca.[71] He took five of us kids. We were so excited. We sat in the grandstand about halfway up. During one of the most exciting moments in the show, we heard Dick give out a strangled cry. We looked down and saw that Dick was hanging by his neck. He had slipped out of his seat and through an opening behind the seat in front of us. My father got him out and held him on his lap for the rest of the show. Dick wasn't really hurt, but if he had fallen all the way to the ground beneath the stands, he might have been.

One more event I recall is when Marge pressured me into going to the opera with her. She had made a plan for three guys to go along with her and two of her girlfriends. One of the girlfriends had backed out at the last minute, and Marge couldn't find anyone else to take her friend's place. She asked Mother if I could go. Mother agreed, but I didn't want to go. It seemed too much like a formal date setting for a girl my age, and the whole idea made me nervous. I knew I wouldn't know how to act. But Marge and our mother kept coaxing me until I finally gave in and agreed to go. Well, the boys showed up, and the six of us started off down the street. I knew that one of the finer points of etiquette was that the man is supposed to walk on the outer part of the sidewalk closer to the curb, so when we came to the first corner, I stepped behind the guy to go toward the inside. My date then informed me that the man was supposed to pass behind the woman when it came time to change. This was enough to embarrass me, and the evening just went downhill from there. I'll admit that the opera itself wasn't as bad as I thought it might be. It was called *Lilac Time*.[72]

After the show, we all started to walk back down the street toward home, but we hadn't gone very far when I realized that Marge, her girlfriend, and the two other guys had disappeared. This left me walking the long way home with a strange boy in a

---

71 This could not have been Buffalo Bill's Wild West Show, which went bankrupt in 1913. Even most of its imitators closed down around the time of World War I. It could have been the "Miller Brothers 101 Ranch Wild West Show", which was the last of the wild west shows to go out of business.

72 I know almost nothing about opera, but for what it is worth, *Lilac Time* is described as an English-language adaptation of a Viennese operetta with a story line based on a fictionalized version of Schubert's romantic life, and much of the music comes from Schubert. I am uncertain where opera performances were held in Ithaca in those days. Probably it was one of the theater venues near downtown, so Jessie's uncomfortable walk home with a fellow she didn't know was likely fifteen minutes or more.

setting more formal than I was accustomed to. Strangely, the one thing I remember about the guy was that he had beautiful teeth. When we got to the front of our building, I wondered what was supposed to happen next. It was just as well that Bill happened along at just that point and gave the guy a very dirty look. That hastened our parting. If this was my first official date, it was a big flop. I suspect the guy thought much the same thing about the experience. When Marge finally got home, I told her in no uncertain terms what I thought of her for leaving me alone to walk home with the poor guy. I told her I would never let her talk me into doing anything with her again. She tried to make up with me, but it was a long time before I forgave her for that one.

Chapter 4—Binghamton

We moved to Binghamton the spring after I was fifteen.[73] I hated to leave my friends, but my father got transferred. The house we moved into was a lot like the one in Scranton because it slanted toward the back. There were four rooms on the first floor, including a living room and a little sitting room, plus a kitchen. There was a wrap-around porch and a good-sized back porch. Upstairs there were three bedrooms—one for my parents, one for the three boys, and a large front room that had to hold two full sized beds for us girls. Off of this room was a small balcony that of course made me think of Romeo. There was a small entrance hall. We had a large cellar and outside there was a trap door that let to what we called the root cellar.

After we got settled in as much as we could that first day, Claire and I asked permission to take a walk around the neighborhood. Mother said it would be alright, but we had to be back at nine o'clock. Claire and I walked down the street, and we found a bunch of kids about our ages. We started talking about school and exchanging names, and the time just seemed to fly. We realized it might be getting late. One of the kids had a watch and we were horrified to find it was ten minutes after nine. Claire and I flew down the street to our new home. When we got there, the front door was locked. Claire said she would try the back door, and I went to try the side door. That was locked too. I could see my father sitting at the dining room table, typing one of his stories. I knocked on the door. I could see him getting slowly to his feet. I was shaking in my shoes. I knew I was in for something because of the look on his face. *He was mad!!!*

He yanked the door open and, grabbing me by the hair, he dragged me into the room. He backed me up against the wall and started to bang my head against it. I wet my pants. By this time, I was really crying, and I could hear Claire knocking on the

---

73 The spring after Jessie turned fifteen means that the family moved from Ithaca to Binghamton in early 1927. In the publicly available records around that time, there is some inconsistency as to their house number on Conklin Avenue, but what she describes from the start is the house at 387 Conklin Avenue, on the corner of a minor side street leading about 100 yards downhill almost to the south bank of the Susquehanna. We can be sure that for the whole time they were together in Binghamton the family was living in that same three-story house built on a lot sloping quite steeply down to the back.

In the early 20th Century, it still seems to have been the norm to expect railroad men to live close to the railyard if possible, and I am not sure whether William had a car when they first moved to Binghamton. Perhaps these factors were what led them to choose to find a house in the southeastern corner of the city. It is true that the DL&W railyard just outside the city limits in the Town of Conklin was almost a mile or a twenty-minute walk from the house even to reach the closest part, but at the time, this was a relatively sparsely populated part of town, and there may not have been a suitable house available any closer. In relative terms, it was convenient for William.

Well before 1927, even before the family moved to Ithaca, Helen had married Jack Hawley and Mary had married Ralph Clark, and they were already starting their own families. Therefore, as of the spring of 1927 when they moved into 387 Conklin Avenue, the Davenport household had long been down to nine members. Father (William) was forty-three, Mother (Elizabeth) was forty-four; Bill nineteen, Marge seventeen, Jessie fifteen, Claire thirteen, Carmel eleven, Jim nine, and Dick seven.

back door. He finally let me go and told me to get upstairs. When he let Claire in the back door, all he did to her was give her a boot in the pants as she ran by him.

We ran up the stairs, and when we got into our bedroom, Claire and I collapsed on the bed from laughing so hard. I whispered to her that I had wet my pants and hoped that Father got his feet wet and would catch cold. Just about that time Mother called from her room to say we should get down on our knees and say our prayers. We did, but I don't remember doing much praying, as Claire and I giggled the whole time we were on our knees.

Mother made homebrew for my father and root beer for the kids. We had to wait several weeks until it was aged enough to drink. She bottled it in quart bottles. It was always wonderful on hot days to have a glass of ice-cold root beer to drink. But after a few days the root beer would be all gone, or so we thought. We sat around moaning over the fact that we had drunk it all. We would be wishing for one more bottle when Jim and Dick would come around the corner of the house, and each of them would have a big bottle of root beer in his hand. They would go running around taking big swigs from their bottles. We girls would put up a holler, but all we got was a small glassful. Then the boys would go to their hiding places and finish their bottles. For the longest time, we didn't know where they hid the stuff. We finally found out they were hiding bottles in the root cellar. They would dig out the dirt walls and hide them in there. They would hide at least six or seven bottles. They would snitch one bottle at a time so we wouldn't miss them, and that was how they built up a stash. For a few days they would enjoy root beer with us, and when we ran out, they would have their secret supply. They weren't so smart though. If they hadn't brought out the bottles to torment us, we wouldn't have looked for their hiding place, which we eventually found. But they got such a big kick out of tormenting us that they couldn't resist doing so, and thereby foiled their own scheme.

I was sitting in the back yard one day when Jim and one of his friends came along. Jim told me to hold out my hand as his friend had a surprise for me. Without thinking, I held out my hand, and the boy dropped a handful of fishing worms into it. I jumped up screaming. I wanted to get ahold of Jim and really let him have it with the back of my hand, but he was too quick for me and got away. By the time I saw him again I had calmed down. Jim would come running to me, put out his finger, and yell, "Pull my finger, pull my finger." From the look on his face, you would think he was in real pain, so I would pull his finger, and he would break wind. He pulled that trick on me for years, and I'd fall for it almost every time.[74]

I think Jim was the mastermind behind all the mischief that went on. Dick followed him in most schemes. He was Jim's shadow. They seldom fought each other. I remember one day Jim did something that got Dick mad, and he went charging after

---

74 Doesn't it seem that in some families, the way a younger brother bonds with an older sister is by playing pranks on her, and she might enjoy the process as much as he does? This likely explains why Jessie kept falling for the same silly trick.

his brother. He was yelling that he was going to kill Jim. Claire and I hung onto Dick and all he kept saying was, "I can't fight unless I'm mad, and I am mad now, so let me go." That was the only time I saw Dick get that angry with Jim. A few years later Jim was in the hospital with a body cast from his chest to his knees. Dick was so worried he would go to the Catholic church on his way to the hospital and pray for his brother to get well.[75] They were best friends all their lives.

When I was sixteen, my mother was supposed to go to Shamokin for her nephew's graduation. I don't remember why she couldn't go, but she sent me in her place. My father drove me in his car, and I wasn't looking forward to making conversation with him. I hadn't wanted to go because I would have to stay with Cousin Agnes. As I discussed in the Ithaca chapter, I detested her. My father delivered me there on a Tuesday night, and on Wednesday, Agnes and her friend, Catherine, took me to a park that had all the popular rides—roller coaster, Ferris wheel, etc. I had never been on a roller coaster, and Agnes wanted me to try it. I was afraid to go on the darn thing, but I didn't want Agnes and her friend to know how I felt. They waited until a car came along with one man in it and told me to get in. "Tell him you have never been on one before and to please hang on me," they said. Well, I got into the car and told him what they had said. The poor man put his arm around the back of the seat and took hold of my shoulder. By the time the ride ended, I was buried in the front of his shirt. I had grasped his tie in my hands, and he was lucky I didn't choke him. I never got on a roller coaster again after that.

After the fiasco with the roller coaster, they took me to a dance. The dance hall had benches around the wall, and we sat down. The girls told me that if I was asked to dance, then I should do so without worrying about them, since they would soon get dance partners too. It wasn't long before a young man came up and asked me to dance. I didn't know how to dance and had never been on a dance floor. But I didn't want Agnes and her friend to know that, so I kept my mouth shut. I thought it looked easy, but did I ever fool myself about that! I slipped and slid all around the dance floor, and every time I stepped on my partner's toes, *he* apologized. My face was burning. I must have been beet red, and I know I was slightly damp with perspiration on my face and back. When the dance was finally over, the man took me back to my seat and thanked me for the dance. I sat on the bench refusing any more offers to dance. I waited for Agnes to take me home. If she wanted to get even for the things I did to her when she

---

75 It must have seemed unfortunate to much of the family that they lived quite far from the nearest Catholic church. This would have been decades before the St. Andrews church was built in that neighborhood. The only Roman Catholic church on the South Side (and again now that St. Andrews has closed as a Catholic church) was St. John the Evangelist on Vestal Avenue. It was well over a mile and a half, part of it uphill, from their house. There was likely a streetcar or bus route that made it a little easier to get there when they didn't have the use of a car. St. Mary of the Assumption on Court Street near downtown might have been slightly closer. Still, if we assume that Jim was a patient at Binghamton General Hospital, then St. John the Evangelist would have been on the way there, so that is likely where Dick prayed for his brother's recovery.

visited Ithaca, she couldn't have found a better way. Of course, she hadn't actually planned in advance for all this to happen, but when I told her I had never been on a roller coaster before, I'll bet she thought it was too good to pass up. Thank goodness she was too busy to notice that I had made a fool of myself on the dance floor.

I only saw Agnes once more after that. It was when my parents celebrated their anniversary.[76] All the relatives from Shamokin were there, and Agnes brought her girlfriend, Catherine. My boyfriend was there, and we all stayed in the kitchen. We had to run to the cellar and fill up the beer pitcher, and we dared each other to drink some whiskey and wine.[77] I had more than Agnes because I filled the pitcher more often and I always managed to get in a few extra swallows of beer. About two in the morning that night Bill was walking me up and down the street, stopping now and then to hold my head as I was violently ill. I finally went to sleep some place, I don't remember where, and at the time I don't think I cared very much.

My mother was very sickly during these times and would go to the hospital in Scranton quite often where she would stay for a week or more. I really don't know what her illness was. Anyway, I had to stay home and take care of the kids. You would think that being brought up in a house full of kids, I'd know something about cooking. Sadly for the kids, I didn't know much. I could boil and mash potatoes, and I could make sandwiches. Goodness, I'd been making them all my life. I could cook hot dogs and scrambled eggs. I remember one time I tried my hand at making pancakes. Remember, this was before mixes, so I had to start from scratch. Those pancakes were awful.

My father had a fit when he found out that the grocery bill was over thirty dollars [for the month?]. He said if I could keep the bill under thirty dollars, we would give me the difference. I really tried and the bill was only twenty-eight dollars. I never did get the two dollars difference. In fact, he never even mentioned it.

---

76 I have not yet found an exact date for the marriage of William and Elizabeth, but it must have been about 1903, meaning that this special celebration was probably for their silver anniversary.

77 Considering that this was during prohibition, where did all this beer, wine, and liquor come from? The wine might be easiest to explain. Grape juice concentrate sold in large quantities during prohibition, with very detailed warning labels explaining what steps must be avoided at all costs lest the grape juice should turn to wine. Interestingly, the Volstead Act was enforced more strictly for homebrewing of beer than it was over home winemaking or cidermaking, but I was informed (by my grandfather) that homebrew supplies were readily available in Binghamton at that time. Indeed, the city directories have adds for businesses specializing in malt products and hops. Earlier in the chapter, Jessie explains that Elizabeth made homebrew for William on a regular basis at the same time she made root beer for the children. It might seem that the hard liquor would have been hardest to obtain, but maybe it was not really so difficult to find illicit sources dealing in imported bootleg whiskey or moonshine. In fact, there was rumored to have been a log cabin near the foot of Felters Road that had a still and sold illicit liquor. Historians also claim that portable stills were quite common for home use, though that seems unlikely here. If the Davenports had one of those, Jessie would probably have mentioned it somewhere. In any case, there was clearly a lot of booze available at the anniversary celebration.

The poor kids had to pay the price for me not having money on hand. I remember Claire had holes in her shoes and her stockings weren't much better. The soles of her shoes were coming apart from the uppers, and when Claire ran to school, they made flapping noises. As she was always late, she did a lot of flapping around. One Saturday the grocery man came to the house to take our order for the weekend. Mother would always order a five- or six-pound roast, so thinking that dried or roast, quantities of beef are equivalent, I asked the grocer for six pounds of dried beef. The grocer was a little shocked and finally talked me down to one and a half pounds, which was still a lot of dried beef.

One night I invited my boyfriend to supper. I was fixing Swiss steak. (I knew how to cook that.) And for dessert I had bought some little chocolate cakes with marshmallow and chocolate icing on top. I fed the kids first and gave each of them a cake. I told them that after my friend left, they could share any cakes that were left.

I set the table and placed the dish of cakes in the middle of it. The kids were fooling around and started to march around the table singing a song. A girlfriend of Claire's named Anna was there too. They kept this up for a while until I hollered at them to stop, and they went into the den.

I noticed then that some of the cakes were missing. I yelled at the kids to tell me who had taken the cakes, but they only laughed at me. I was furious and went out on the back porch to find a stick. I marched into the den where they were all standing around looking innocent. I went up to Carmel, who towered over me by that time, and demanded to know who had taken the cakes. She only laughed at me. I said, "If you don't tell me what you did with them, I'll whack you with this stick." They laughed harder. I reached out with the stick and hit Carmel on the arm. It was only a light tap and couldn't have hurt her. The next thing I knew, I was flat on my back on the floor with Carmel straddling me. I was so humiliated to have an outsider see me like this. I told Anna to go home, but the kids said she didn't have to. Defeated, I crept out of the room. I found a dark place in the living room and shed tears of humiliation. They weren't bad kids. They were only teasing me because I was so bossy. I didn't have too much trouble with them in general, but I had learned a lesson. Never go after a younger sister who has grown bigger than you.

I sometimes acted recklessly. One time only Bill and I were home. It was a cold day, so Bill built a fire in the furnace. He had to go out for a while, so he told me to go down into the cellar and put some coal on the fire in about half an hour. Well, I got to reading and forgot about the furnace until I felt the cold. I ran down the stairs, but it was too late. The furnace was out. I was really scared. I knew Bill would be furious when he came back. How could I get out of this mess? I had been reading a mystery story, and in the story a person who thought he was going to be killed wrote a note saying who the killer was. I decided to write a note too, because I was sure Bill would kill me when he came back. I wrote a note saying, "If you find me dead, Bill did it." Bill came home and he was furious. He had to build another fire. And, of course, he never laid a hand on me. He just said I was a stupid ninny, and one of these days I would be in real trouble for not doing what I was told. I really loved my brother, and I often look back and think what if I had fallen down the stairs and broken my neck. Poor Bill would have been blamed. I tore up the note and was very thankful Bill hadn't seen it. He would have really thought I was stupid.

I always loved the winter and the snow. One winter I had a terrific crush on a young man who was older than I. I never thought he would give me a tumble. He had a younger brother who was my age. He asked me if I would like to go for a ride in a horse-drawn sleigh. Of course, I jumped at the chance. I didn't want to go with him alone, so I cooked up a plan with Claire to go along with us. Just as we were about to leave, who should show up but the older brother. We all piled into the sleigh. Claire had to sit on the driver's lap as the sleigh was only a two-seater. The older brother sat on the arm of the sleigh on my side. He had to put his arm around my shoulders, so I really had a good time. How his brother liked it, I don't know, and at the time I didn't care.

One Friday night after school, one of the girls who lived on a farm asked a bunch of kids to come and stay overnight at her house. She was having a sleigh-riding party. The big farm wagon that her father hitched his team to had the wheels taken off and runners put on. The two big farm horses were to pull the wagon. For a wonder my mother said I could go even though there would be boys there too. Krissy had several brothers, and they had invited some of their male friends. They helped to load the back of the wagon with piles of sweet-smelling hay for us kids to sit on. We could snuggle down in the hay out of the cold wind. After supper, we all piled into the wagon and started down the frosty road. Krissy's parents sat on the high front seat. It was a most wonderful experience. The air was cold, and a few snowflakes drifted down. They fell softly and quietly. They just seemed to flutter along, touching my cheek for a cold instant. We were all snuggled up in the hay with quilts. We were giggling and laughing just for the joy of being alive. Some of the kids started to tell jokes, and then they started to sing, but I just leaned back in the hay and listened to the bells making twinkly music. The bells were strung along the sides of the wagon, and some were on the horses' harnesses. If I had my way, we could have gone on all night. About ten o'clock we got back to the farmhouse and had hot cocoa and fresh doughnuts. We didn't get much sleep that night, and I'll always remember that night as a very special experience of my youth.

One night I went to the movies with a boy I really liked. After the movie, we waited for the streetcar. There was a candy and ice cream store nearby, and he left me for a moment after stating that he had to get something. I watched him as he went into the candy store, and I knew he was going to buy a box of candy. Sure enough, when he came out again, he had a package under his arm. All the way home, I waited for him to give me the candy. It wasn't until we were standing at my front door that the package slipped, and I grabbed it with both hands. I said good night and thanked him for the movie and the candy. I thought he looked like he wanted to say something, but my father was home, and we knew I couldn't be late coming inside. I went into the house and upstairs to my bedroom where I opened the package. Inside was a beautiful pink box with a silver ribbon that said in raised blue letters, "HAPPY MOTHERS' DAY". I realized that the next day was Mothers' Day, so obviously the candy was intended for his mother. The next time I saw him, I tried to give the candy back, but he said he had already bought another box for his mother.

The fall that I was sixteen, Mary wanted me to come and stay with her as she wanted to do some shopping for Christmas, and she needed me to babysit. I had been writing to Dick C., and when he found out that I was going to be at Mary's, he asked me if I would go to the movies in Scranton with him. My mother said it would be alright, so I went off to stay at Mary's. Saturday night, Dick picked me up in his car, and we drove to Scranton and to the movie. I was thrilled to be out with Dick at night. It was a rare occasion. After the movie we went and had ice cream sundaes, and I began to feel the call of nature. I thought I could wait until I got back to Mary's house. Dick had other plans. He wanted me to meet his mother at her apartment. I was too shy or too stupid to ask her if I could use her bathroom, so I sat in agony. I don't think she thought I was very bright as I didn't have much to say. We finally got on the road again. If you have ever driven on a country road, you know they are full of potholes, and we must have hit every one of them. I was sure the next bump would embarrass me, and I would flood the car.

Luckily for me, we reached home before that could happen. I ran into the house, telling Dick to wait in the living room. I raced up the stairs to the bedroom. We had no indoor plumbing, so I grabbed the pail from the boys' room and let loose. The noise that made as it hit the empty pail was loud, and the worst of it was that there was a hole in the living room ceiling. A pipe from the stove in the living room was supposed to go through that hole. It hadn't been hooked up as yet, so the noise I made was clearly heard down in the room where Dick was waiting. I came down the stairs as though nothing had happened, although I knew Dick must have heard that awful noise. The next day my brother-in-law, Ralph, who slept in the downstairs bedroom, said that I had woken him up, and he thought a cow was in the house.

The swimming hole in Binghamton was the river. I don't believe anyone swims there today because of the pollution. To get to the river, we would cross a big field in back of our house. Then we came to the railroad tracks. We had to cross the tracks, go down a steep bank, and there was the river. We called the place Slippery Elm.[78] There were trees, and we'd take a picnic lunch and spend the whole day there. As you walked

---

78 No matter what town she was living in, clearly swimming was among Jessie's favorite activities. Anyone who grew up near that neighborhood certainly knows exactly where Sandy Beach is. It is a little ambiguous though where she means by "Slippery Elm". It seems like she is describing going straight back from her house to the river, but that would not involve crossing tracks and seems too far from Sandy Beach to fit. Most likely then she means walking diagonally across the field and crossing the part of the tracks just before the trestle.

up the river, there were two other places that were swimming holes. One place had a lot of sand and later became known as Sandy Beach. When it became a public swimming hole, it was a nice tidy place, but back when I first saw it, there was tall grass growing almost to the water's edge.

One day, one of the boys and I decided to swim up the river to Sandy Beach. I wasn't an expert swimmer, and I was taking a chance, but I was young and willing to try. We made it to Sandy Beach and dragged ourselves from the water. All I wanted to do was rest. Naturally, youth being what it is, we started to fool around; wrestling and pushing each other. We rested for a while and then swam back down the river to Slippery Elm. It was a lot easier going with the stream than against it.

That evening just about dusk, a car pulled up in front of the house. There were two men in the car and one of them asked Jim if my father was at home. Thank God he wasn't, so my mother went out to the car. Apparently, these men knew my father because they also worked for the DL&W Railroad. They were up in the observation tower that afternoon and were using binoculars when they spotted me and the boy I was swimming with up at Sandy Beach.[79] They saw us fooling around in the grass and thought my father ought to know. Mother called me up to the car as soon as the men started to tell her about me. I felt sick. I tried to tell them that we were just resting from our long swim up the river, and we weren't doing anything wrong. I don't know if they believed me or not. I just think they had dirty minds. I don't know if they ever told my father. If they did, he never said anything to me. All l know was that I stayed out of the tall grass from then on, and I kept as far away from the sight of the railroad observation tower as possible.

I learned to smoke the summer I was sixteen. I was out in a canoe on the river, and the boy I was with offered me a cigarette.[80] I didn't know how to smoke, but he showed me. After a few times of choking when I inhaled, I got the hang of it. I thought I was really something as I leaned against the back rest in the canoe and puffed away. When we reached the shore and I got out of the canoe, I couldn't walk straight. I had smoked three cigarettes, and I felt drunk. Every time after that, when I went out on a date, I smoked. My poor mother complained about my clothes smelling of cigarettes, but she thought it was because the boys smoked. I smoked for forty years, and then gave it up.

I remember one time when Mary was very ill. I had to go down and stay with her to help with the kids and the housework. Mary had a history of rheumatism from the

---

79 It is unclear where exactly the observation tower was at that time. If we assume there were fewer trees in those days to obstruct the view, Sandy Beach could have been observed from a tower at any point between the northern end of the railyard to somewhere near the trestle. It might also have been on the far side of the river, leaving an unobstructed view.

80 Social historians inform us that during the 1920s for the first time it was becoming socially acceptable for women to smoke. Also at that time, cigarettes were becoming more popular than other forms of tobacco use.

time she was a small child. Poor Mary—her bones were so stiff and painful that she couldn't reach up and scratch her own ear. We had to do everything for her, even to taking care of her personal needs. She never complained, but one day she got very angry with me. It happened on a Saturday, which meant clean-the-house day and giving the kids a bath. I scrubbed the kitchen floor while the two oldest girls did the dishes and helped me with the younger kids. I bathed Diana first. After her bath, I dressed her in clean clothes. I had to do something for Mary, so it was a while before I got back to bathing Jessie.[81] When Diana saw me putting clean clothes on Jessie, her older sister, she wanted me to dress her in another clean dress. I said "No, one clean dress a day is enough."

A little later, Diana went into the pantry for a drink of water. The pail of water was on a shelf. She climbed onto a chair, got a dipper of water, and spilled it down the front of her dress. As I changed her clothes, I said, "I'll bet you did that on purpose so I would change your dress." I was only joking, but apparently Mary didn't think so, because she hollered out from the bedroom that Diana wasn't old enough to think of a scheme like that. I could tell by the sound of her voice that she was pretty upset, but I had to start supper, so I didn't try to find out what was bothering her.

Ralph came home with a beautifully cooked ham for Sunday dinner. It made my mouth water. I had made stew for supper. Ralph fixed Mary's tray that included a slice of the ham. Earlier when I was setting the table, I had asked Bud to fill up the sugar bowl and the saltshaker. Somehow, he must have gotten them mixed up, because when Mary tasted the tea, she said it tasted salty. Ralph blew his top at Bud, and I couldn't get a word in edgewise. Mary would not eat her supper, and I had to face an evening with a sister who was angry with me and a brother-in-law who was angry with everyone.

We were expecting Mother and Bill to come down that night, and I couldn't wait for them to get there. I was sitting in the window looking out and I wanted to relieve the tension, so I turned to Ralph and said, "I feel like the lighted lamp in the window." All he did was lower his paper and glower at me. At ten o'clock I gave up and went upstairs to bed. I had no sooner crawled in when I heard a car pull into the driveway. I was downstairs in a flash. I was never so glad to see anyone as I was to see my mother that night. I hugged her and Bill.

Later, after things had quieted down, Mary called me into her room. She said she was sorry for the way she had behaved. She had watched me and the two oldest girls running down the path to the privy. We were laughing at the way we raced against each other. Mary wanted to be with us so badly, and she couldn't, so she got angry, and when I told Diana that she had spilled the water on purpose, that made her even more angry.

---

81 This is a little confusing. Here Jessie may be describing an occasion that actually happened long after she was married, or perhaps she is confused about which little girls she was bathing. Diana and Jessie Clark, the youngest children of Mary and Ralph were not born until 1937 and 1934, respectively. And yet Elizabeth died in 1929, so my grandmother is remembering incorrectly in some way, probably conflating in her memory two incidents that happened several years apart.

She didn't mean to act the way she did, but she was so tired of feeling helpless. I understood her feelings, and whenever she needed me, I would go and help her.

One other time when I was staying with Mary, she was sitting on the porch. The kids and I were playing on the lawn. Diana had taken off her shoes. She was about four years old at the time, so you can imagine how small her shoes were. I got the bright idea of putting Diana's shoes on my toes and went dancing around the lawn. Mary was laughing at my antics. It finally dawned on me that she was pointing toward the road. I turned around and there in his wagon sat a farmer, his wife, and a couple of kids. Apparently, while I had been busy doing my ballet with those small shoes on my toes, the farmer and his wife had been enjoying the floor show.

One summer when Mary was getting over one of her bad spells, she was sitting in a chair outside of the kitchen door while Diana played in the grass nearby. Diana tired of playing by herself and came and stood by her mother's chair. She wanted Mary to tell her a story. As Mary started a fairy tale, Diana looked toward the corner of the house. Her eyes got big and round. She stared past Mary. When Mary saw the look on Diana's face, she quickly turned to see what Diana was staring at. It was a *big bull*. His head was down, and foam dripped from his mouth. Pain was forgotten as Mary grabbed up Diana and fled into the house. Luckily, the other kids were in school. Finally, some farmers came and got the bull who had broken a fence and got out of the field. Mary told me about the bull, and for years I had nightmares always about bulls or cows chasing me, and I'd be trying to close doors that would never quite close.

I remember when we lived in Binghamton we made a few friends—a girl named Jessie, who was my age, and a girl named Ann, who was between Claire and Carmel in age. We got together with our friends and formed a club. Our idea was to be like the girls in the *Little Women* books, so we decided to put on a show like they did. We were going to make costumes and everything. Jessie's mother gave us a bolt of taffeta that was a beautiful shade of pink. We were so excited, planning what kind of costumes we would make. Much to our sorrow, the taffeta was so old that it cracked every time you tried to make a seam. Every time we tried to push a needle through it, it made a big hole. We were so disappointed. We finally gave up on being little women and went back to being little hellions.

Looking back, I remember one time when my father really surprised me. Ann was having a Halloween party at her house, and of course all us kids were going. The evening of the party my father came downstairs dressed as a bum. He had blackened his face and his clothes were ragged and torn. He had a tin can fastened to his rope belt. We were very surprised when he announced that he was going to the party with us. We all went to Ann's house, and my father was the life of the party. He played the guitar and sang funny songs. That was a Halloween party we talked about for years.

Marge was always being held up to me as an example. I admit that she never lost a grade in school as I did. My father and mother expected great things from Marge. Naturally, I grew to resent hearing how wonderful Marge was. She shadowed my life.

I thought she knew everything—how to behave in company, and she wouldn't be embarrassed to eat out in a restaurant. Underneath my brashness I was really very insecure. If Marge had been younger or not as smart, I might have turned out a very different person. Well, I can't go back and change that.[82]

One time I had bought myself a leghorn hat.[83] It was a large, floppy hat, cream in color, with a polka dot band. I wore it to church. When winter came, I put it away until summer. A boy who lived in Endicott had given me a gold ring with a ruby cross in it. The ring was too big, so I wrapped string around the ring so I could wear it. Well, Marge came home one weekend, and when she left, she took my ring and my beautiful hat back to college with her. She said they wanted to use my hat in a play. I don't remember why she borrowed the ring. Weeks went by, and the play was over. I kept asking Marge to bring back my hat and ring. Finally, she told me that the girls in her sorority house had been using my hat as a football. She said she was sorry, but she couldn't do anything about it. As for the ring, she said she had lost it.

When we moved to Binghamton, I got a job in the five-and-ten-cent store. I needed a new coat. I had saved fifteen dollars for it. I knew just the coat I wanted. It was a red coat that was double-breasted, with a flared skirt. Marge had one that was double-breasted, but hers was brown with a velvet collar. I loved her coat, but the red one was really my color. When I told my mother about the red coat, she said fifteen dollars was too much to pay. She said for me to wait until Marge was home on the weekend, because Marge had such good taste.

Marge came home, and we were supposed to go shopping on my lunch hour. On Saturday she came into the store carrying a big box. My heart skipped a beat. I had told her how much I wanted the red coat and had asked her to talk mother into letting me have it. She opened the box and took out a single-breasted cream-and-brown shadow plaid coat with a rabbit skin collar. She had bought the coat before I had even seen it,

---

82 It is indeed clear that the family believed Marge to be more capable of academic achievement than Jessie, and it might be fair to say that Jessie had more reason than most people do to be resentful of a sibling. Marge graduated from Ithaca High School in 1927, and by 1928 was pursuing post-secondary education—specifically at Cortland Normal School (teachers' college). It was certainly a higher level of education than any of her siblings. Based on what Jessie writes a little later, it is clear that Marge came home only on weekends and lived at the sorority house during the week. This turns out to be a sorority called Arethusa, and their house was at 45 Church Street in Cortland. Jessie, on the other hand, had a much more limited education. She mentions elsewhere in the chapter being pressured by her father when they moved to Binghamton to get a job rather than continuing with school. If she was fifteen at the time and had been held back a year as she mentions a few times, this means she was being told to discontinue her formal education at around the eighth or ninth grade level. This is quite a disparity with the sister who was two years older. It is clear, from what she writes both here and the Ithaca chapter, that Jessie feels that Marge also had the edge on her in terms of poise, style, and self-confidence. That must have put even more of strain on the sisterly bond.

83 I had never heard the term leghorn hat before. I gather that it was generally interpreted to mean any elegant and stylish type of straw hat for either men or women. There was usually some sort of attractive fabric hatband.

and what is more, had paid fifteen dollars for the darn thing. I was so disappointed. I wore the coat for one week, and then Marge suggested that we exchange coats for the week. So, I wore the brown coat, which I loved almost as much as I would have the red one. The next weekend, I had to go to the store, so I wore [the borrowed] coat. It was raining a light misty rain and a few sprinkles got on the collar. Marge threw a fit and said she wouldn't take back her brown coat because she said I had gotten a stain on the skirt. I probably did, but I didn't let her know how happy I was to get her brown coat. I hated the one she had bought for me.

I never liked to be laughed at when I was a kid. I always wanted to play the piano, but there was no money for lessons. I had gotten a harmonica one summer, and I went around for days trying to play a tune. It never seemed to come out right, but I kept trying. I hit some very sour notes. I was home alone one day, except for Helen, who was visiting and was reading in the living room. I sauntered into the room still playing on my mouth organ. After I had played the same thing two or three times, making the same mistakes each time, Helen started to laugh and asked me what I was trying to do. When I told her I was playing "Bye Bye Blackbird" she laughed so hard she almost cried. I was so mad and hurt that I threw the harmonica against the wall. I never tried to play the thing for years.

As I've said before, I didn't have much love for my father. As I grew older, I tried to change the feeling, but it didn't work. I was thinking about the time, the only time, that I talked back to him. I was seventeen, and I worked in a grocery store. I only got ten dollars a week for a six-day week, and I had to be there at seven in the morning until six at night. My mother had traded with this store ever since we had moved to Binghamton, so we had a store bill. The first week I applied my weekly wage towards the store bill. The second week my mother said I could take the money and go shopping. It was rare that I had ten dollars in my hand. Claire came along with me on the shopping spree. We bought Mother some silk undervests. Claire and I got some new collie coats and slippers. I can't remember what we got Carmel, but I got hats and ear warmers for Jim and Dick. That seems like a lot, but in those days, a dollar really went a long way.

The third week I had to go to the dentist. One noon when I came home for lunch, my father was there. As usual, he didn't have much to say to me. For a while he only growled now and then. Then suddenly he demanded to know what I was doing with the money I earned. So, I told him how it had been used and finished with the statement that I had gone to the dentist because if I didn't pay for it, no one else would. That was like waving a red flag in front of a bull. He ranted and raved and shook his fist, holding a fork almost in my face. For once I didn't dissolve into tears. I went on calmly eating my lunch, although inside I was shaking like a leaf. After he got through yelling, he left the room. Claire, who had been standing by the stove, said to me, "I thought he was going to hit you and knock you through the wall." I laughed and shook my head. I said, "He wouldn't hit me, because he'd be afraid I couldn't go to work."

128

We hadn't lived in Binghamton long before I had a boyfriend named Tim. He worked for the milk company as a driver's assistant. After we got to know one another better, I would often find a bottle of cream or a bunch of flowers in the mailbox. This happened every day, and one of the bright moments of the day was looking in the mailbox. He worked in the morning and would have the rest of the day off. We could go swimming or hiking with the other kids. One day he left a bottle of perfume. Another day, it was hand lotion. These little gifts went on all summer long, and then one day he left a little chain with two clasps at the ends. I didn't have the faintest idea what it was used for, so I asked my mother. She told me that they were supposed to hold your slip straps from slipping off your shoulders. She didn't think I should accept such gifts from a boy. I was going to give it back that afternoon, except we had visitors. It was Tim's mother and sister. His mother talked to my mother, and then she talked to me. It seems that some of the gifts that Tim had given me he had stolen from his mother. I felt terrible, but luckily the cosmetics were still unopened. I was so embarrassed. I really felt sorry for Tim. If he had just stuck to cream and flowers, we could have remained friends. After that, I never found anything in the mailbox except mail, and that wasn't always welcome.

A frightening experience happened one summer night. I had an idea that the couch downstairs would be cooler than sleeping in the bedroom. We had a little dog who settled in at the foot of the couch. It must have been around two in the morning when she woke me up. She was crying and shivering like a leaf. I heard a deep growl down in the cellar. I ran upstairs and woke up my mother. I told her there was something in the cellar and asked if I should wake up Bill. She told me to go back to bed, and we would look down in the cellar in the morning. In the morning, we didn't find anything in the cellar. That afternoon we heard that a lion had gotten loose from the circus that was in town. The lion had been wandering the countryside. They found him, but to this day I am glad that Bill didn't go down in the cellar in the middle of the night. I swear I heard that lion![84]

---

84 Jessie's experience here relates to a particularly colorful episode in local history, though apparently, she never got the complete story. It happened in early July of 1929, only about a month and a half before Jessie and Harold married. A Cortland resident named Leon Carrington had a collie named Rover, apparently a rough collie who seemed to be suffering in the summer heat due to his long coat. Carrington decided to shear the dog and decided it would be fun to make Rover look like a lion by leaving a mane around his neck and a tuft of hair at the end of his tail.

A short time later the man decided to visit his brother living near Endwell to celebrate the 4th of July together and took his unusual looking dog along on the visit. Poor Rover was frightened by the fireworks that night and ran off. Over the next several days, dozens of sightings of a lion on the loose poured in both from inside the Binghamton city limits and at various points to the north as far away as Castle Creek. The state police were skeptical at first, but many of the sightings were at close range by people who swore they knew what a lion looked like and were certain that's what they'd encountered. A woman haying on Prospect Mountain claimed the lion came within 15 feet of her, but she managed to scare it away by throwing her wooden hay rake at it. The news spread, and even the *New York Times* reported that Binghamton seemed to have a lion on the loose, apparently one escaped from a circus. The community was in panic. Most people were afraid to leave their houses. The exceptions

Almost a year after we moved to Binghamton, I went back to Ithaca for a weekend visit. I remember I wore Marge's new winter coat. It was dark blue and had a silver fox collar. I felt gorgeous in it. I was going to stay with my friend Helen W. I was so excited. Helen had a boyfriend named Ozzie, and that evening he and a friend took us to a party. I had a wonderful time. I think my whole weekend would have been wonderful except for a few things that I found out about my old friends. Helen worked in a little smoke shop that was in the hotel. I went there with Helen on Saturday afternoon. Business was slow that day, so we had plenty of time to talk. We were chatting away when Helen asked me if I had ever done *it*. I knew right away what she meant. I said of course I hadn't. Then she shocked me by saying that I ought to try *it*! She said *it* hurt a little at first, but then it was wonderful and worth it.

I was confused. In one short year my friends had changed. That morning I had called Dorothy only to have her mother tell me that Dorothy was in the hospital. I went to see her there later that day. Everybody thought she was in the hospital to have her appendix out. But she really had had an abortion—not at the hospital. It was done somewhere else, but they had botched the job, and Dorothy landed in the hospital as a result. She was in trouble with the law too. I was so shocked about Dorothy, and when Helen told me what she had been doing, I felt *sick*. I went home on Monday wishing I had never made that visit and was still in ignorance about what my friends were doing. I never saw them again.

The clay down by the riverbank inspired me to try my hand at sculpting. I spent one afternoon dragging up little buckets of so-called clay. I took a small board and sculpted a bust of George Washington. Well, it was really more of a bas-relief than an actual bust. It was flat in the back with just the face built up. I thought it was pretty good. I placed it in a safe place to dry. The other kids made fun of me, and one day one of them picked up the board and dropped it on the floor. The head of George Washington was in a million pieces. After all, it wasn't real clay and had dried into dirt. I was so mad, and if I had gotten my hands on those kids, I would have smacked them good, but they had taken off, and I couldn't catch them. That ended my sculpting career.

Kids today think they have to work too hard, but they don't realize how easy they have it compared to what it was like in the twenties. I was not trained for anything. When we moved to Binghamton, my father said I couldn't go back to school. I was fifteen. He said I would have to go to work. We moved in on a Tuesday and on

---

were bands of well-armed men trying to hunt down the lion. It was surely at this time that the Davenports heard the news.

Eventually Rover wandered back to Carrington's brother's house in Endwell and was reunited with his owner in Cortland. When state troopers went to Cortland to see Carrington and Rover as part of closing out the case, they reported that the shearing had indeed been done in such an artful way that the dog really did look remarkably like an adult male lion in every respect except size. No doubt, the imaginations of all the people who saw him made him seem much bigger than he was.

Jessie either didn't read how the story turned out or forgot that part. We don't know what the growl was coming from the cellar and how much danger Bill might have been in had he gone down there in the middle of the night, but we can be pretty sure it was not a lion.

Thursday I had a job at Woolworth's. It only lasted a short time. My mother would soon have a sickly spell, and I would be needed at home to help with the kids and the housework. We didn't have a washing machine, and I had to scrub clothes on a scrubbing board. It was nice to see the wash blowing in the wind and to take them down smelling of sunshine, but it was hard work. We had to heat our flat irons on the stove, so in the summer we had to keep a fire going in the kitchen stove. We finally got an electric iron and a washing machine with a wringer.[85] It was great not having to wring the clothes out by hand.

It was about this time that Ray came back into our lives.[86] He was working in Binghamton, and to our surprise, he was married. He had married a girl that he had known from childhood. She had gotten into trouble and had been sent to a school for girls when she was fourteen years old. When she reached the age of eighteen, she was released, and she and Ray got married. They were going to have a baby. They were living on the East Side of Binghamton. My mother was at their house almost every day before the baby was born. Ray's wife wasn't very well. The baby was born after a hard delivery, and he only lived for two weeks. In that time, women had to stay in bed for ten days, so mother stayed at their house during this time. I would go there every day and bring home the washing. I was so grateful for that electric washing machine. I don't know how long they stayed in Binghamton, and when they moved away, we lost track of them.

I don't remember how many jobs I had between my fifteenth birthday and the time I was seventeen. I worked in five-and-dimes. I worked for a grocery store. I worked for two weeks at the telephone company. In between jobs, I was helping my mother or Mary, and I had several babysitting jobs. I remember one such job. The lady I worked for had just had a baby, and she needed someone to help with her three-year-old daughter and the housework. Her husband was really nice. He'd go to work in the morning, and when he came home at night, he would fix dinner, do the laundry, and listen to his wife complain. I'd get there about seven in the morning, and I'd sweep and dust and do the dishes. I had to dress and take care of the little girl, but most of the time I was running around, doing things the lady wanted me to do. She had an inside privy, and she would get into a rocking chair and have me pull her to the privy when she had to use it. I guess that was better than cleaning bed pans. My mother had a fit when I told her.

---

85 In the present era those of us living in developed countries might take washing machines for granted. They are one of the greatest labor-saving devices of all time, and in the 1920s, their use in homes had not yet become common. If anything, the Davenport household was ahead of most homes in having one then, but for a large, busy family, it was surely well justified. Electric irons were also then a new labor-saving device that not everyone had.

86 It is not entirely clear who this Ray is, but it would seem to be the close friend of Jessie's brother Bill who she discussed in the Ithaca chapter, the one who kissed Jessie at Buttermilk Falls. She seems to suggest there that Ray became a friend of the entire family and her mother thought highly of him.

One day the little girl was acting up. She was very spoiled and couldn't understand why her mother didn't get up and take care of her. Finally, about two in the afternoon I put her in her crib for a nap. She kept standing up in her crib and crying and screaming at the top of her lungs. I finally had enough, and I made her lie down. I said to her that if she didn't quiet down and go to sleep, I would spank her. It was the wrong thing to say. Her mother heard what I had said and yelled from her room, "Oh no, she won't." Of course, with that kind of backup, I was lost. The kid was smart enough to know all she had to do was run to her mother. At the end of the week, I collected my five dollars with a sigh of relief. She wanted me to come back for another week, but was I glad when my mother said no to that!

I had a lot of jobs like that. None paid more than five dollars except the rich family I worked for. The baby's nurse was off for a week, so I had the job for just that one week. They were rich snobs who thought it was alright to run around in their underwear in front of a young girl as if I was invisible. I worked for the poor and the dirty, but most of them were better to work for than those with money.

My mother always behaved like a lady. There was no swearing around our house. Even my father very seldom said anything off color. That is until one day when my mother got really upset. The phone had rung, and she thought she was talking to her good friend, Mrs. Bushnell. She had just found out that the cat had done its business behind the couch. Mother was so mad that when she answered the phone, she just let it out in a rush of words, "That damned cat got behind the couch and shit all over the floor, and I have go clean it up, and it stinks to high heaven!"

To Mother's horror, a small voice said, "Is this Mrs. Black? I'm calling for the nuns at Saint Mary's." Mother quietly hung up!

Claire had borrowed a black cape from Helen to wear to a Halloween party. One Saturday night in early November, we were going to babysit for Helen's two little girls. Claire thought this would be a good time to return the cape. We left our house about four o'clock. We had to take the streetcar that took about an hour to get to Endicott. When we got off at our stop, it was getting really dark. We had to go through Ideal Park.[87] Ordinarily, there were a lot of people around, but in November it was getting cold, and most of the mothers had taken their kids home by this hour.

Going through the park, Claire and I got into an argument. It was just a silly

---

87 Ideal Park was what is now called En-Joie Park, and it had not yet been turned into a golf course. It was one of the many amenities the Endicott-Johnson Company built for the benefit of their employees. This is quite far west in Endicott near what would later be the IBM Glendale Labs. As is common for young married couples, Helen and Jack moved several times. Apparently, by this time, Jack had the job with the forging company in Endicott, and they had moved into one of the houses on the far side of the park. Streetcars tended to have routes that would take passengers to popular parks, so it is not surprising that there was a line going as far as Ideal Park. By 1930, Jack and Helen must have moved again to another part of Endicott, since in that year records show them at 1500 North Street, only half a block from where much later I lived as a three-year-old. It was only later that they moved to Binghamton, eventually to the house on Vestal Avenue on the South Side.

thing, but I got mad and walked in front of Claire. After I had walked a few yards, I turned around, but couldn't see Claire. I thought she must have taken another path. I reached a part of the path where the trees were thick on both sides, and I began to feel a little uneasy. There were streetlights all through the park, but they only gave a weak light on the dark path. I heard a noise behind me, and my heart jumped into my throat. It must be Claire I thought to myself, and I slowly turned my head to look behind me. Instead of Claire, I saw a horrible monster running down the path toward me. It had fangs, and a black cape billowed behind it! It was reaching out its hand toward me and making weird noises. I was so frightened I turned and ran, forgetting what might have happened to Claire. I could hear a voice as I ran saying, "Stop. It's only me." I kept on running until I came out of the park into a brightly lit street with lots of people around. I stopped and looked behind me. The monster was coming out of the dark and into the light. I could see it was only Claire with Helen's cape streaming behind her. She reached up to her mouth and took out two short sticks. They were the fangs of the monster I thought I saw. Claire was laughing so hard, she had to sit on one of the benches.

"Boy! Did I scare you!" she said.

"Oh no, you didn't," I replied. "I knew it was you all the time." I had my fingers crossed behind my back to ward off the evil spirit that would get us for telling such a big lie.

I probably could think up a lot of other things that happened in my young life, but that would take me into my adult years. I got married very quietly one August night. I didn't know that I was to lose my mother barely two months later.[88] If I had known I was to lose her so soon, I wouldn't have gotten married when I did.

I am almost eighty years old now, and I wonder what the future holds for me. I wonder when I go to the place in the sky if I will once more see those what have gone before—my mother, Helen, Mary, Bill, Marge, Camel, and Dick.[89] I think it would be so wonderful to see them all again. I might even see my father, and I'm sure I would be very glad to see him too.

THE END

---

88 Jessie married my grandfather on Wednesday, August 21st in 1929. Elizabeth passed away on November 21st of the same year, not two, but three months to the day later.

89 That she mentions being almost eighty means that this was written sometime around 1990. She lists Helen's name next to those of several family members who were already deceased suggesting that Helen too had passed away. Since Helen died at the end of July 1990, we can conclude that Jessie wrote this, or at least finished writing, sometime after then, but still before her eightieth birthday in October of 1991. Mary had passed away in 1942, Bill in 1969, Marge in 1984, Carmel in 1986, Dick in 1930, and her father, William, in 1971. Elizabeth, Mary, Bill, and especially Dick all died far too young. Claire would live until 2010 and Jim until 1993. Jessie herself would pass away shortly before Christmas in 2000.

Afterword

After reading a true story, it is natural to wonder what happened next. If we feel connected to the characters, we may even want to know some of the details. We have seen that Jessie chose to end her narrative in 1929, and just barely mentioned the two major events for her that happened that year—the beginning of her first marriage in August and the loss of her mother in November. No one alive today can tell us everything about what happened to Jessie and the other family members in the years that followed, and we don't really need to know it all anyway. But if we are even a little curious, it is worth exploring what we can.

Before moving too much ahead from 1929, we might back up a little to cover one topic that Jessie intentionally avoided in her Binghamton chapter, or at least avoided being explicit about. That is my grandfather, Harold Lewis, and anything relating to his family or the details of their wedding. Two or three of the incidents she mentions that relate to anonymous boyfriends in the Binghamton chapter probably refer to Harold. Also, most likely the grocery store she mentions her family doing business with and where for a time she had a job was "Geo. F. Lewis & Son, Grocers" at 33 Saratoga Avenue. That store was a partnership of my great-grandfather and grandfather. Only a tenth of a mile away, this was by far the closest shop to the Davenport home,[90] and in the days of neighborhood grocers, when families depended on cars less than now, proximity was a major factor.

My great-grandfather, George Lewis, had left the family farm near a hamlet then called Tiona to seek employment in what for him might have seemed the big city of Binghamton. This was about 1890 when he would have been twelve years old. According to family memory, he worked first as a bellhop in a hotel, and he had a variety of other jobs following that. No later than 1900 when he was seventeen, he had his first long-term job working in a factory of the Endicott-Johnson Shoe Company in the suburb that was then called Lestershire and is now Johnson City. He met Alida Deming there, also a shoe factory worker, and they were married in 1901.

George and Alida were of similar family backgrounds. For many generations their ancestors had been small-holding farmers or practiced relatively solitary crafts such as carpentry or blacksmithing. They had been the early settlers of the hilly country of south-central New York State. The Demings arrived here from Connecticut, having been a purely Connecticut Yankee family since early colonial times all the way back to the founding of an English colony there in 1635. The Lewis stock arrived from both the Hudson Valley and Connecticut, as a mix of Welsh, Dutch, and English descent going back to early New Netherland and early colonial New England. They had no history in Pennsylvania, either as a colony or a state. They had never engaged in mining, and before taking jobs in the shoe factory, they had never been involved in

---

90 The second closest store was one operated by Horace VanKuren, nearly a half mile to the west at 308½ Conklin Avenue. That store was also still there when I was a child and we called it "The Sugar Bowl".

large-scale commercial endeavors. They were all Protestants going back for centuries. What is more, Alida and especially George were pious Evangelicals and took matters of faith very seriously. They were generally Puritanical in their outlook. Their families had never lived in big cities, or even small ones. In terms of overall patterns, the nature of their background was different from that of Jessie's family.[91]

Harold was born in Lestershire in March of 1905, the second of George and Alida's five children. A few years later, the family moved to Binghamton, and around 1909, with the aid of a senior partner who put up much of the capital, George was able to open a shop and start working for himself as a grocer in the downtown area. There were several ups and downs in the grocery business over the next several years. In 1911 the family moved to a house on High Street on the South Side, just across the Susquehanna from downtown, a location where they would live for over a decade. When Harold and his older brother were old enough to finish the eighth grade, they took jobs of their own. Among Harold's early skill set was driving automobiles, and much of the time he worked as a delivery van driver for a variety of businesses including a flower shop.

Based on what we can piece together from available records, by 1927, the last of George's downtown stores had closed, and George, Alida, and most of their children had moved further east within the South Side of Binghamton. It was apparently in that year, when my grandfather was twenty-two and my great-grandfather was in his mid-forties, that they formed a father-and-son partnership and erected the building at 33 Saratoga Avenue. This is the small building that is still there, and it must have been somewhat cramped because it appears that the family was living in the upstairs, including George, Alida, Harold, and the three younger children, then adolescents; and the ground floor was the store.[92] Geo. F. Lewis & Son, Grocers as a business lasted only a few years, and sometime in 1929 they sold the shop, and my great-grandparents moved about a half mile to a hillside just outside the city limits. There they owned several acres that they ran as a part-time farm. From that time and for the rest of his working career, my great-grandfather worked for a Binghamton wholesale bakery business called Spaulding. It is a coincidence that the period when the father-and-son grocery was in business almost exactly corresponded with the period the Davenport family was living on Conklin Avenue in Binghamton.

Assuming it is correct that all references Jessie makes in the Binghamton chapter to a neighborhood grocery are to that little shop on Saratoga Avenue, then it suggests a quite significant connection to the Lewis family since early 1927. It would be the store her mother "traded with ever since we had moved to Binghamton" and where she had "run up a bill". It would be where Jessie tried to order six pounds of dried beef and had the "grocery man" [Harold?] talk her down to a pound of half. And presumably it is the shop where later, when she was seventeen, she worked six days

---

91 My mother's ancestry was generally like that of the Lewises and Demings, and thus Jessie represents the unique part of my family history.

92 The building is now just a residence, but when I was a child, it was still a shop—by then mainly a candy store with a clientele mainly of children.

a week for ten dollars meaning she would have been working then for her future father-in-law and husband.

It is at least clear that the story of how my grandparents first met relates to that store. I am sometimes doubtful of stories passed down in families, but this one has the ring of general accuracy about it. It was routine in those days to expect the neighborhood grocer to make home deliveries. One time when my grandfather was delivering groceries to the back door of the Davenport home on Conklin Avenue, he saw a pretty girl in the back giving the family dog a bath in the tub of a washing machine. Surely these were the small dog and the washing machine that Jessie mentioned in the Binghamton chapter. To me, it seems a practical and resourceful idea to make use of the family's washing machine as a container in which to bathe a small dog. Perhaps to Harold it seemed intriguingly original, but one way or another, first meeting a girl in this way sparked his interest in her.

Whatever the mutual attraction between Jessie and Harold, clearly their parents or anyone else trying to be objective about it would have considered them something less than an ideal match. The two more obvious red flags were the age difference and the difference in the faiths in which they were raised. A six-and-a-half-year age difference need not be an issue if both parties were already clearly adults. A thirty-year-old man marrying a woman not quite yet twenty-four, for example, is a scenario most people would view as entirely appropriate. But a twenty-four-year-old man and a still-seventeen-year-old girl is not quite the same thing. It might be fair to argue that based on her previous experiences Jessie was emotionally mature for her age, both in the sense of having been forced to take on adult-like responsibilities in her family and in the sense of being somewhat worldly wise. Still, it must have seemed to some that the expression about *robbing the cradle* applied here.

Having come of age during the social and sexual revolutions of the 1920s, it appears that at that period in their lives neither Harold nor Jessie considered matters of faith to be a particularly important issue. They probably were underestimating the potential long-term impact of the differences in their belief systems. Though William was not Catholic at that time, Elizabeth was very strong in her Catholic faith and still expected Jessie to conform to the kind of upbringing she had. Harold's parents were equally strong in their Evangelical Protestantism and placed similar expectations on him.

The term generation gap may not have been in widespread use then, but it is useful in describing what was going on in both the Lewis and Davenport households. Clearly it was a contributing factor in why Harold and Jessie decided to marry despite what their parents or other family members surely advised. Social histories of the early 20th Century[93] inform us of what a radical departure the 1920s were from what had come before. Some of the trends, especially for women, were toward behaviors that would have been unthinkable just ten years earlier—drinking by women, smoking by women, short hairstyles, knee-length skirts, racy magazines, being kissing before

---

93 A particularly good description of this moral revolution can be found in Chapter 5 of the 1931 book, *Only Yesterday*, by Frederick Lewis Allen listed in the bibliography. See other sources as well. The societal changes of the 1960s seem mild by comparison.

being at least engaged, being out at late hours with boys, "necking" or "petting parties", psychoanalysis, etc. Jessie certainly didn't embrace all the new trends, but her Ithaca and Binghamton chapters describe participation in some of them. In any social revolution, there are those who champion the traditional values as worth preserving, and Elizabeth was clearly an excellent example of this. Jessie's father and even her older brother probably had much the same sentiments. Though Jessie did not openly rebel against her mother's guidance, it is clear from her narrative that she conformed to the modern trends as much as she could get away with. Similarly, Harold would not be openly rebellious against his parents' Victorian standards, but with his naturally mischievous attitude and charismatic personality, he knew how to skirt the rules. His father would enthusiastically go to a revival or a prayer meeting. Harold would be equally enthusiastic about entering a pool hall.

We can understand the probable reasons that any reservations the family had about the match would have little effect on the decision of Harold and Jessie. At twenty-four, Harold would have long since felt he was an adult with the right to make his own mistakes. As for Jessie's case, there may have not been much interaction with her parents during this period. Elizabeth's health was in decline, and she may have been in a hospital for part of the time. And as was true at most times, William was traveling for the railroad more often than he was home at night.

So, beyond the mutual attraction and the carefree lack of constraints that came with the era, what else could have made Jessie and Harold decide they were ready to marry? Obviously, we have no direct knowledge of how my grandparents thought and behaved when they were young, but we can make reasonable conjectures based on what we know of them and their circumstances. Having read Jessie's memoir, we already know a lot about her mindset. We know, for example, that she was a romantic of the first order, which means that if her heart told her to do something, any practical considerations would be ignored completely. We also know that she was attracted to older boys/men, or more precisely, she was flattered by the attention of older males. She was probably weary of the role she was playing in her family and may have thought that if she had to bear up under so much responsibility anyway, she might as well have a family of her own. Harold's thinking is a little more difficult to imagine. He was a young man who enjoyed having a good time. He was not only quite handsome, but he had extraordinary charisma. Even when he was in his nineties, he would still have an ability to charm and flirt with his nurses that was uncanny. Perhaps he just felt some pressure to marry and settle down. His older brother, having married at twenty-one, was already four and a half years into domestic life. And perhaps Harold felt that if it was time for him to marry too, it might as well be with a gal who intrigued him partly because she was different from what people expected.

Based on the available information,[94] we can know some, but not all, of the details of their wedding. Jessie and Harold were married during the evening hours on

---

94 The marriage license and the entries in the New York State marriage index are not too hard to find, but the marriage certificate has not turned up. Jessie gives us very few clues in what she wrote, and I don't know of anyone alive today who can remember hearing them describe this wedding in detail.

Wednesday, August 21st, 1929, in Port Dickinson.[95] Apparently, it was a civil ceremony officiated by the Town of Dickinson Justice of the Peace. The bride's and groom's ages and dates of birth are recorded accurately on the marriage license, but I found no evidence relating to parental consent. It is possible that we simply don't have the record where one of Jessie's parents signed. Or it could be that at that time exceptions were sometimes allowed in New York State to eighteen being the minimum marriage age without parental consent. If we knew who the witnesses were who signed the marriage certificate, we would have a better clue as to whether any family members were there, or if this was entirely an elopement. Clearly, a Wednesday evening after work would not be the time anyone would plan a wedding of the type that was intended to be a major event for the larger family. There is one suspicious aspect to the information listed on the marriage license. The address Jessie listed for her residence up to the time of the marriage is a location in the Town of Dickinson. We know (for example based on the false lion incident in July of 1929) every indication was that she was living with her family in the house on Conklin Avenue at least almost up to the time of the wedding. Would there have been some circumstance that would have caused her to make a temporary move (perhaps staying with a girlfriend) just for the last few weeks before marriage? Or was there some reason the couple felt they had to be deceptive about where she had been living? As for where the newlyweds intended to live immediately after marriage, they listed an address for an apartment on Bevier Street on the North Side.

Whether or not they did inhabit the Bevier Street address for the first few months, we can be sure that Harold and Jessie did start married life as apartment dwellers within the more urban parts of Binghamton. Like many newlywed couples, they may have moved quite frequently from one rented home to another. The first record I can find of a specific address for them is in April of 1930, which shows them on Isbell Street in Downtown, near the current YMCA. They were living in the apartment next door to that of Harold's older brother, Charlie, and his wife and baby daughter. Harold, then twenty-five, was working as a truck driver, and probably this already meant he had the job driving the delivery van for the laundry-service company, a steady job he would hold for several years. Jessie was then about six months pregnant with their first child. Elizabeth Carmel Lewis, my Aunt Betty, would be born July 24th, 1930. Clearly, she was named after Jessie's mother and youngest sister. We'll come back to the married life of Jessie and Harold presently, but it is now a good place to discuss the other family members.

We do know that Elizabeth passed away due to an extended illness during the nighttime hours on Thursday, August 21st, 1929, but beyond that, I don't have any

---

95 Port Dickinson, New York is an incorporated village just north of Binghamton along the east bank of the Chenango River. The population in 1929 was about 1800. Though far from the sea or even a large lake, it was called a port because in the days of the Chenango Canal (1834-1878), it was the first stop for passenger boats going north out of Binghamton (followed by Chenango Bridge, Port Crane, Chenango Forks, Greene, and several more stops on their way up to Norwich and possibly as far as Utica where the Chenango Canal joined the Erie).

details. We can easily find her listed in the New York State index of deaths, but the actual death certificate has not turned up, and neither what Jessie wrote, nor anything contained in the vaguely written obituary mentions a specific disease. Clearly, she had been seriously ill for several months, and there may have been several complicating factors from multiple maladies. Though Jessie mentioned that her mother sometimes sought treatment at a hospital in Scranton leading up to this time, sources make it clear that it was in Binghamton where she died. Whether this was at their home or at a Binghamton hospital I don't know.

The funeral for Elizabeth was held the morning of Monday, the 25th, and I can imagine that not only family, but many of her friends were there. It may have been that the reason the funeral was not held sooner was to give time for relatives from Shamokin to make travel arrangements to be there. Elizabeth was laid to rest in Calvary Cemetery in Johnson City, one of the largest Catholic cemeteries in the Binghamton area. Apparently for several decades the grave was unmarked until one of Elizabeth's granddaughters, a daughter of Jessie's younger brother Jim, arranged for a stone to be made and placed there. Like most of Elizabeth's grandchildren, my father was not born until years after she died. In the spring of 2022, when he was well into his eighties, my dad suddenly asked that I help find the exact location of his grandmother's grave so we could visit. Finding a specific grave in a huge cemetery, especially one that is older and where the plot numbering system was not always well organized, is not a trivial task. With some help from my seven-year-old grandson, George, a great-great-great-grandson of Elizabeth, we did find her grave. And with the help of some local relatives, we will be sure flowers are planted there every spring from now on.

Over the years after Elizabeth's death, it becomes a little more difficult to follow exactly where all the family members were at times, let alone to understand exactly why they did what they did. This certainly applies to the father, William. We do know that he continued as a locomotive engineer, and sometimes fireman, for the DL&W Railroad for most of his working career. Whether it was at his request or strictly for the needs of the railroad, they transferred him to be based back in Scranton sometime within a few months after the death of his wife. In terms of his actual place of residence, city directory and census records indicate that he shifted quite frequently from one address to another within Scranton over the next few years. In fact, the first location I see for him, he is just a lodger in a boarding house.

None of his six unmarried children moved to Scranton with William. This includes even the younger ones. Claire, Carmel, Jim, and Dick were only sixteen, fourteen, twelve, and ten, respectively at the time of their mother's death. It might be appropriate to view this as a case of parental abandonment on William's part. I do not deny that there is at least some validity to that viewpoint, and I do not intend to take the role of trying to explain away all of William's actions. Nonetheless, it seems obvious to me that the situation may have been a complicated one. First, it would not have been convenient for all the children to drop everything and move to Scranton with him, especially the ones who were already adults. Bill was already making a living in Binghamton and would have his own circle of friends there. Marge apparently hoped to continue her college education in Cortland. If just the younger children would be moving to Scranton with their father, there were some obvious logistical difficulties. Given that he was still traveling for the railroad more nights than he was home and further given that his first residence was just a boarding house, bringing just the younger children along would have been a plan unlikely to work. Besides that, the idea of changing schools in the middle of a school year would not have been popular. It could have been that William planned from the start that leaving the younger children behind in the care of the older ones was just a temporary measure, and once he had established himself in Scranton the younger ones would join him there.

Aside from the logistical considerations, is it possible that the unmarried children as a group felt estranged enough from their father that in this time of grief that they preferred not to live with him? And having a father who was so much of the time away from home for his work, they may have assumed they would be largely on their own anyway whether they moved all the way back to Scranton with him or not. Bill and Marge likely considered themselves already responsible adults. Bill especially had long been assuming a major responsible role for the family, so taking charge for their younger siblings may not have seemed a major change. We might also keep economic factors in mind. The stock market panic came in October and November of 1929, and even though the full dimensions of the impact on ordinary working people of the coming depression might not have been fully evident in early 1930, people would have had a sense that their financial well-being would take a turn for the worse. Even before the onset of the depression, William was perpetually in debt anyway. I'll come back momentarily to what happened to the children, but first a little more about William.

I do not know exactly when, but I believe it was in about 1932 that William married a nurse named Mary Nabor (1894-1968) as his second wife. They continued to move from one rented home to another in Scranton, and William continued working for the Delaware, Lackawanna & Western Railroad until for health reasons he left their employ in 1946. He was sixty-two then, and I wonder if he may still have been suffering the effects of being stabbed in his twenties. It is not entirely clear, but the impression I have from what is in his personnel file is that the railroad was trying to push him out without having to pay him a pension. After quitting the railroad, he got jobs working in the boiler rooms of first the Clarks Summit State Hospital and later another hospital. He eventually had to retire completely, again due to health reasons, in about 1956 at the age of about seventy-two. The elderly couple continued to live mainly in Scranton for the rest of their lives. The best we can tell, William continued to have financial struggles until his death in 1971 at the age of eighty-seven. Mary had died three years earlier at the age of seventy-four.

We know for certain from the available records that William was raised in a Methodist family. And we know from Jessie's comments and other sources that at least as late as the 1920s, he did not consider himself Catholic. Yet late in life he and Mary were both practicing Catholics, so an obvious question is when did he convert? My best guess is that it was around the time he remarried. Maybe having one wife who was Catholic was not enough reason to convert, but having a second Catholic wife was. In any case, near the ends of their lives, both William and Mary were members in good standing of St. Peter's Cathedral in Scranton, and they are buried there in Cathedral Cemetery.

Jessie's eldest two sisters, Helen and Mary, had each already been married for several years by 1929, and it is relatively easy to trace what was happening in their lives in the time that followed. At the time of their mother's death, second daughter, Mary, was already six years into married life and had her first four children. She and her husband, Ralph Clark, were living on a small farm in Scott Township, Lackawanna County, north of Scranton, and Ralph had a job at a nearby feed mill. Elizabeth's eldest daughter, Helen, had been married to Jack Hawley for five years and they had their first two children. They were living in Endicott where Jack worked in a forging company.

We can verify that Helen and Jack continued to live in Endicott at least through 1930 and Jack continued to work for Endicott Forging Company. For the period from 1931 to 1941, I have not yet found information on exactly where they lived. The three of their children born during this period all indicate Pennsylvania births, but that hardly pins down a locality. Jack was a native of Montrose, so the most likely scenario is that they lived either in that borough or somewhere else in Susquehanna County during this time. That would make it plausible that Jack commuted from there by car and continued working at the same forging company. If, on the other hand they had moved back to the Abingtons where they lived early in the married life, it would suggest that Jack found another way to support his family during this time and was rehired by Endicott Forging only after returning to the Triple Cities in the 1940s. In any case, we know for certain the family lived within the City of Binghamton from 1942 on. Some still remember that during the war years they lived over a tavern near the north bank of the Susquehanna. It was just above the Rockbottom Dam at the intersection of what were then South and Tudor Streets, what today is part of North Shore Drive. Records available from 1942 to 1944 verify this location.

By sometime in 1945, Helen and Jack had purchased the house at 1312 Vestal Avenue, at the corner of Rollins Street, two blocks up the hillside on the South Side. They would live there for the rest of their lives. They had three daughters and two sons born from 1925 to 1937. Don, their youngest, and my father enjoyed the times they spent together in their early adolescent years. They were first cousins, close in age, and lived almost exactly two miles or about a forty-minute walk away from each other, so there were many opportunities to play backyard sports, take hikes in the woods, and so on. Some of Jack and Helen's children and grandchildren moved south to warmer climates, but the majority seem to have stayed within the local area and probably visited the couple often in their later years. I am not certain in what year, or even if, Jack retired from Endicott Forging. We do know he died in February of 1972, just short of this seventieth birthday. Helen passed away at the age of eighty-five in July of 1990.

The adult life of Mary, the second sister, was hard and tragically short, but the way Jessie described her, Mary was the kind of person to find a certain joy in life all the same. Mary and Ralph had three sons and five daughters from 1924 to 1937. Jessie described in her memoir the births of her first two nephews, Buddy (Ralph Jr.) and Richard. We have seen that Mary's married life began at the age of seventeen when she eloped with Ralph Clark and lied about her age. They lived and raised their children in Justus, Pennsylvania for the rest of their lives together, and Jessie described the house there as quite basic in terms of modern amenities. It was a working farm, and undoubtedly produced much of the sustenance for the growing family and probably some cash crops as well. But Ralph's main source of income seems always to have been his job at the feed mill. Mary died of heart disease at a hospital in Scranton in September of 1942 at the age of just thirty-six years and six months. Her eight children would have ranged in age from four to eighteen at the time. As far as I can tell, Ralph never remarried, and continued to raise his children on the farm. Later in life he moved to Binghamton and held a variety of jobs there. I am not sure what the circumstances were that took him to Los Angeles where he died in 1972 at the age of sixty-eight. He is buried though back in the Scott Valley Cemetery as are many of the other family members.

I believe that the eldest sons, Buddy and Richard, served in the military in World War II. I know for certain that Richard was in the Navy from August 14th, 1943, just a little after his eighteenth birthday, through April 30th, 1946. Of the eight children all of them married and started raising families, so Ralph must have had many grandchildren. The majority of his offspring settled somewhere in Pennsylvania or New York State, though some moved as far away as Kentucky or Idaho. To mention one example from the family, the fourth child, William Lincoln Clark, served in the Korean War and later married and settled in Binghamton, where he held management posts with Broome Transit and the Tri-Cities Warehouse, as well as being a prominent member of the Park Avenue Baptist Church.

It is more complicated and difficult to follow over the next few years what happened in the lives of the six siblings who were not yet married when Jessie's narrative ended in 1929. There is sometimes enough documentary evidence and handed-down stories to know where they went, but we can generally only speculate why they went there. By four and a half months after their mother's death, we find that all six of them had moved into part of a house they were renting on Central Avenue in Cortland for thirty dollars per month. The records seem to indicate that Bill was the only one working for pay, sometimes as a truck driver and sometimes as a painter, an occupation he previously had in Binghamton. Surely, Marge and the other sisters were helping take care of them all. All five except Bill were listed as attending school. For Marge, then aged twenty, this must mean she was still attending Cortland Normal School (teachers' college). Claire, Carmel, Jim, and Dick, aged sixteen down to ten, would have been in primary or secondary schools in the Cortland public school system. It is possible that some of the other siblings could have had part-time jobs, and we don't know what, if any, financial support William might have been sending from Scranton. But on the surface, it looks like Bill was the primary means of support for all these siblings. Interestingly, his age is listed in the census as twenty-seven, whereas he was actually still short of his twenty-third birthday. Though it is possible that this is a simple error on the part of the enumerator, it seems more likely that Bill lied about his age to make it seem he was more capable of taking responsibility for his young siblings.

It is not surprising that the six siblings would move out of the house on Conklin Avenue, but we might wonder why it was to Cortland. Why were they moving to a smaller city forty miles to the north at about the same time their father was moving to a larger city fifty-some miles to the south? The only previous known connection that any of them had with Cortland was that Marge was going to college there. Perhaps she suggested to Bill and the others that Cortland would be a good location for all of them, and not just because she hoped to continue her studies there. She may have been aware that there would be more job opportunities there whereby Bill could support the rest of them. Or perhaps cost of housing was a little more affordable than in Binghamton. Another possibility is that they as a group had a falling out with their father of such a serious nature that they did not want him even to know where they were. In those days, moving to another city would have made it harder to be found.

The plan for the six siblings to stay together as a family unit must have eventually proved unsustainable, and though I have not been able to trace exactly why or when the arrangement broke down, we find that within a matter of months it did. We know for certain that Bill was settled back in the Binghamton area and married there in June of 1932. Even earlier, the evidence suggests that Marge had moved to Massachusetts and married there by early 1931.

Bill's bride was an eighteen-year-old Binghamton-area girl (though native to Unadilla) named Catherine Smith. For the earliest years of their marriage, they lived with her parents at their house on Frederick Street in Binghamton. Bill soon had a steady job with Sears and Roebuck and was eventually promoted to a manager there. It was in about 1942, when he was in his mid-thirties, that he left Sears and took a job with IBM, eventually becoming a manager there as well. He and Catherine had two daughters and they eventually settled into a house in Conklin in a house right across from the old Julius Rogers School. Bill died in June of 1969 at the age of sixty-one. Catherine lived until 1999.

All three sisters; Marge, Claire, and Carmel; soon moved to Massachusetts, specifically to Cape Cod, and spent most of the rest of their lives there. It is not surprising that they would have moved away from Cortland, Binghamton, and Scranton, but I do not know the exact reason they chose Cape Cod as their destination. My guess would be that Marge moved there first, and then the younger two sisters, still in their teens, followed her, since she may have been the surviving family member with whom they still felt the closest bond. But that still leaves the question of why Marge left for Cape Cod in the first place. It may be that somehow by about the end of 1930 she had already met and decided to marry her Massachusetts-born future husband. It is unclear how he, as a working man, would have met someone going to teachers' college in Upstate New York, but stranger things have happened. The wedding was somewhere in Barnstable County on the cape in 1931 and seems to have been very early in that year. His name was Joseph Moruzzi (1907-1989) and he was born in Bourne in the Upper-Cape (the part closest to the mainland) into a family that had immigrated from Italy just two years earlier. Among jobs he held, we was a crane operator for a drop-forging company and a carpenter in a home-construction business. He served in the army from 1943 to 1946. The couple lived on the cape for much of the 1930s and probably had their one daughter and one son there. But by 1940, they moved to the Springfield area, likely for better job prospects. They apparently moved back to the cape later on, because that is where Marge died in 1984, aged seventy-five. Joseph lived until 1989.

I do not know at present whether Claire and Carmel followed Marge quickly to Cape Cod or whether it was a few years later, but we can know for certain they were in Falmouth by 1935. From the 1940 census, we can see that twenty-six-year-old Claire and twenty-four-year-old Carmel were still single and they were both working as "salesladies" in a "chain store", which I imagine to be a department store or perhaps a five-and-ten. The record shows that Claire had had two years in high school and Carmel only one. They were lodging with an Italian immigrant family in West Yarmouth in the Mid-Cape.

Youngest sister, Carmel, at the age of twenty-six, married Gil Sousa Condhino in October of 1941. They traveled back to Scranton to have the wedding. Gil was born on Sao Miguel Island in the Azores, a territory of Portugal, in 1908. His family immigrated to the US when he was about eighteen months old and soon settled in coastal Massachusetts. This was a second marriage for Gil. He had married a Portuguese woman (Zulmida Jacinto, 1912-1997) about ten years earlier and had at least two children by her. They divorced sometime before 1940. When Gil met Carmel, he was living with his parents in the Town of Barnstable where he was a truck driver, and his father was a farm worker. Gil enlisted in the army in December of 1942, about a year after Pearl Harbor and about fourteen months into his marriage with Carmel. The 1944 Springfield city directory shows Gil in the army and Carmel working as a welder, no doubt as part of the war effort. By sometime in 1945 at war's end, they were both able to go back to the cape. Carmel and Gil had a daughter during the war and a son a few years after the war was over.

Claire, the sister just two years younger than Jessie and the one who had been Jessie's sidekick especially during their time in Ithaca, did not marry right away. In 1950, at the age of thirty-seven, she married Francis Wyman (1907-1967). Perhaps Claire continued to work in a department store in the meantime and may have participated in the war effort in some way. Francis was from a family that had been on Cape Cod for at least a few generations, though they seem to have had a short sojourn in Ohio before returning to Massachusetts. Francis was a skilled auto mechanic. He was in the army during the war, but it was only for a period of months in 1943. Perhaps he was discharged for a health-related reason. Claire and Francis had one daughter and one son, born in 1951 and 1952, respectively. Though her husband died quite young in 1967, Claire outlived all her siblings by a decade or more and did not pass away until 2010 at the age of ninety-six on her beloved Cape Cod.

As far as I can remember, Aunts Claire and Carmel were the only two of Grandma Jessie's siblings that I ever met, and that meeting was when I was too young to have anything more than a faint memory of them. Our family was of limited resources, but my dad still wanted to have chances for us to travel, so he developed the quite practical strategy of taking us to see relatives who lived in other states. I think it was in 1961, the summer that I turned five, that he took us to Cape Cod where we spent a few days staying at Claire and Carmel's cottages and swimming in a lake nearby.

I have not yet found much documentary evidence to help trace what happened over the next few years to the youngest brothers, Jim and Dick. With the exception of census records, the evidence we can readily access online generally does not tell us much about minors. A second cousin informed me that she knew, from what her grandfather (Jim) had told her, that Jim and Dick were placed in a Catholic orphanage for a time and that it was a quite miserable experience for them. In terms of timeframe, this must have started right after the arrangement with the six siblings living together in Cortland broke down, perhaps starting in late 1930 or early 1931. Jim might have still been thirteen, and Dick eleven. Bill was then a young adult, but with the depression at hand, it may not have been possible to find steady work and have an income that could be counted on. If we assume Marge, Claire, and Carmel might have already moved to Massachusetts, there was less of a household together anyway, so I can well imagine that the older siblings simply thought putting the two young brothers into an orphanage was the only viable option.

The next question is where was this orphanage? I have not found anything about a history of orphanages in Cortland. It is possible that it could have been a Catholic orphanage in the Scranton area. But my best guess is that it was in Binghamton. Anyone who knows much at all about local history has probably heard of the Susquehanna Valley Orphans' Home in a part of the South Side that was until the early 20th Century mostly open farmland. But that was not specifically a Catholic orphanage. Until I started researching this, I was not aware that there was another orphanage in town known as St. Mary's Home or St. Mary's Orphans' Asylum. This was on the West Side located on what is now part of the grounds of Seton Catholic Central High School. The number of children there varied and was generally somewhere around one hundred. There may be a way to gain access to the records of that orphanage, but I have not yet discovered it. Since Bill was moving back to the Binghamton area at about this time, it may have seemed to him that if he couldn't care for his young brothers himself, the next best thing would be to place them in a Catholic orphanage nearby.

I was also informed that there was a particular reason the stay of Jim and Dick in the orphanage came to an end. It was that when their father found out they were there, he felt embarrassed about having sons of his in an orphanage and decided out of a sense of pride he had to take them out of there and into his own home. Whether that was the whole reason, or some other factors were at play, I don't know, but this must mean that Jim and Dick spent part of their adolescent years in Scranton. City

145

directories did not list the names of the minor children, at least until they were old enough to have jobs of their own, so we don't get a clue from those. Thus, we can't be sure exactly when the two young sons were staying with William and his second wife as they moved from place to place in Scranton during the 1930s. We also don't know how Mary would have been as a stepmom. There is at least one bit of documentation indicating that Dick was in Massachusetts in 1935, when he would have been about sixteen. This is evidence that he, and likely Jim as well, spent part of their teen years staying with, or at least living near, one or more of their sisters on Cape Cod. Jim was already almost an adult by then.

The earliest record after that that I have found for Jim was when he enlisted in the army in December of 1939 at the age of twenty-two. Since this is exactly two years before America entered the war and was theoretically at peace, I wonder if this gives an indication that he was already exploring the idea of staying in the army long-term. In any case, it did indeed become his career, and he served for over thirty years until his discharge in February of 1970. What records I have found give only an incomplete picture of his service, but we can know from these at least some points along the way. Jim was part of the 64th Coast Artillery for most of his early years in the army, based both at Fort Barrancas in Pensacola and at Fort Shafter in Honolulu as an anti-aircraft unit. In April of 1940, we know he was at Fort Shafter in the headquarters battery of the 1st Battalion of the 64th. I don't yet know if he was still there in December of 1941 fighting off the attack on Pearl Harbor. Apparently for much of the war he was stationed at Fort Barrancas. We know that on October 10th, 1942, when he was twenty-five, he married Helen Olivia Antoine (1918-2009) in Pensacola. Helen grew up near Scranton in the Clarks Summit area. Their first child was born in Florida in September of 1944. It was at Fort Barrancas that Jim re-enlisted as a master sergeant in the post-war army in December of 1945, which probably means that by then he was quite sure the army would be his career. Fort Barrancas has quite a history. The Spanish built it in 1698. In American hands, it played an important role in the War of 1812. It was not deactivated as a US Army base until 1947. Obviously, Jim was posted at several different bases in the course of his career. A record for 1952 shows him at Kaiserslautern, Germany.

Jim and Helen had two daughters and two sons, born between 1944 and 1956, all while he was in the army. In 1950 Jim and his family lived near Chesapeake Bay in Anne Arundel County, Maryland, and he worked at one of the bases nearby. They may have lived other places in the meantime, but by the 1980s, Jim and Helen were living as retirees in West Virginia, eventually near the town of Hedgesville in the rural eastern panhandle of the state. Their four children and their families all lived within a few hours' drive in Maryland, West Virginia, and Pennsylvania. Model railroading became a hobby, and Jim called his setup the RTMS Railroad, though I don't know what that was an acronym for. It appears that Jim and Helen made a good life for themselves. He passed on in 1993 at the age of seventy-five, and Helen lived on in West Virginia until her passing in 2009 at the age of ninety-one. They are buried back in Pennsylvania in Mount Bethel Cemetery near Clarks Summit.

The adult life of youngest brother, Dick, was a sadder story. After his period in

Massachusetts around 1935, he must have moved back to the Southern Tier of New York State by his late teens. It was in Waverly, New York in September of 1937, when he was eighteen, that he married Ella T. (1918-1993). Ella was a native of Waverly, a small town right on the border with Pennsylvania. When she was small, her parents divorced, and her mother quickly remarried. Ella grew up with a stepfather and several younger stepsiblings on just the other side of the border in South Waverly, Pennsylvania.

Dick and Ella's only child, Rochelle, was born in Pennsylvania in 1938, and it seems almost certain this meant in the hospital in Sayre. They probably already lived near Binghamton by this time, and Ella had gone back to her hometown to have the baby near her mother or just because they preferred Robert Packard Hospital. For sure they were living near Binghamton by the following year, and Dick had a job at the Crowley's milk plant, maintaining the processing equipment there. Multiple sources remember them living a little outside of Binghamton, near the Julius Rogers School in the Town of Conklin, and for at least part of the time, Ella's mother was living with them there. People remember both Ella and her mother as obnoxious toward everyone. Dick and Ella must have moved around a few times because they were in an apartment near Downtown for part of 1940 and in an apartment on the East Side for part of 1941. Dick's job at Crowley's seems to have been a steady one during this time, and it appears that he often worked long hours there.

Tragically, Dick and Ella's marriage broke down during this time. According to some sources they were living in Conklin at the time they decided to separate in 1943. What seems to be the official divorce record though is in Escambia County, Florida in 1944. This would be in the Pensacola area, and it is a little bit of a mystery why the divorce is registered there. Could it be that Dick was based there in connection with his work in the merchant marines? Could it have something to do with his brother being stationed there at Fort Barrancas, and it was somehow convenient to make the divorce official in Florida? Though improbable, it is possible that this record is for a different Richard and Ella Davenport.

Dick by this time had stomach ulcers and other health issues as well. This prevented him from joining the military at the start of the war, so hoping to help his country in another way, he joined the merchant marines. We will never know all the experiences he had during the war, but we do know quite a bit about the most arduous hardship he faced, because some family members remember clearly what they heard from him about this. Somewhere west of the Azores, the cargo ship on which he was working was torpedoed by a U-boat and sank. The surviving crew members were not quickly rescued, so Dick and some of his crewmates spent all of twenty-eight days on a life raft with little food or water. After several days, they encountered a Portuguese ship, that had also been torpedoed, and though it didn't sink, it was so severely crippled that they refused to take Dick and his crewmates aboard. The only supplies the Portuguese captain was willing to spare for the shipwrecked men were some oranges and canned tomatoes. These were enough to keep those on the life raft alive, but the acidic foods were far from the best thing for a man with ulcers. It is also remembered that Dick suffered long-term problems with his feet from having them immersed for so long in the seawater in the bottom of the raft. We believe that Dick never fully recovered from the further damage to his health caused by the severe privations of this misadventure.

At this time, I know only part of the story of what happened to Dick after the war. He did stay for one extended period in the home of my grandparents, Harold and Jessie, while they were living in the nice house on Emmett Street in Binghamton. My dad, then a pre-teen, spent a lot of time with his Uncle Dick during this period. It was also during these postwar years that Dick was successful in having some of his short stories published in one or more major national magazines. Unfortunately, I have not yet been able to find these. The only remaining clues from the records I have found relate to his death in December of 1950, at the age of thirty-one. These show he died in Bourne, Massachusetts and was residing at the time in nearby Falmouth, on the Upper-Cape. He is buried in St. Peter's Cemetery in Sandwich. The reason he was living on Cape Cod at the time possibly could have something to do with some continuing connection to the merchant marines,[96] or it could be that living near some of his sisters made as much sense as any other choice of a place to live. Maybe, despite his bitter experiences, he was accustomed to living near the sea.

People in the family remember Dick's only child, Rochelle, as "Peaches", which must be a nickname she often went by. Though generally I am avoiding going into detail about the generation of Jessie's nieces and nephews, more than one person in the family has asked me repeatedly, "Whatever happened to Peaches?" I only have some of the facts about her life, and it generally seems a sad story like her father's. If you're sure you want to know, here's the little that I have found. Very soon after the divorce, Ella married a considerably younger man from Horseheads named David W. who worked in restaurants and grocery stores. They lived in the Waverly area, and they soon began having children. Thus, like her mother, Rochelle grew up with a stepfather and younger stepsiblings. Apparently, a few years later, the W. household, including Rochelle Davenport, moved to Horseheads, and during her mid-teens moved again from there to East Smithfield, Pennsylvania. Peaches graduated from high school there and appears to have been an active and popular student.

Shortly after graduation, Peaches moved on her own to Syracuse and in 1958 at the age of nineteen, she married a man about the same age named William L. As far as I can tell, they had no children together, and were divorced by sometime in 1963. In November of that year, she married in Syracuse a man originally from New Hampshire named Stanton Hancock. Stanton was twelve years her senior and had been divorced twice before. He had been a marine during the Korean War. They soon moved to rural Sullivan Township in Tioga County, Pennsylvania, a little to the east of the borough of Mansfield. The saddest part comes next. On January 10th, 1966, at Robert Packard Hospital in Sayre, Peaches gave birth to a baby girl. The next day, the baby died of "severe erythroblastosis fetalis", meaning the condition of Rh factor incompatibility. As far as I can tell, Peaches and Stanton stayed together until his death in 1998. There is no record of any other children, probably because

---

96 The Massachusetts Maritime Academy is adjacent to Bourne, for example.

they would have feared the same result. I have not found records that give a hint as to what occupations Stanton or Peaches might have had to earn their living. I am not clear on all the places they might have lived, but from at least 1994 onward, they lived in a trailer park in Horseheads. Fifteen years after her husband's death, Peaches died there in 2013 at the age of seventy-five.

Finally, we come back to our heroine, Jessie. Where we left off, she had married twenty-four-year-old Harold on August 21st, 1929, while she was still seventeen. This turned out to be three months to the day before her mother's tragically early and unexpected death. Harold and Jessie were soon living in an apartment near the center of Binghamton at 26 Isbell Street in the same building as Harold's older brother and his family and paying $22.50 per month in rent. Geo. F. Lewis & Son, Grocers had gone out of business by this time, and Harold was driving the delivery van for a commercial laundry, a job he would hold for several years. The couple's first child was born on July 24th, 1930, and they named her Elizabeth Carmel, surely to honor Jessie's mother and youngest sister. The family always called her Betty.

Apartment living in the downtown neighborhood of a small city in 1930 on a workingman's wages might not seem comfortable compared to the conveniences and luxuries we have now, but it was probably not so bad for the times. Unfortunately, as the Great Depression set in, even this level of comfort would not last. When it began to be clear that the economic downturn would not be over soon, saving money had to become an obsession for almost everyone. There is no way of knowing now the exact details of the financial circumstances of this young couple, but we do know that from 1929 to 1932 overall weekly earnings across the country went down between thirteen and forty-five percent in most industries.[97] This was due to wage cuts even though many people were still working fifty or sixty hours per week. It is a good guess that Harold experienced a significant cut in wages about this time, though he may have felt lucky still just to have a steady job. It is not surprising that Harold and Jessie might have decided that in order to provide for their other needs, rent was one expense they could no longer afford.

I don't know the exact month, but it was sometime around 1931, and certainly no later than 1932, that Harold decided to build a small structure on part of his father's land on a hillside location just outside the southeastern corner of the City of Binghamton with the goal that the family could live there rent-free. The word "cottage" sounds too cozy, and though honest, it is uncomfortable to call it a "shanty", so let's just use here the term "small house". The best anyone can remember now, the internal dimensions of this single-story house were about twelve by fifteen feet.[98] It was rather roughly constructed, probably of rough lumber and other materials that

---

97 See Wolman, Leo, 1933 in the bibliography.

98 At first blush a twelve-foot width seems too small for a house to be divided into rooms, but having lived in houses in Japan, I am sure it is not. Harold later added an additional five-section out back.

were available for little or no cost, and so it was completely uninsulated and quite drafty. It was a limited protection against the cold of Binghamton winters, especially when strong winds blew unimpeded across the valley to strike this north-facing hillside. There were then fewer than five other dwellings this far up or higher on this hillside, but the small house was directly across the road from the home of Harold's parents, youngest siblings, and handicapped uncle. It was on a dead-end side road. It was not altogether inconvenient in the sense that it was only about two and a half miles from there down to the center of Binghamton, and in those days, one would have passed relatively few houses for the first mile or more.[99]

The amenities in nearly all homes then were much less than we have now, but in this little house they were particularly basic. Fuel for cooking, heating in winter, and warming water for bathing and cleaning was coal and wood. Being close to northeastern Pennsylvania, coal in Binghamton of course always meant anthracite.[100] In addition to the cooking stove in the kitchen, there was a small potbellied stove in the living room for use in the colder months. Even with these, it was sometimes hard to keep the house warm. At first, electrical power was out of the question. Power lines did not yet extend that far up the hillside from inside the city. Sometime around 1936, power lines did make it up the hill, but even then, the connection was only made to Harold's parents' house and not over to the little house. Harold corrected this situation by attaching a wire to the main line at his parents' house and extending it across the road on his own. To keep the wire from drooping too much, he propped it up with forked poles cut from saplings in the same manner once commonly used for propping up clotheslines. The wire was still only about eight feet above the road surface. There was no reason for large trucks to go up that dead-end road in those days, and I suppose that they could just take the hay wagon around another way. This didn't mean they had many electrical appliances to use, but it did make a radio possible as well as electric light and a washing machine. Even after they had electricity, they did not get a refrigerator until 1943 when they got the used one when Dick and Ella broke up. Until then, Harold brought home a block of ice when needed for the icebox.

One of the more surprising issues was water sources. I am not naïve about earlier living conditions and have always been well acquainted with houses without running water from stays at my maternal grandparents' farm in Pennsylvania. I do know that getting household water by means of a handpump was still common, especially in rural locations. And even today in many parts of the world, people must

---

99 Today there are literally about one hundred times as many people living on that hillside as there were in 1930. For most of my childhood I lived there on "the Hill", as we called it, within one hundred yards of my grandfather's house.

100 At the beginning of the 19th Century no one knew how to use anthracite effectively until it was discovered that it would burn well provided it sat atop a grate of some kind to allow enough oxygen from beneath. When used in this way, it was cleaner burning than the bituminous coal that much of the rest of the world had to use. When I first examined anthracite in our coal bin as a small child, I remember thinking it was so hard and shiny that it seemed more like black glass than something that would burn, not like the dirty soft coal I heard about from stories. Naturally, homeowners also had to keep a supply of kindling wood on hand in a coal-fueled house.

go outside their homes to get access to a communal well. But in that neighborhood at that time, there were no wells at all. It was not a matter of just having to pump by hand or going outside to use a public well. It wasn't all bad since George and Alida's house across the road had a system for collecting rainwater off the roof into a huge cistern under the back porch, with a handpump for moving the stored water from cistern to Alida's kitchen. It was a relatively minor inconvenience for the household of Harold and Jessie to have to buckets across and into the bigger house to be supplied with water for drinking and cooking. The problem was that the cistern would be quickly depleted if both households used it as their water source for washing and bathing as well. That meant the creek had to be the source for the greywater needs of both households. If a creek ran somewhere near their doorsteps, this would not seem so inconvenient, but it did not. Getting water on laundry day or at other times when large quantities were needed meant carrying large buckets or milk cans a tenth of a mile down a steep road, and then scrambling down a very steep bank to a creek bed about fifteen feet below the road level. After scooping water out of that small stream, obviously, the hardest part was carrying the heavy buckets all the way back up to the house. My Great-grandmother Alida, then in her sixties, was a remarkably strong woman. I wasn't there to witness it, but I am told that on washing day she would routinely carry two milk cans filled with water up the steep road at the same time, one in each hand, each weighing about eighty pounds. It is quite understandable that Jessie wasn't up for that and had to get help when it came to fetching water.

Another difficulty was that Jessie was still a city girl in most respects. It is true that young Jessie loved hiking, swimming, hay rides, and being outdoors in general, life on a small farm still wasn't something she was prepared for. Besides being fearful of creatures like snakes, she had a general phobia of cattle, even gentle old family cows. It seems that Jessie made a good effort to adapt to these living conditions, but she couldn't be blamed if she felt she had already suffered too many hardships in her childhood, and this was like going from bad to worse in terms of the basic struggle of daily life.

The physical hardships of their life and the emotional strain of depression-era family finances would naturally put a strain on any marriage, but religious and cultural challenges might have been even more formidable for the young couple. Harold and Jessie may have had a carefree attitude about differences in the backgrounds, but that doesn't mean these wouldn't eventually catch up with them. If they had continued living in apartments some distance away from other family members, the difficulties might not have become so pronounced, but once Jessie was living just across from her in-laws, differences must have come more readily to the surface. In addition to being of differing faith traditions, the generational differences in attitudes about morality, coming as they were out of a decade of revolutionary social changes which were the 1920s, must have been significant. There were parallels between Jessie's situation of living next door to in-laws and that of her father a generation earlier when William and Elizabeth as a young couple lived in Coal Township in a cottage adjacent to Elizabeth's parents' house. Very likely, George and Alida at most times made an effort to get along with their daughter-in-law, and vice versa, but even so, the differences in their belief systems must have made harmony more difficult and added substantially to the stress of their lives and on the marriage. Surely, Harold felt a strain as well, as the one between the two sides.

We should keep in mind too that for most of the 1930s Jessie was largely on her own in terms of connections to her family of origin. As far as I can determine, for most of the depression years, her only sibling living in the Binghamton area was Bill, and she may not have seen him very often. At least at times, she must have felt cut off from her roots and wishing she had more sources of moral support.

Jessie and Harold had probably not moved into the little house before Betty came along, but their other three children were born there. Their second child arrived on January 5th, 1934, and they named her Jean Ann. Their third was my father, Harold Jr., born January 15th, 1936. It wouldn't be until several years later, after his kid sister was born, that "Bub" would become his nickname within the family. The fourth child, Amy Louise, would be born March 31st, 1943, in the middle of the war years and a few months before the family would move into a much larger and more comfortable house in the city. I wonder if the first and middle names of Jean and Amy were inspired by some of Jessie's favorite stories since we do not find similar names in either hers or Harold's family histories.

In the midst of the hard life that they endured during the depression, the family did have happy memories too. We humans come programmed in such a way that we sometimes remember even our struggles in fond ways. I am told that on the worst days of winter, when the temperature outside was below zero on the Fahrenheit scale, and the northwesterly winds were blasting against the drafty little house, my grandmother would open the dampers on the potbellied stove and stoke it to make it so hot it glowed cherry red. Then she and the children would sit around the stove wrapped in blankets while she read them stories from her numerous books.

We know from her narrative that Jessie enjoyed spending time outdoors, so it is not surprising that pattern continued into adulthood. Most winters there was plenty of snow on the ground, and their hillside location was ideal for sledding. It became a frequent activity for Jessie and her children on the winter days when it was not so cold. This was still an era when women always wore dresses or skirts in public, but Jessie was not shy about borrowing a pair of her husband's trousers when that was more practical, and of course she and the children would be bundled up well against the cold. There were very few houses and next to no car traffic then on that whole hillside, so the roadways were just as much fair game for sledding as my great-grandfather's fields were. When Harold Jr. was a toddler, Jessie would lie on her tummy on a sled, have him sit on her back, and they would ride on the roads that way for the nearly half mile down to Conklin Avenue.

There were plenty of things to do in the summer months as well. In addition to helping with the farm chores and simply playing outside in the way children naturally do everywhere, they could hike in the woods or along the creek. Shoes cost money, and during the war years they were rationed as well, so there was no sense in unnecessarily wearing them out. The kids went barefoot all summer and put on shoes and socks again only in September when it was time to go back to school.

152

And the family was probably eating healthier and tastier food than they would have in the city. Food preservation technology had improved by the 1930s, but was not as advanced as today, and quality standards were not as uniform, so store-bought food might not always be as wholesome as what we expect now. It was still generally true then that country people ate more wholesome food than city people, a clear advantage of living on a small farm. Even if you didn't produce sufficient cash crops to make a livelihood out of it, your family could at least eat better, and eat quite well even when the economy was bad. But, of course, there was a lot of work involved. The family aided in George and Alida's farming efforts, especially as the children got old enough to help substantially with the chores. In addition to the obvious vegetable garden, there was a family cow, and some years they raised a pair of pigs for slaughter in the fall. And for both eggs and meat, there were so many chickens that my father had the luxury of complaining that he was sick of eating chicken all the time. In the early years, the cow was just kept in a small shed, which meant that the hay for the winter months had to be stacked outside. Years later, George added a hay mow, so it became more like what could be called an actual barn. Balers were not yet common, so we are speaking here of loose hay. Harold Jr. did learn well from his grandfather how to make a proper outdoor haystack, and he helped care for the cow and the chickens, but he never quite got the knack of milking well by hand.

Based on the stories many in my generation have heard, it is probably fair to assume that Jessie was the main disciplinarian with the children. Harold had sometimes been severely punished by his parents when he was a boy, even horsewhipping on at least one occasion. But he was of such an easygoing character and had such a laissez-faire approach to childrearing that it just did not come natural to him to mete out corporal punishments much at all to his own children. Unlike Jessie's father, Harold did not have the kind of job that kept him away from home for days at a time, but most jobs at that time required more than a forty-hour work week, so it is probably true that he was home a little less of the time that would be typical of dads today. It also seems fair based on stories we have heard to assume that Harold Jr. was the one most pampered by his mother at least until his baby sister was born seven years later. It might have come natural to Jessie to make a special fuss over the one who was then the youngest as well as being the only boy.

We know that neither Harold nor Jessie came out of the Roaring Twenties with a particularly spiritual mindset, and they were not inclined toward formal religious observance to any large degree. Therefore, even though the one had been raised Protestant and the other Catholic, this did not become a particularly significant issue at first in how to raise the children. There were no churches of any type particularly close by anyway, so there was even less reason to worry about it. For some years the young family did not attend church on a regular basis. George, Alida, and Harold's only sister, Arlene, on the other hand, took spiritual matters very seriously. George found he was drawn to the preaching an Alliance church on the North Side, nearly four miles away. He had driven horse-drawn vehicles his whole life[101] and never learned to

---

[101] This included the delivery van he drove for his grocery stores, drawn by his standardbred gelding, Midget, who had been retired from harness racing.

operate a motor vehicle. Harold had access to a car and made his living as a driver, so obviously the best way to get across town to the church every Sunday was to have him drive his parents and sister there.[102] Auntie Arlene was never one to hold back when it came to giving advice, and soon she was lecturing her older brother. If he was driving all the way to the church anyway, why didn't he care for the souls of his children enough to take them along for church and Sunday school as well? That is how Harold Jr. and his older sisters got their first formal religious training according to the doctrines of the Alliance denomination. Jessie acquiesced to the Protestant ethos surrounding her for the sake of getting along, but never converted to it despite pressure from both her father-in-law and her eldest daughter, Betty, who quite a spiritual little girl.

By 1940, the country was coming out of the worst of the Great Depression, and though the war years would bring their own set of hardships, people at least had more opportunities economically. It appears that Harold, thirty-five years old in that year, was still working for the laundry company, though perhaps no longer primarily as a driver. For a fifty-hour work week his wages provided him with an annual income of just about one thousand dollars. Fifty-eight-year-old George was working nearly the same number of hours in the bakery, and his income was also about one thousand. These were about average earnings among grown men in their neighborhood who held full-time jobs. I have heard that the owner of the laundry company was of less than savory character, but despite his moral failings, he apparently ran his business reasonably well and paid wages on time. Harold might have preferred a different job for any number of reasons, but he had little choice but to stick with a steady job during the depression years. George and Alida's house and lands were valued at $1800 according to the 1940 census, and Harold and Jessie were continuing to live rent-free in the little house on part of that land. Though they probably felt they were on a little bit more solid ground financially than they had in the preceding years, they were still not ready to move into anything more modern or spacious.

When America entered the war, more opportunities opened. Harold was of the in-between generation—far too young to fight in World War I, and a little too old to join the military when World War II broke out. So, the family of Harold and Jessie could stay together during the war. But like all Americans then, they were participating in the war effort in a variety of other ways. Construction of Air Force Plant #59 on a thirty-acre site in a part of Johnson City known as Westover began in 1942. Harold was able finally to quit his job with the laundry company and get a construction job there with The Defense Plant Corporation. This was for the quickly constructed 600,000-square-foot factory that later generations in the area knew as the GE Plant. Later still it was occupied by Lockheed-Martin and BAE, before it was finally demolished after the major flood of 2011. But from 1942 to 1945, Remington-Rand occupied it and

---

102 At one point, Harold bought a Pierce-Arrow seven-passenger touring sedan, specifically so he would be able to transport all these family members to church and for visits to relatives. Surely, it was a used one, since Pierce-Arrows were among the most expensive luxury cars in their time. Perhaps he got a bargain from a previously wealthy person who lost big in the stock market crash.

produced aluminum aircraft propellers for war planes there.

As the construction was nearing completion in 1942, Harold was able to land a job with Stowe Manufacturing Co. in Binghamton. This company, established in Binghamton in 1875, specialized in machines using flexible shaft technology, and during World War II, they made cables and other products for the war effort. It may have been good, steady work, but the downside in July of 1943 when Harold suffered a serious workplace injury there. A large spool of cable fell on his foot. At the hospital they amputated his big toe and part of the next toe on one of his feet, and he was laid up for a while in the little house. He was awarded five-hundred dollars compensation for this injury. Jessie, Harold, and their children had endured life in the little house for about a dozen years. They had longed for a house in the city with a few more modern conveniences and especially with more spacious living arrangements. As it turned out, five-hundred dollars was just the right amount for making a down payment on such a house. Just a few months later, they had secured the mortgage, completed the purchase, and were moving into a large, pleasant house on Emmett Street at the corner with Eldridge Street, just past the railroad tracks in the near North Side. Once he recovered, Harold was able to go back to work at Stowe, and at some point, Jessie got a job at a nearby ice cream parlor to help with expenses, including certainly the mortgage payments.

Compared to what they were accustomed to, the house was luxurious, and the entire family was overjoyed with the move. Harold and Jessie put effort into renovating the place to make the house still better. Even in terms of convenience it was a big improvement. Jean and Harold Jr. could attend Thomas Edison, which was then the public elementary school for the neighborhood located near the corner of Robinson and Chenango Streets, less than a quarter mile away. This was much closer than how far they had had to walk just to catch the bus to Julius Rogers, and what is more they didn't have to walk uphill on the way home. They could even come home for lunch. Betty was then junior high school age, and East Junior was less than a fifteen-minute walk. There were at least two small groceries within a three-minute walk. Even if they chose to walk to the center of Downtown, that was only about a mile. With so many more people living close by, the children could form a more expansive network of friends their same age, and on Halloween Jean and Harold Jr. had the experience for the first time of going trick-or-treating.

A particularly significant factor was that St. Paul's Church was also within a few minutes' walk, and Jessie apparently felt this was the right time and the right opportunity to reassert her Catholic heritage in her family. She saw to it that Betty, Jean, and Harold Jr. attended there and studied their catechism. The children were at least a little confused. This has to remind us of the folk song, "The Orange and the Green". Obviously, the situation was not an exact fit in the sense that their father had no heritage associated with Ulster, and more to the point, that song is too light-hearted for expressing their exact situation. But it was indeed the sort of "mix-up" the song describes. There was a parochial school right there as well, but, given how much Jessie hated her experiences at the Catholic school in Ithaca, sending her children to a Catholic school was not an option she considered.

It was about this time that Harold Jr. was given the nickname "Bub", which as the story goes was based on Amy's attempt when she was a toddler to pronounce the word "Brother". From that point on, none of his closest family members ever referred to him as anything other than Bub, and since that is less cumbersome than Harold Jr., I will use that here as well.

Surely, the family of Harold and Jessie celebrated the same sense of joy and relief that most Americans did at the end of the war, but the most significant immediate practical change in their daily lives was that Harold had a change of employers. There were two factors at play for why he could no longer continue at Stowe Manufacturing. First, most of the company's defense contracts were cancelled. Second, both by law and by custom, returning GIs were given priority to be rehired into their old jobs. It was inevitable that Stowe would lay off most of the employees hired during the war. Once again, solid work was hard to come by, and Harold may have been stuck doing odd jobs for a while. But it was apparently not too much later that he was hired by Spaulding Bakery,[103] likely with some influence from his father, who had been working there for over a decade and a half by then. George would continue working there until he retired, which I believe was about 1948 when he was about sixty-six years old. Harold would continue to hold his job there for several years after that.

It was not long after the war that Jessie's youngest brother, Dick, came to stay with Harold and Jessie's family for an extended period at the Emmett Street house. Though Dick would still have been in his twenties, his health had declined due to the horrendous period on the life raft. Betty, Jean, and Bub were in their teens or preteen years, and naturally formed a special bond with their Uncle Dick. They would be particularly saddened to learn of his loss a few years later. Later in life, several decades after the divorce, my grandmother once told me that one of the things she had to give my grandfather credit for was his exceptional hospitality toward her family. Harold's easygoing nature was such that he never begrudged her siblings or even her father anything they asked for, and she wanted me to know that. The stay by Dick might have been one example she was thinking of. During the first few years after the war, Harold did modifications to the house such that the upstairs could be used as a separate apartment. A family of returning GIs lived there. The wife as well as the husband had served in the military during the war, and they had a small child at that time about the same age as Amy. Overall, it was a busy household, and some aspects of the immediate postwar period must have been cheerful.

---

103 Spaulding (not to be confused with the still existing Kentucky bakery with the same name) started small in 1896, selling a few loaves of bread per day baked by Mrs. Spaulding in her home on the South Side, but within a few decades it became a major regional producer of baked goods, primarily bread and donuts. They continued to be based in Binghamton, but also had large bakeries in several other towns and a distribution region that included virtually all of eastern and central New York State and eastern Pennsylvania. Some old-timers remember the delicious aroma halfway along on Exchange Street as they headed toward the center of the city. Among their best loved products were Country Squire Bread and Spaulding Krullers. After Spaulding filed for bankruptcy in 1982, long-term rival, Williamsport-based Stroehmann, bought the Spaulding Kruller brand name, but unfortunately, not the recipe, and locals claim the krullers were never the same.

156

But one of the most unhappy chapters in the whole story came in 1947, culminating in the divorce of Harold and Jessie in October of that year. It would be inappropriate here even to attempt a detailed diagnosis of the breakdown of the marriage, first because it would be ugly to read about, and second because it would involve excessive speculation on my part. Third parties never understand on a detailed level what is going on in someone else's marriage, and this is all the more true in a case that is two generations removed. I will only go so far as to say that the clues I have indicate that the story may have involved frigidity, followed by serial infidelities, followed by revenge infidelity. Enough said on that subject.[104]

Besides the rapid completion of the formal divorce proceedings, the practical result was that Jessie quite suddenly left the household. I do not know the exact sequence of events, but not long after she was cohabiting with the new man in her life, Anthony Joseph Raimondi (1922-1986). A year and a half later, in April of 1949, they had their first child, my aunt, Mary Evelyn Raimondi. Jessie was then thirty-seven, and Tony was almost exactly eleven years younger.[105] They may have been living in other locations in Binghamton previously, but at least by 1950, Tony, Jessie, and baby Mary were living in a large apartment building then at 60 Susquehanna Street. This is very close to where the Binghamton YMCA is now located, a few dozen yards away from the building where Jessie had lived twenty years earlier. The official records indicate that Jessie and Tony were wed in August of 1950 in the Borough of Susquehanna. It is not clear whether it was a civil or church wedding, and the reason for crossing over the state line to marry in Pennsylvania is also unclear. Information about Jessie's divorce in New York State is recorded accurately on the Pennsylvania marriage license, and the only intentional falsehood is that Jessie fudged her age a little, claiming to be thirty-four, no doubt to decrease the apparent magnitude of the age difference.

Tony was born in Williamsport to parents who arrived from Italy several years earlier. Philip and Mary Raimondi must have been a typical hardworking immigrant couple well on their way in their pursuit of the American dream. Philip (Filipo in many of the records) had a job in a foundry, and they seem to have owned rental properties as well as their own home in central Williamsport. Like most families during the depression, they experienced a downturn in their fortunes. Shortly after Mary died of tuberculosis in December of 1939, Philip along with Tony and his siblings moved to Binghamton. Tony and his siblings held a variety of occupations there, and Tony

---

104 Though divorce was less common in the past than it was in recent generations, it was far from rare even at the time of Jessie's childhood. By 1915, one in seven American marriages ended in divorce. (See especially Schlereth's *Victorian America*, pp. 280-281.) It is always a tragic outcome, but not an unusual one that out of the nine Davenport siblings' first marriages, two—Jessie's and Dick's—ended in divorce. On the Lewis side even a generation earlier, divorce was a part of the family history. Harold's father, George, had four siblings. Only two of them ever married. In both cases, those first marriages ended in divorce, certainly a high percentage for the times.

105 It is perhaps a strange thought, but one that adds perspective to consider that when Jessie married Harold, Tony was still a six-year-old getting ready to start first or second grade in a Williamsport school.

served in the army in World War II. By the time he married Jessie, Tony was sometimes a warehouseman and sometimes worked construction.

By 1952, Tony, Jessie, and their toddler daughter, Mary, had moved from Susquehanna Street to Pearne Street on the North Side. This was to a house on a part of that street that has since been torn up to make room for a large apartment complex. Tony then had a steady job as a custodian. In November of 1953, they had their second child, Tony Joe Raimondi, Jr. He was less than three years older than I and seemed more like a cousin than an uncle when we were growing up.[106] Years later, we got to know him well when my father took us to visit Grandma Jessie. He was a fun-loving kid, and quite good at luring my brothers and me into his mischief-making schemes. We were always surprised how lax his mother was in disciplining him compared to how strict our parents were with us. He had a talent for working with mechanical and electrical devices and enjoyed tinkering with them. Years earlier than that, in 1957, when I was about one year old, my parents took an apartment on Pearne Street, immediately adjacent to that occupied by my grandmother, Tony, and little Mary and Tony Joe Jr. We stayed there only for a matter of months before moving to an apartment elsewhere, but it was during this time that my mother got to know her mother-in-law quite well and formed a bond to some degree. Of course, I was too young to remember any of this, but my mother later talked about this period in our lives quite often.

By 1959, Tony and Jessie bought a house on Linden Street further up on the North Side. Jessie would live there for the rest of her life. I don't believe I ever saw my grandmother anyplace other than within those four walls. I do not know if it was ever officially diagnosed as such, but in her later years my grandmother seemed to suffer from agoraphobia. I believe that Mary, and sometimes Tony Joe Jr., ran all her errands for her, and she never had to leave the house. I also remember the dog she had for many years there—a medium-sized mongrel. Many dogs bark when strangers approach their house, and we were all well acquainted with that, but that dog barked so persistently and in such a viciously threatening way that it was quite remarkable. Grandma always had to shut it up in one of the bedrooms whenever anyone came to visit her.

During the early days there, Tony Sr, was usually around, and during our occasional visits, he and my father would always find interesting topics to converse on. I remember, for example, that for a while Tony was taking judo lessons. They both enjoyed it when he demonstrated some of the moves to my dad. Of course, they weren't really that far apart in age. In fact, Tony apparently wanted to emphasize that he was still young. My brothers and I were taken aside and coached that we should be careful never to refer to him as a grandfather. I restate my intention always to avoid thinking I know much about what is happening in other people's marriages, but I will go as far as noting that there were hints that the marriage of Jessie was not entirely peaceful. Tony Joe Jr. explained to my brothers and me once that the reason a lot of the knick-knacks in the house had been broken and glued back together was that his

---

106 My father enjoyed confusing people by explaining that he had "a half-brother and three and a half sisters".

158

parents tended to throw things around when they quarreled. Tony wasn't around most times when I visited in later years, and Grandma Jessie hinted that they had decided to live mostly apart. Tony was sixty-four when he died in December of 1986. He is buried in Calvary Cemetery on the hillside in Johnson City with a stone that emphasizes his army service in the war. Jessie was cremated when she died in 2000.

The story would be incomplete if I were to omit any discussion of the emotional impact in the family, no matter how difficult it is to write about. It is obviously a topic of great subjectivity, and I am sure that even my best efforts to describe it fairly, I still might be at fault for missing the mark.

Abandonment is a potent word that should not be used too casually, but it is a word that is at least hinted at across three generations of Davenports. We might remember that when James Davenport left Shamokin in about 1911 to move across the state to McDonald, Pennsylvania, it is possible to argue that he was abandoning his family. But that characterization is at least a bit of a stretch. His wife had been dead for five years and their youngest child was at least seventeen. She was nearly a grown woman, and furthermore had other relatives, important people in the community no less, looking out for her. His only other surviving child was a son in his late twenties, William, with already four children of his own.

We also noted earlier that it would not be quite such a stretch to use the label of abandonment a generation later when William Davenport moved from Binghamton back to Scranton in early 1930, within a few months of when his wife died. At the time, he had six unmarried children who ranged in ages from twenty-two down to ten. There were no older relatives in the same community or with whom the children would have felt a close bond at that point. It was a case where the older unmarried children, just into adulthood themselves, were left to care for their younger siblings the best they could, which indeed makes it a good case for claiming that William abandoned them. But as also noted earlier, we do not know all the circumstances and should be a little circumspect in how we apply the word "abandonment".

One more generation on, how should we view Jessie's departure from the home of her children and husband in 1947? Is it fair to call this abandonment? The circumstances are even more difficult to sort out objectively, and they are messy in a way that I would prefer not to know them all anyway. Instead, I will simply consider what my perception is of how her children viewed the question. Recently I asked the question outright to one of my aunts, "Is it fair to say that when your mother left, she was abandoning your family?" It is not easy to ask this kind of question such that it comes across in a completely unprejudiced way. But my rapport with my aunt is such that she knew that I had no preconceived expectation of whether the answer should be "yes" or "no". Her reply was a bit roundabout, but nonetheless clearly in the affirmative. Of the four siblings, I have the least sense of what Betty thought on this question. She was seventeen at the time, already moving into the adult phase of her life, and she would marry the next year. As for the other three: Jean, Bub, and Amy were thirteen, eleven, and four, respectively, and they experienced their mother's abrupt departure in a raw way. The sense of confusion over where to place the blame made it all the worse, as is always true for young children in a family breaking apart.

In discussions with my aunts and cousins, when the subject of Grandma Jessie comes up, a feeling often expressed is that aside from the legacy of her departure itself, much of the lingering resentment is over the long-term aftermath. Jessie often gave evidence of caring much less than she might have about the offspring from her first marriage. Jessie routinely forgot the birthdays of her first set of children, even when they visited on the day. One of my aunts told me of taking her newborn first child to show to her mother. She left with the feeling that Jessie had in no way welcomed the experience. There was understandable pain in my aunt's voice when she said, "Mother didn't even want to hold her." This kind of experience is where the concept started that Jessie cared more for her doll collection than she did for actual children.

Grandma probably did not think of all grandchildren in just the same way. In my case, I did not feel discrimination against me, and she often seemed interested in what I thought, but her treatment toward me might not have been exactly what is expected of a grandmother either. Maybe the kind of connection we had was a subtle mix of mutual awkwardness and mutual curiosity.

Incidentally, some family members compare Jessie's apparent lack of caring later in her life to a similar attitude in her father. During his senior years, William came back to interact more with his children and met some of his grandchildren for the first time. And yet, he gave no evidence of being truly interested in them as people or caring about them. His universally negative reputation in the family may have more to do with his attitude later in life than any of his acts when he was younger.

Naturally, life changed for Harold and the children in a variety of other ways. The house in the city was sold, and the family moved back up on "the Hill", not to the little house this time, but rather, into the house with Harold's parents, thus, making it a three-generation household. Selling the house might have been primarily for financial reasons, but there may have been other motivations for the move as well. George was approaching retirement age and Alida, as the grandmother, could be an adult female presence in the daily lives of the children. The family was again living a rural lifestyle and helping with the farm chores. Harold continued to work for Spaulding Bakery. He could be at home a little more than would have been possible in the past, since the forty-hour work week had become the norm for many wage earners in America. The children officially transferred out of the Binghamton City school system. Bub would be going back to the little Julius Rogers School in Conklin, and Amy would go there as well when she was old enough. At the secondary level, it didn't matter so much in practical terms because the Susquehanna Valley School District had not yet built its own junior high and high schools, and instead was paying the city district tuition to allow their students to attend East Junior and North High. A high school was finally built just in time for my Aunt Amy. She was in the very first graduating class of SVHS in 1962 and had some of the same teachers I had there twelve years later.

Obviously, each family member had to make a variety of different adjustments to their new life, some major and some minor, and some must have been easier than others. The grandparents' house was large compared to the little one they had once lived in across the road, "large" here is only a relative term, and there was quite a houseful at first. George's never-married older brother had already been living with the George and Alida since the 1930s when George's parents died. Uncle Warney was mentally handicapped and by then was an exceptionally cantankerous man in his seventies. He became a less-than-ideal roommate for both Harold and Bub who had to share a bedroom with him.

Perhaps the largest challenge though was that Arlene, Harold's only sister, and her husband were also living there at the time. She had married the West Virginian Lee Gibson near the end of the war in Texas where he was stationed with the army at the time. They had decided to move to Binghamton and in with her parents after Uncle Lee was discharged, and he had a job as a mail and freight handler at the Binghamton railroad depot. To understand the scope of this as a problem, it is necessary to know something about Auntie Arlene.[107] She was a very religious woman and full of good intentions, but for those very reasons she was an insufferable menace throughout her life. Among other issues, despite never having children of her own, she viewed herself as the ultimate authority on the science of childrearing, and she never was one to hold back in imparting her wisdom to others. She simply didn't understand that her enthusiastic, but unwelcomed, efforts to guide and discipline her older brother's children at this time were excessive interference. And this was in addition to the problem of overcrowding. They soon were able to fix up a room where Arlene and Lee could sleep downstairs that at least relieved slightly the congestion in the small upstairs bedrooms. And over the next year or so, Uncle Lee was able to build a house out back from George and Alida's, but that was still too close for complete relief from Auntie Arlene's meddling.

On a brighter note, the children had the opportunity to form a closer bond with their grandparents. One of the many happy memories they have is coming home from school to a house filled with the smell of their grandmother's bread and rolls just coming out of the oven. The youngest child, Amy, was still small when the family moved into the household of her grandparents, and she stayed there the longest. She still remembers her grandfather with extraordinary fondness. With their mother's departure, the children mostly left the Catholic elements of their upbringing behind. They drifted back toward Evangelical Protestantism, though some became more fully committed to it than others.

While acknowledging that anything I think I know about their lives then is strictly second-hand knowledge, some points come through quite clearly from the oft-repeated stories I have heard. One of the general patterns was that, except for Auntie Arlene's efforts, discipline was quite lax. As already mentioned, Harold, despite his own strict upbringing, grew up to be a man whose natural tendency was to be easygoing, fun-loving, and nonjudgmental in most circumstances. The best I can tell, he had a rather laissez-faire style of parenting. George and Alida strove as always for high moral standards, but with the wisdom of age and the natural indulgency of grandparents, they were no longer strict disciplinarians either. The children, especially

---

107 She was the only relative I knew who preferred to be called "Auntie" rather than "Aunt".

Bub as the only boy, could feel quite free to do as they pleased, and even safety was not always the highest concern. Bub was restless. He did continue his schooling and did hold down part-time jobs, but he also spent some of his time engaged in mischief. He and his friends went in for wild antics, some involving firearm and some involving motor vehicles long before they were old enough to have drivers' licenses—nothing criminal, of course, but certainly bending the rules a bit. Bub also had a travel lust and by the age of fourteen he was already hitchhiking all over the northeastern United States, sometimes with friends and sometimes entirely on his own.

Life went on for Jessie's first family. Eldest daughter, Betty, married in December of 1948 at the age of eighteen. Jean was still sixteen when she married in June of 1950. Bub married in 1955, two months after his high school graduation. Youngest child, Amy, was the only one to break out of the pattern of marrying as a teen. She married in June of 1967 at the age of twenty-four. Of these four marriages, only Betty's would end in divorce, and that would be much later. Over the course of a few decades, Betty and Phil DeGroat would have four sons; Jean and Leonard Baker had four daughters and one son; Bub and his wife Ethel Jane had two daughters and four sons; and Amy and Frank Komorny had two daughters, one lost in a tragedy. Thus, there were in total seventeen grandchildren from Jessie's first marriage, and there would later be many great-grandchildren and beyond.

It was three and a half years after the divorce that Harold remarried. The previous fall, one of Harold's younger brothers married the woman who had been a live-in maid in the grand home of George W. Johnson, who by that time was chairman of the board of Endicott-Johnson Shoe Company. At that wedding, Harold met Mabel Dailey, who was the live-in cook in the same household. Mabel grew up on a large farm in the still very rural and sparsely populated Farmington Township in Tioga County, Pennsylvania. The roots of the Dailey family go back to early colonial times in Rhode Island, and they had been among the first families to settle and start farming in Tioga County. After a courtship of only a few months, Harold and Mabel married in a church in Conklin in March of 1951. He was forty-five at the time and she was thirty-five. Mabel never had children of her own. She is justly remembered as a devoted and caring stepmom and step-grandmother. Betty and Jean had already married, but Bub at fifteen and Amy at eight were still at home. Mabel also faithfully aided in the care of Harold's aging parents and uncle. Alida passed away in 1958, George in 1962, and Warney in 1963. Harold and Mabel were an especially loving couple and were devoted to each other until Harold's death just after his ninety-eighth birthday in March of 2003. Mabel died almost exactly one year later.

If you have gone to the trouble to read all or parts of this book, I pray that you got out of it some of what I got from the effort of putting it together. This would include a little better general understanding than before of what small-town American life was like for someone growing up a century ago. It might also include a greater respect for how fascinating and devilishly complex the family histories are that lead to us mongrel Americans. Despite the myths in the family that my grandmother was of entirely Irish roots, and as such her ancestors were always oppressed and impoverished, the real story was much more complex than that.   Maybe the biggest lesson of all that comes from the effort is a deeper appreciation of the overwhelming complexity and near unpredictability of the connections between cause and effect in the cycle of life.   We make life-altering decisions largely on the basis of what we have experienced already in our lives, and the outcome of those decisions is what determines the experiences the next generation will have.

Hal Lewis
Berkshire, New York
March 2023

Topical Bibliography

Anthracite Mining:

Bartoletti, Susan Campbell, *Growing Up in Coal Country*, Clarion Books, 1999.

Fitzgerald, John, *Dirty Mines: Coal Mining in Pennsylvania,* Createspace Independent Publishing Platform, 2015.

Leonard, Joseph W., III, *Anthracite Roots: Generations of Coal Mining in Schuykill County, Pennsylvania,* The History Press, 2005.

Miller, Donald L. and Richard E. Sharpless, *The Kingdom of Coal: Work, Enterprise and Ethnic Communities in the Mine Fields,* 1985.

Richards, John Stuart, *Early Coal Mining in the Anthracite Region,* Arcadia Publishing, 2002.

Scotney, John, *Ireland - Culture Smart: The Essential Guide to Customs and Culture,* Kuperard, 2016.

Early Twentieth Century History:

Allen, Frederick Lewis, *Only Yesterday: An Informal History of the 1920s,* Perennial Classics, 2000 (based on 1931 edition).

Allen, Frederick Lewis, *Since Yesterday: The 1930s in America,* Perennial Library, 1972 (based on 1940 edition).

Captivating History, *The Roaring Twenties,* CreateSpace Independent Publishing Platform, 2018.

Erbsen, Wayne, *Manners and Morals of Victorian America,* Native Ground Books & Music Publishers, 2009

Gilbert, Martin, *History of the Twentieth Century Volume I: 1900-1933,* Harper Perennial, 2001.

Green, Harvey, *The Uncertainties of Everyday Life: 1915-1945,* Harper-Collins, 1992.

Kyvig, David E., *Daily Life in the United States 1920-1940,* Ivan R. Dee, 2004.

McCutheon, Marc, *The Writer's Guide to Everyday Life from Prohibition through World War II,* Writer's Digest Books, 1995.

Schlereth, Thomas J., *Victorian America: Transformations in Everyday Life 1876-1915*, Harper Perennial, 1992.

Wolman, Leo, "Wages During the Depression", *Bulletin of the National Bureau of Economic Research*, May 1, 1933.

Irish-American culture:

Coffey, Michael, *The Irish in America*, Hyperion, 1997.

Dolan, Jay P., *The Irish-Americans: A History*, Bloomsbury Press, 2008.

Maguire, John Francis, *The Irish in America*, Forgotten Books, (original 1873) 2017 reprint.

McNally, Frank, *Xenophobe's Guide to the Irish*, Oval Books, 2008.

O'Donnell, Edward T., *1001 Things Everyone Should Know about Irish American History*, Gramercy, 2006.

Osborne-McKnight, Juliene, *The Story We Carry in Our Bones: Irish History for Americans*, Pelican Publishing, 2015.

Szabados, Stephen, *Irish Immigration to America*, Independently Published, 2021.

Literature of John O'Hara (examples):

O'Hara, John, *Appointment is Samara*, Penguin Classics Deluxe Edition, 2013.

O'Hara, John, (ed. Frank MacShane), *Collected Stories of John O'Hara*, Random House, 1985.

Local history, Scranton:

Flanagan, Thomas F., *Northern Electric Railway: Scranton, Montrose and Binghamton RR Co.*, B. Rohrbeck Traction Publications, 1980.

Kashuba, Cheryl A., *A Brief History of Scranton, Pennsylvania*, The History Press, 2009.

Stoddard, Dwight James, *Prominent Men: Scranton and Vicinity*, Forgotten Books, 1905 (2018 reprint).

Wenzel, David J., *Scranton's Mayors*, Tribute Books, 2006.

Local history, Other:

Bruce, Harry, *Illustrated History of Nova Scotia,* Nimbus Publishing, 1997.

Lindermuth, John R., *Digging Dusky Diamonds: A History of the Pennsylvania Coal Region* (Shamokin), Sunbury Press, 2013.

MacGaffey, Janet, *Coal Dust on Your Feet: The Rise, Decline, and Restoration of an Anthracite Mining Town* (Shamokin), Bucknell University Press, 2015.

Ward, Leo L. and Mark T. Major, *Pottsville,* Arcadia Publishing, 1995.

Ward, Leo L. and Mark T. Major, *Schuylkill County,* Arcadia Publishing, 1996.

Pennsylvania-Germans ("Pennsylvania Dutch"):

Kuhns, Oscar, *The German and Swiss Settlements of Colonial Pennsylvania; A Study of the So-called Pennsylvania-Dutch,* Heritage Books, 1989 (reprint of Henry Holt & Co., 1900).

Speaker, Thomas B., *Here Come the Pennsylvania Dutch: A Family Saga of Emigration and Early American History,* CreateSpace Independent Publishing, 2005.

Szabados, Stephen, *German Immigration to America: When, Why, How, and Where,* Independently Published, 2020.

Tolzmann, Don Heinrich (ed.), *The Pennsylvania Germans: James Owen Krauss Jr.'s Social History,* (1922), Heritage Books, 2014.

Railroading:

Canfield, J.R., *Lackawanna Memories: A Mid-Twentieth-Century Diary of a Great Railroad,* Biographical Publishing Co., 2021.

Casey, Robert J., *The Lackawanna Story: The First Hundred Years of the Delaware, Lackawanna and Western Railroad,* McGraw-Hill, 1951.

Crosby, David, *Lackawanna Railroad in Northeastern Pennsylvania,* Arcadia Publishing, 2014.

Harris, Henry J., "The Occupation Hazard of Locomotive Firemen", *Publications of the American Statistical Association,* Vol. 14, No. 107, (Sept. 1914), pp. 177-202.

Langone, Louis C., *Railroad Days: Memories of the Delaware, Lackawanna and Western Railroad,* Outskirts Press, 2015.

MacLeod, William, *Harper's New York and Erie Railroad Guide Book of 1851*, New York Historical Review, (reprint) 2014.

Orr, John W., *Set Up Running: The Life of a Pennsylvania Railroad Engineman, 1904-1949*, Penn State University Press, 2003.

Trains Magazine, *The Historical Guide to North American Railroads*, Kalmbach Publishing Co., 2014.

Westwood, John and Ian Wood, *The Historical Atlas of North American Railroads*, Chartwell Books, 2011.

Scots-Irish History and Culture:

Charles River Editors, *The Scotch-Irish: The History and Legacy of the Ethnic Group in America,* independently published, 2020.

Ford, Henry Jones, *The Scotch-Irish in America,* Princeton University Press, 1915 (2016 reprint by Books Ulster).

Leyburn, James G., *Scotch-Irish: A Social History,* University of North Caroling Press, 1989.

McCarthy, Karen F., *The Other Irish: The Scots-Irish Rascals Who Made America,* Fall River Press, 2011.

Szabados, Stephen, *Irish Immigration to America,* Independently Published, 2021.

Webb, Jim, *Born Fighting: How the Scots-Irish Shaped America*, Broadway Books, 2005.

Made in United States
North Haven, CT
19 April 2023

35641321R00102